Narrative and Social Control

SAGE ANNUAL REVIEWS OF COMMUNICATION RESEARCH

Editor
Dennis K. Mumby

Narrative and Social Control: Critical Perspectives

Sage Annual Reviews of Communication Research
Volume 21

SAGE Publications
International Educational and Professional Publisher
Newbury Park   London   New Delhi

Copyright © 1993 by Sage Publications, Inc.

For information address:

SAGE Publications, Inc.
2455 Teller Road
Newbury Park, California 91320

SAGE Publications Ltd.
6 Bonhill Street
London EC2A 4PU
United Kingdom

SAGE Publications India Pvt. Ltd.
M-32 Market
Greater Kailash I
New Delhi 110 048 India

Printed in the United States of America

Library of Congress Cataloging-in-Publication Data

Main entry under title:

Narrative and social control : critical perspectives / edited by
    Dennis K. Mumby
            p.   cm.   —(Sage annual reviews of communication research ;
        v. 21
    Includes bibliographical references and index.
    ISBN 0-8039-4931-6. — ISBN 0-8039-4932-4 (pbk.)
    1. Discourse analysis, Narrative. 2. Discourse analysis—Social
aspects. 3. Social Control. I. Mumby, Dennis K. II. Series
P302.7.N366   1993
401'.41—dc20   93-5203

93 94 95 96 10 9 8 7 6 5 4 3 2 1

Sage Production Editor: Astrid Virding

CONTENTS

INTRODUCTION:
NARRATIVE AND SOCIAL CONTROL

Dennis K. Mumby

THIS INTRODUCTION GIVES me the opportunity to provide the reader with some insight into the orientation of this book. Although ostensibly its title might appear fairly self-explanatory (it is about how narratives function as a form of social control in diverse communication contexts), at a more fundamental level there are a host of issues embedded in the title that belie its simplicity. Many readers will no doubt have been attracted to this book because of the appearance of the term *narrative* in the title. Indeed, Walter Fisher's (1984, 1985) invocation of a "narrative paradigm" has alerted many scholars to the possibilities inherent in the development of a more literary, aesthetic approach to human communication. The articulation of social actors as *homo narrans* provides one alternative to the model of rationality that has characterized Western thought from Descartes to the present. The most recent iteration of the latter paradigm is best represented by the social science model, with its quest for testable and verifiable observation statements about human behavior.

Although we might question Fisher's claim that his narrative approach warrants the status of a paradigm, there is little doubt that what might broadly be referred to as "narrative theory" has contributed significantly to the "crisis of representation" (Jameson, 1984, p. viii) in contemporary thought. This crisis is founded in the challenging of "an essentially realistic epistemology, which conceives of representation as the production, for subjectivity, of an objectivity that lies outside it [and] projects a mirror theory of knowledge and art, whose fundamental evaluative categories are those of adequacy, accuracy, and Truth itself" (Jameson, 1984, p. viii).

1

Although some scholars might be profoundly disturbed by this crisis (and others may be unaware that such a crisis even exists!), I would argue that it provides us with a tremendous opportunity to explore alternative ways of making knowledge claims and hence to develop new ways of seeing the world. Indeed, I see the recent controversy over so-called political correctness as in part an expression of the tension that exists between those who want to maintain a monopoly over the rules for what counts as legitimate knowledge and those social groups who have been largely disenfranchised in terms of their ability to shape our understanding of the world. It is no accident that political conservatives in various realms (including academia) have appropriated the term *political correctness* as a way to denounce any efforts to breach the monolith of truth claims that makes up the body of Western thought. The attempts by various social groups (women, racial minorities, gays, environmentalists) to articulate a voice within the domain of Western orthodoxy is therefore framed by the Right as a threat to both the political and intellectual stability of democratic society. Thus, for example, postmodernism is considered anarchic in its rejection of rationality, gays and single mothers on welfare represent the undermining of family values, and environmentalists threaten the most cherished "democratic" principle of all—free enterprise.

The reader may indeed wonder what such issues have to do with a book on narrative and social control. My answer is that there is an integral relationship between the kinds of knowledge claims that we can make in a particular society and the quality of that society. In this sense, the crisis of representation works on at least two interrelated levels. First, as Jameson states above, it involves a casting into crisis of Cartesian notions of foundational Truth. But second, and just as important, it is a crisis about the process of political representation and about who gets to play a role in the constitution of societal meaning systems. Following Laclau and Mouffe (1985), I would therefore make the case that the current challenge to Western orthodoxy represents not a threat to intellectual and political freedom; on the contrary, it must be viewed as an expansion and (potential) radicalization of it. The plurivocity of the discourses that may arise out of the "decentering" of the Cartesian subject may in some sense be destabilizing, but at the same time such a destabilization process relieves us from the burden of discovering "essential" truths and creates a context for "thinking the unthought" in terms of political and intellectual possibilities.

Thus, the focus on narrative in this book also operates on two levels: narrative is both a communication phenomenon that is worthy of intellectual scrutiny and (epistemologically speaking) it represents a particular orientation toward the study of social phenomena. In the remainder of this introduction, I want to provide an orientation toward narrative in the context of the issue of social control. In particular, I want to suggest a characterization of each of the terms *narrative, social,* and *control* that provides a rough set of guidelines for the reader in exploring the chapters in this book.

Framed epistemologically, the concept of narrative has emerged as a way of challenging the foundational premises in which most knowledge generation is grounded. The most (in)famous current articulation of this challenge is provided by Lyotard in *The Postmodern Condition* (1984). Written as a report on the status of knowledge in the postindustrial, information age, Lyotard argues that science does not simply consist of a neutral body of knowledge claims about the world but rather "produces a discourse of legitimation with respect to its own status, a discourse called philosophy" (p. xxiii). Lyotard uses the term *modern* to designate "any science that legitimates itself with reference to a metadiscourse of this kind making an explicit appeal to some grand narrative, such as the dialectics of Spirit, the hermeneutics of meaning, the emancipation of the rational or working subject, or the creation of wealth" (1984, p. xxiii).

To Lyotard, however, "the grand narrative has lost its credibility, regardless of what mode of unification it uses, regardless of whether it is a speculative narrative or a narrative of emancipation" (1984, p. 37). As such, the advent of a postmodern sensibility requires a different approach to legitimation through narrative. Lyotard thus argues the case that the postmodern involves "an incredulity toward metanarratives" (1984, p. xxiv) and conceives of knowledge as paralogical; that is, as searching for and creating instabilities in dominant views of the world. Postmodern thought therefore consists of *petit récits* ("little narratives") that continuously challenge the stability of received knowledge.

In what sense, then, are the chapters in this book consistent with this postmodern orientation to knowledge? Although not all of the chapters articulate an explicitly postmodern voice (certainly Clegg, Ehrenhaus, and Nakagawa are explicitly postmodern), each embodies in its own way a critique of any foundational conception of knowledge. Narrative is examined not as a fixed and stable communication phenomenon but rather as part of the complex and shifting terrain of meaning that makes up the social world. What is perhaps most striking about the chapters in this regard is their willingness to recognize the open-ended nature of knowledge claims; to recognize the difficulty (impossibility?) of making any universal claims about the nature of the human condition; and to acknowledge the extent to which, as theorists and researchers, we are never neutral, dispassionate observers of behavior but are always heavily implicated in the construction of the narratives (petit or grand) that provide insight to the social reality that we inhabit.

This is perhaps never more apparent than in the chapter by Porter and Catt. Their orientation toward the intersection of narrative and knowledge claims is best represented by the postmodern ethnographer Stephen Tyler when he states:

> Because post-modern ethnography privileges "discourse" over "text," it foregrounds dialogue as opposed to monologue, and emphasizes the cooperative and collaborative nature of the ethnographic situation in contrast to the ideology of the transcendental observer. In fact, it rejects the ideology of "observer-observed," there being nothing observed and no-one who is observer. There is instead the mutual, dialogical production of a discourse, of a story of sorts. (1986, p. 126)

Tyler's position encapsulates well the struggle that unfolds as we read Porter and Catt's chapter. It is highly self-reflexive in its attempt to wrestle with the essential question of the authorial standpoint (i.e., author-ity) of the researcher. Porter and Catt are forced to struggle with one of the most fundamental questions faced by critical-interpretive researchers—that is, how does one frame the so-called observer-observed relationship? From the standpoint of the traditional canons of social scientific rigor, this relationship is unproblematic because knowledge is produced only through the careful bifurcation of observer and observed. From this standpoint, Porter and Catt's chapter is nothing more than a series of interesting anecdotes that have about as much to do with knowledge claims as the cup of coffee that helps the researcher through the day.

However, I think (I hope) we have grown enough as a field to recognize the problem in allowing the epistemological underpinnings of the scientific method to dictate to us what constitutes knowledge. Porter and Catt struggle with the (very postmodern) question of how one negates the authorial voice of the researcher enough to allow space for the multiple play of voices that constitute the context of study. The Gordian knot that confronts them seems almost impossible, but the chapter has great value as a treatise on the kind of sensitivity that researchers must bring to their domains of study and on the problems associated with privileging a particular narrative voice.

The question of the "social" is of equally central concern to the chapters in this book. At a very broad level, all of the authors focus in various ways on how narratives function to construct the social reality that constitutes the lived world of social actors. Thus, Langellier and Peterson argue that the social unit we call "family" is not a pre-given entity but is rather partly constructed through the various narrative structures that family members articulate. Similarly, Nakagawa deconstructs narratives of the Japanese-American internment experience to show that such narratives do not simply retell an already preformed experience but actually play a constitutive role in the (divided) self-identity of the Japanese-American community.

In general, then, each chapter assumes an integral link between narrative and the social. Narrative is a *socially* symbolic act in the double sense that (a) it takes on meaning only in a social context and (b) it plays a role in the construction of that social context as a site of meaning within which social actors are implicated. However, there is no simple isomorphism between narrative (or any other symbolic form) and the social realm. In different ways, each of the chapters belies the notion that narrative functions monolithically to create a stable, structured, social order. Indeed, one of the prevailing themes across the chapters is the extent to which social order is tenuous, precarious, and open to negotiation in various ways. In this sense, society is characterized by an ongoing "struggle over meaning."

The idea of the precarious nature of social order is perhaps best expressed by Laclau and Mouffe (1985; Laclau, 1991) with their rather counterintuitive notion of the "impossibility of society." With this notion they suggest not that society as such does not exist but rather that we need to abandon the notion that society is a complete, fixed totality. Thus,

> the incomplete character of every totality leads us to abandon, as a terrain of analysis, the premise of "society" as a sutured and self-defined totality. "Society" is not a valid object of discourse. . . . If the social does not manage to fix itself in the intelligible and instituted forms of a *society*, the social exists, however, as an effort to construct that impossible object. Any discourse is constituted as an attempt to dominate the field of discursivity, to arrest the flow of differences, to construct a centre. We will call the privileged discursive points of this partial fixation, *nodal points*. . . . *The practice of articulation, therefore, consists in the construction of nodal points which partially fix meaning; and the partial character of this fixation proceeds from the openness of the social, a result, in its turn, of the constant overflowing of every discourse by the infinitude of the field of discursivity.* (Laclau & Mouffe, 1985, pp. 111-113; emphasis in original)

I quote Laclau and Mouffe at length because I think that their position accurately characterizes the central thrust of many of the chapters in this book. In essence, many are concerned with the ways in which narrative functions in attempts to construct the "impossible object" (society). In this sense, each chapter is about "nodal points"—about how narratives attempt to "arrest the flow of differences" and "construct a center" around which certain kinds of social relations form. A good example of this process at work is provided by Ehrenhaus's chapter on narratives that characterize the legacy of the Vietnam War. Through a deconstructive analysis, he demonstrates that the "therapeutic motif" functions as an articulated "nodal point" of discourse that attempts to "fix" the meaning of the Vietnam legacy. This motif "dominates the field of discursivity" by articulating "healing" as the natural response to the aftermath of Vietnam (with the Vietnam Memorial at the center of this narrative construction [a physical nodal point?]). As Ehrenhaus incisively demonstrates, this therapeutic motif functions as a narrative strategy of containment that effectively provides a totalizing and "sutured" reading of the Vietnam legacy and hence precludes the possibility of a political, resistant reading that enables critique of U.S. foreign policy.

But as Laclau and Mouffe indicate, the impossibility of society means that, even though discourses are articulated in powerful ways to construct nodal points of meaning, the "infinitude" of discourse means that such nodal points are always open to contestation and change. As Hall (1985, p. 113) states: "Ideology . . . *sets limits* to the degree to which a society-in-dominance can easily, smoothly and functionally reproduce itself." Indeed, Ehrenhaus points out that despite the pervasiveness of the therapeutic motif surrounding the Vietnam War, oppositional discourses have emerged that challenge the dominant narrative and provide the potential for an "ideological crisis" through which America's Vietnam experience can be more fully explored.

The issue of "control," then, is tied integrally to the question of the social, insofar as the social and the political are largely interdependent. In this sense, the social construction of meaning does not take place in a political vacuum but rather is a product of the various constellations of power and political interests that make up the relationships among different social groups. This is the central thrust of Witten's excellent chapter. Building on the literature on power in sociological theory, she makes a compelling case for the idea that control in the workplace is exercised not through direct, coercive means but rather through the discursive construction of a workplace culture that maintains and reproduces the prevailing system of power relations. In this sense, the construction of social reality is not spontaneous and consensual but is the product of the complex relations among narrative, power, and culture. The relationships among social actors in institutional settings are thus as much political as they are social.

The issue of control pervades all of the chapters in this book in the sense that each takes the social construction of reality to involve a struggle over the ways in which meanings get "fixed." As such, the social construction of meaning is inevitably a political process. In this context, it is useful to quote Laclau's distinction between the *social* and the *political*: "The sedimented forms of 'objectivity' make up the field of what we will call the 'social.' The moment of antagonism where the undecidable nature of the alternatives and their resolution through power relations becomes fully visible constitutes the field of the 'political' . . . the boundary of what is social and what is political in society is constantly displaced" (1991, p. 35).

In every instance, then, the chapters in this book attempt to deconstruct the relationship between the social and the political. In other words, the focus of analysis is both (a) the process of sedimentation that leads to the reification of the social and (b) an attempt to show how such reification potentially hides (political) antagonisms and mutes the articulation of alternative worldviews by groups at the margins of political power. Thus, for example, "The Family" is "denaturalized" and deconstructed as a social, political, and economic configuration that potentially marginalizes women and children (Langellier & Peterson); the social construction of the news-gathering process is analyzed as a response to a legitimation crisis (Zelizer); and, at a metatheoretical level, modern conceptions of power are shown to be the products of specific—historical, theoretical, and political—narratives (Clegg).

At its heart, then, this book is about the relationship between narrative (as both a theoretical perspective and a communication phenomenon) and politics. It is an effort to illuminate the myriad processes by which attempts are made to overcome "the impossibility of society." The myth of "society" means that efforts to "fix" meaning are always political and always ultimately doomed to failure, given the "surplus of meaning" that always characterizes hegemony-at-work. But it is important that we understand these efforts and thus develop a sense of how we, as members of particular social formations, are more readily able to accept some "realities" than others and sometimes become imprisoned by these realities.

If the "impossibility of society" is a leitmotif for this book, is its perspective not ultimately pessimistic in regard to possibilities for human action and emancipation? Laclau provides the best answer to this question:

Opaqueness will always be an inherent dimension of social relations and . . . the myth of a reconciled and transparent society is simply that: a myth. We have therefore upheld the contingency of social relations, the ineradicability of power relations, and the impossibility of reaching a harmonious society. Are these not pessimistic conclusions? . . . [F]ar from being the cause for pessimism, they are the basis for a radical optimism. . . . [I]f social relations are contingent, it means that they can be radically transformed through struggle, instead of that transformation being conceived as a self-transformation of an objective nature; if power is ineradicable, it is because there is radical liberty that is not fettered by any essence; and if opaqueness is constitutive of the social, it is precisely this which makes access to the truth conceived as an unveiling (*aletheia*) possible. (1991, pp. 35-36)

Each of the chapters in this book, I would argue, views power as ineradicable while simultaneously recognizing the radical liberty and transformational possibilities implied by a contingent view of society. It is thus in the spirit of *aletheia* that these chapters are written.

FORMAT OF THE BOOK

Although clearly each chapter in this book can be read independently, there is a real sense in which it forms a coherent whole. First, in Part I, Stewart Clegg provides an excellent overview of many of the issues that are taken up in subsequent chapters. Clegg's chapter is a narrative itself and provides a metatheoretical historiography of the concept of power that is both nuanced and wide-ranging. Basically, he maps out two separate and often conflicting narratives about how power functions in society. The first, "sovereign" view, narrates power as a largely mechanistic, causal, agency-oriented phenomenon. Rooted in Thomas Hobbes, this narrative is traced by Clegg through to the pluralists and neo-Marxists of the 1960s and 1970s. The second, "disciplinary" perspective, conceives of power as simultaneously enabling and constraining. Born of a postmodern sensibility (see particularly the work of Foucault, 1979, 1980), the origins of this narrative, however, can be traced back as far as Machiavelli's work on strategies of power.[1] Finally, he intertwines these two narratives through his model of "circuits of power" (see also Clegg, 1989) and demonstrates its utility through its application to a specific organizational context—a construction site (see also Clegg, 1975).

The first major section of the book, Part II, addresses the role of narrative in diverse communication contexts. First, Langellier and Peterson examine the constitutive relationship between narrative and family. Critiquing the prevailing tendency in the communication literature to treat "family" as an unproblematic, monolithic phenomenon (i.e., as a "container" for communication events), they demonstrate the important role of narratives in the ongoing construction of particular family formations and relations of control. Thus, "Stories and storytelling both generate and reproduce 'the family' by legitimating meanings and power relations that privilege, for example, parents over children, males over females, and the white, middle-class family over alternative family structures" (p. 50).

Second, Peter Ehrenhaus's analysis of post-Vietnam public discourse demonstrates the "tyrannizing power of the therapeutic motif" (p. 82). He convincingly suggests how this motif functions as a strategy of political containment by "psychologizing" the Vietnam veteran and creating "a context that defines the warrior as cripple, and muzzles the warrior as witness" (p. 89). As such, voices that challenge the dominant therapeutic narrative are marginalized and rendered ineffective as a means of developing alternate readings of the post-Vietnam experience.

Third, Marsha Witten adopts a neo-Marxist perspective to examine the relationship between narrative and social control in an organizational context. Drawing on recent work in the fields of sociology and communication, she shows how legitimation and control is not a static—structural or individual—organizational phenomenon but is rather achieved "ongoingly through symbolic processes" (p. 101). Looking specifically at storytelling in two different organizations, Witten shows how a "culture of obedience" is not simply imposed by management but rather arises dynamically through the active constitution of organizational reality by members.

The next section, Part III, contains chapters addressing the relationship between narrative and race. Teun A. van Dijk adopts a discourse-analytic approach in examining how racist views emerge through the structure of storytelling. The importance of this chapter lies in its ability to show how storytelling is not linked simply to the cognitions of specific individuals; rather, stories are "a major discourse genre for the reproduction of culture and society" (p. 125). Van Dijk thus examines specific stories to demonstrate how, through the application of conventional storytelling practices, social actors articulate and reproduce the prejudices that exist at the macro-social level.

Gordon Nakagawa's chapter adopts a very different approach to the question of the relationship between narrative and race. Adopting a Foucauldian perspective, Nakagawa examines narratives of the Japanese-

American internment experience. Through an analysis of internee narratives, Nakagawa shows how they "chart a 'political anatomy' of the Nikkei [ethnic Japanese American] subject, a grid of power relations whose coordinates are deployed across the body of the internee" (p. 149). This chapter poignantly demonstrates the extent to which institutionalized practices of discipline and surveillance exercised in the internment camps "normalized" the Nikkei population; this normalization process, Nakagawa shows, is reflected by the internees in their narrative expression of space, time, and movement.

Finally, W. Marc Porter and Isaac E. Catt's chapter is framed around a critical racial incident on a university campus. Using the narrative form, they document and analyze the emergence of different constituencies and a narrative of "narcissism" in the debate over race that develops as a result of the incident. As I indicated earlier, the authors problematize authorial voice insofar as they adopt a "hermeneutics of vulnerability," taking a standpoint of radical contingency in terms of their ability to make "truth claims" in light of their analysis.

The final section of the book, Part IV, contains chapters that focus on the relationship between narrative and the media. First, Barbie Zelizer examines narratives of self-legitimation that emerged in the writings of journalists in the aftermath of the shooting of Lee Harvey Oswald. Zelizer focuses her analysis on two different narratives articulated by the journalistic community, each of which constructs a different relationship between that community and the issue of journalistic excellence. The juxtaposition of these two contrasting narratives allows Zelizer to examine "the cultural authority that American journalists have come to embody as authoritative spokespersons for events of the 'real' world, and the control this gives them . . . in narratively determining preferred versions of those events" (p. 190).

Finally, A. Susan Owen's chapter on the television series *China Beach* argues that although the series conforms in many respects to the format of traditional television melodrama, moments of radical opposition are embedded in the narrative structure of the series. She shows how the producers of the series use the marginalized voices of women and "feminized" black males to speak the radical discourse of rage, despair, anguish, abjection, and horror that is the lived experience of many Vietnam veterans. She further argues that, given the political economy of the television medium, such cleverly crafted resistance is worthy of our attention.

Clearly this book has a wide appeal. My hope is that, in addition to being sympathetically received among the highly diverse and pluralistic community of communication scholars, its themes will also resonate with those scholars who pursue similar concerns in fields such as sociology, anthropology, political science, and literary studies. Each of these disciplines is struggling with precisely the same issues that I have addressed in this introduction regarding questions of representation, knowledge, control, society, and so forth. This book's engagement with the concept of narrative will hopefully provide readers with an enlightened approach to posing questions regarding these issues, even if definitive answers have not yet been articulated.

ACKNOWLEDGMENTS

My father once told me that if people knew how movies were made, they would never go and see them. Perhaps the same could be said of books, both academic and otherwise—people would never read them if they knew how the editorial process worked. But I think that this is a rather naive view of how an apparently seamless narrative is created. Books and movies are compelling precisely because there is a disjunctive, aporetic, and often serendipitous process of creation that goes on behind the scenes. This is certainly no less true of this book; many people have contributed to its "final" form in both an intentional and serendipitous fashion. In its early stages, Joe Turow helped greatly in shaping the perspective of this collection. Along the way, I was lucky enough to be able to draw upon Linda Putnam's extensive editorial experience. Diane Gruber, Ramsey Eric Ramsey, and Patricia Ryden did a superb job with the subject index. Charlie Stewart, my department chair, was gracious enough to provide me with research leave during Fall Semester, 1992. Beverly Robinson and Liz Whitworth were generous with their excellent word processing skills. At Sage, Sophy Craze, Astrid Virding, and Mary Curtis provided excellent editorial support. Finally, I would like to thank my co-contributors for making my editorial duties both challenging and stimulating; their intellectual contributions and support of this project are greatly appreciated. All remaining errors can be attributed to the shortcomings of the editor!

NOTE

1. Although Clegg does not explicitly deal with Machiavelli in his chapter, he does so in detail in Clegg (1989). The reader is referred to this excellent and comprehensive study of power for further information.

REFERENCES

Clegg, S. (1975). *Power, rule and domination*. London: Routledge & Kegan Paul.

Clegg, S. (1989). *Frameworks of power*. Newbury Park,CA: Sage.

Fisher, W. (1984). Narration as a human communication paradigm: The case of public moral argument. *Communication Monographs, 51*, 1-22.

Fisher, W. (1985). The narrative paradigm: An elaboration. *Communication Monographs, 52*, 347-367.

Foucault, M. (1979). *Discipline and punish: The birth of the prison* (Trans. A. Sheridan). New York: Vintage.

Foucault, M. (1980). *The history of sexuality, Vol. 1* (Trans. R. Hurley). New York: Vintage.

Hall, S. (1985). Signification, representation, ideology: Althusser and the poststructuralist debates. *Critical Studies in Mass Communication, 2*, 91-114.

Jameson, F. (1984). Preface to J-F Lyotard, *The postmodern condition* (Trans. G. Bennington & B. Massumi). Minneapolis: University of Minnesota Press.

Laclau, E. (1991). *New reflections on the revolution of our time*. London: Verso.

Laclau, E., & Mouffe, C. (1985). *Hegemony and socialist strategy: Towards a radical democratic politics*. London: Verso.

Lyotard, J-F. (1984). *The postmodern condition* (Trans. G. Bennington & B. Massumi). Minneapolis: University of Minnesota Press.

Tyler, S. (1986). Post-modern ethnography: From document of the occult to occult document. In J. Clifford & G. Marcus (Eds.), *Writing culture: The poetics and politics of ethnography* (pp. 122-140). Berkeley: University of California Press.

PART I

THEORETICAL OVERVIEW

Chapter 1

NARRATIVE, POWER, AND SOCIAL THEORY

Stewart R. Clegg

DESPITE THE EVIDENT differences in topic and focus, the founding theorists of modernity such as Marx, Durkheim, Weber, and Simmel could all tell a good story: about religion and the rise of capitalism (Weber, 1976); about the division of labor and its consequences (Durkheim, 1964); about the rise and eventual self-destruction of capitalism (Marx, 1976); about the individuating consequences of a philosophy of money (Simmel, 1900). Not "ripping yarns," perhaps, but a good read. Each was a grand master of narrative. Indeed, the main thrust of each of their theories was a narrative structure in which a central idea of capitalism, differentiation, Protestantism, individuation, played an ambivalent heroic role.

Later, good stories were to become the cornerstone of an early and influential school in North American sociology, the Chicago School, associated with researchers such as William Foot Whyte (1943) and his *Street Corner Society*. With the development of a sociology based on the hard-hitting style of Chicago investigative journalism that characterized the early contributions, the stories that the sociologist was to tell and the stories of the street were to become inexorably and ethnographically intertwined. In one version of the enterprise, at least, a good story was the basis of excellent sociology. Such sociology was to become a form of meta-narrative about good stories. Of course, this was not only true of the interactionist tradition at Chicago, which sought to show the rationality and integrity of marginalized and other voices (even when it was a tad

AUTHOR'S NOTE: I would like to thank my colleague at St. Andrews, Bob Grafton Small, and also Dennis Mumby, for their helpful comments on an earlier draft of this paper.

patronizing in so doing). It was also the case even during the widespread ascendancy of functionalism.

Functionalism, at its best, as it developed the analysis of "dysfunctions" from Merton (1968), had a classical narrative structure. It consisted of the narrative power of revelation: In classic functionalist studies it is revealed that things are not as they appear to be. The format is familiar: "It is said but it is revealed unto you that . . . " Some examples may serve to make the point. Revelation is evident in works as various as Stouffer et al.'s (1949) *The American Soldier* and Merton's (1940) "Bureaucratic Structure and Personality." Bureaucracy appears an ideal type for rational organization but it is revealed that it needs and produces stunted human beings and this cannot be rational; the U.S. South appears to be the heartland of racial prejudice but it is revealed that, during the Second World War, prejudice was greater in soldiers from the North. In fact, the scientific claims of sociology came to rest, above all, on techniques for confounding common sense. The techniques of factor analysis in Stouffer revealed the unanticipated truth; the techniques of functional theory revealed the irrational core of the apparently rational bureaucratic shell in Merton.

The major theoretical challenge to functionalism did not question the emergent orthodoxy of narrative. Two matters were at issue. Did *conflict* or *consensus* best characterize the stories of everyday life (Horton, 1966)? Did "over-socialized" actors feature in the narrative lines that these stories allowed (Wrong, 1961)? These were the key fault-lines of *conflict sociology*. Much of conflict sociology was an echo of European contexts in which Marx's influence was not as absent as the doyen of functionalism, Parsons (1937), would have had it be. Conflict sociology became the conduit through which many concerns, theorists, and issues, repressed or marginalized by the synthesis of Parsonian functionalism, were to become visible. The high-water mark of the European vogue for Marxist sociology in the late 1960s through the 1970s did not undercut the strong sense of narrative as the central tool of the sociological enterprise, although it did refract elements of its constitution. Instead of the format being one in which "it is said but otherwise revealed," where functionalist science can take an ironicizing attitude towards the mundane attitudes of everyday life, the mechanics shifted. The irony bred of superior convictions was not absent. Now it became displayed not in what people ordinarily said and thought but in what ordinarily they did not say and did not think.

Marxist sociology became an ever more fanciful set of variations to explain why the narrative structure predicted in the classic texts of Marx had not occurred. Orchestration occurred around the themes either of ideology or the role of the state. In the latter the working class was seduced, while their energies were diverted by the sirens of capitalism. The drama failed to reach its narrative conclusion because of the temptations that the Keynesian welfare state had to offer. At least it seemed so, once upon a time before Thatcher, before Reagan. During the 1980s and into the 1990s it became harder to maintain the Keynesian welfare state argument analytically (Clegg, Dow, & Boreham, 1983; Clegg, Boreham, & Dow, 1986) and practically: Inner-city riots from Toxteth and Brixton at the start of the 1980s to Los Angeles and Atlanta at the start of the 1990s seemed to signify that the Keynesian welfare state, after its "fiscal crisis" (O'Connor, 1973), no longer performed the function that the Marxian narrative had once allocated to it.

Was the ideological argument more robust? In this narrative the working class had learned the wrong lines, not those scheduled by the Marxist theory but those of bourgeois aspirations, world-view, and hegemony. Having learned these lines too well they had lost sight of the preferred role scripted for them to play. Significant theories of ideology and hegemony became variations on the theme of working class acquiescence secured through normative incorporation by dominant ideology (Abercrombie, Hill, & Turner, 1980). The narrative was no longer one of revelation but of concealment: Marxist theory, in theory, should have provided revelation in practice—but it did not. Only the theorist could see the unrevealed truth of the mechanisms that, despite and even through resistance, secured and reproduced consent (Burawoy, 1979; Willis, 1977). The subjects of analysis were occluded, incorporated, hegemonized, and falsely conscious and had the nature of their real interests concealed from them. According to the classical script and stage directions what should have been a revelation had transmuted into concealment. The fate of "Western Marxism" was to be able to have the power to see what impotent subjects could not see.

Simultaneously, Western Marxists lacked any agency through which theoretical power could be rendered into practical efficacy because it lacked practical political agency, in a mass political movement or party, that could articulate the truth as they saw it. Therefore, the narrative of concealment could not transcend the theoretical moment of revelation. Western Marxism was impotent at best; at worst, irrelevant (Anderson, 1976). In the West it became increasingly utopian (Bauman, 1977); in the East, increasingly dystopian (Feher, Heller, & Markus, 1983), as the collapse of "dictatorship over needs" lead to its recent implosion.

Outside the rubric of Western Marxism a narrative structure premised on the mechanisms of concealment found a particular resonance in social theory. I will propose that the theory of power began in utter transparency yet it ended with a narrative of concealment. How was this possible? I will argue that it was in the theory of power that the narrative of concealment found its highest expression. There is a story here worthy of inclusion in a text dedicated to "narrative and social control". A supplementary story is what a theory of power might be like that was bathed neither in the pure empiricist ether of utter transparency nor in the dense theoreticist miasma of occlusion.

THEORIES OF POWER AND IDEOLOGY

In its modern form the narrative of power developed from the creative fictions of Thomas Hobbes. Although designed to reinstitute a sovereign basis for narrative order, both practically and theoretically, it has failed to do so (Clegg, 1979). A central narrative in the modern understanding of power sketches a trajectory that stretches from Hobbes to Lukes. In this way, the doyen of 17th-century political theory can be linked to a preeminent power theorist of late 20th-century social science (Clegg, 1989). The narrative that stitched together contemporary political science and a more classical political philosophy centered on concerns with models of causality. These models derived from the new science of mechanics pioneered in the 17th century. It was the "regularity" principles of David Hume that confirmed the adequacy of these conceptions of causality (1902).

The implicit link from Hobbes to contemporary concerns with power is via a common "agency" model, as Ball (1978) terms it, one in which "ontologically autarchic" individuals held sway. Such individuals, conceived on a classical liberal model as natural entities, were at the center of analysis. So, power was something people had, rather than, say, organizations. Explicitly, the formal model developed what has become known as the community power debate. The chief contributor was Dahl (1957, 1958, 1961, 1968), who in a series of publications mapped out a behavioral science-oriented response to the looser methodologies used in the contemporary elite theory of Hunter (1953) and Mills (1956).

The ascendancy of Dahl's pluralist analysis was reached with the publication in 1961 of his empirical study of New Haven, *Who Governs?* The ascendancy was soon under attack, such that it has been the fashion for some time to be highly critical of Dahl's contributions. There is no doubt that much of this criticism is warranted, as the self-denying ordinances associated with Dahl's project definitely rob it of opportunities for insight. Yet, it should always be remembered that the formal model that Dahl produces for the analysis of power, although restricted in scope, was nonetheless deliberately so. It effectively questioned those much looser and less precise research programs associated with the elitist style of analysis that previously had held the center ground of power research. It produced a much sharper model of power than previously, even if its actual representations were not as clearly focused.

Dahl's central essays concerned methodology. The methodology constructed a particular model of formal power. At the center of the methodology was a concern with precision. A methodological focus on the measurement of power, Dahl proposed, could achieve this precision. Instead of measuring what people thought was power it should be measured through "responses." Responses indicated the power that stood as the cause of the measured reaction. Just as a billiard ball colliding with another ball could be said to cause the motion or response of the latter, so the power of an A could be measured through the response of a B. Implicit in this was a mechanical and behaviorist view of the world. Reality was immediately observable. Transparency reigned. Things were as they appeared to be. To appear to be they must be evident, if they were to be observed. Whatever could not be observed could not be said to be. The unobservable was not seen to be a suitable case for treatment as data.

Precision had its costs. The prohibited lines of inquiry pointed toward a less "ontologically autarchic" distribution of power than pluralism was wont to discover. In the pluralist vision, individuals existed in splendid and celebrated conceptual disorganization from each other. In part, it was the excessive individualism of the conception of power, as much as aspects of the real structure of American communities, that oriented researchers towards pluralist conclusions. "Values" were not unimportant either. One has a strong sense of the way in which pluralist models served to license and legitimate postwar American democracy, despite whatever flaws might have been evident in it. In seeing power in America as distributed plurally the democratic ideal could be preserved. The individualism and mechanism of the conception of power used tended to orient these researchers to instances of pluralistic power over more structural conceptions. For many pluralist writers power was something that a concrete individual had to be seen to be exercising. Power prevented another equally concrete individual from doing something that they would have preferred to have done. Power was exercised so that its subjects fell in with the individual preferences of the powerful. Indeed, in these formulations power would be the subordination of others' preferences and the extension of one's own to incorporate these others.

Characteristically, pluralists regarded power as most likely to be dispersed among many rather than few people. It was more likely to be visible in instances of concrete decision making than through reputation and to be more widely dispersed than narrowly concentrated in communities. Presthus (1964) came closest to articulating what an ideal type pluralist analysis would be.

With respect to the concept of power the pluralists made the running. Yet, their rigor is in some respects spurious. Although considerable attention attaches to constructing a precise instrument for measuring power in terms of responses to its exercise, fewer precise aspects of analysis were to be found in the model's application to the empirical analysis of the community of New Haven (Dahl, 1961). In fact, this is to be expected, if for no other reason than that the model itself retains many imprecise and tacit assumptions. The point is not so much that these remained: One would find it difficult to conceive of a formal model on which complete closure could be effected that simultaneously retained much empirical utility. Instead, one might see the precision and tacit assumptions as indicating "fault lines," areas of weakness, in the formal model. As such they are damaging to the terms of closure that the formal model attempts.

Dahl espoused an intellectual position known as *behaviorism*. The central tenet of this position is to treat social explanation as no different in principle from the explanation of a phenomenon that is nonsocial. In practice this amounts to disregarding most of what it is that makes human society possible in favor of a radically constipated conception of behavior expunged of inherent meaning. Given the behaviorism of Dahl's position he is reluctant to consider issues of intentionality; from this perspective, one would obviously be suspicious of any concept seemingly so mentalist and unmeasurable as an intention. Consequently, the considerable criticism that Dahl's approach has engendered has focused on the lack of any criteria for deciding whether an exercise of power was intended. Eventually, in Lukes's (1974) work, this concern was to generate considerable discussion of the question of deciding responsibility for action.

Dahl's model deliberately refuses reference to the intentions that an agent might be said to have. Other writers more concerned with questions of intentionality include Weber (1978), Russell (1938), and Wrong (1979). Weber, in particular, illuminates aspects of the phenomenon of power whose figuration would remain obscured by strict adherence to the formal model of power as Dahl defines it. Despite this, the notion of intention deployed by these writers is not necessarily correct. As a tool for the analysis of power, the way in which these writers conceptualize the notion of intention proves to be very limited.

The limitations of the intentionalist concept of power are evident, revealingly so, in its most sophisticated use in Wrong (1979). Of particular interest is a discussion that concludes with the conduct of sexual etiquette at cocktail parties:

> I do not see how we can avoid restricting the term power to intentional and effective acts of influence by some persons on other persons. It may be readily acknowledged that intentional effects to influence others often produce unintended as well as intended effects on their behaviour—a dominating and overprotective mother does not intend to feminize the character of her son. But all social interaction produces such unintended effects—a boss does not mean to plunge an employee into despair by greeting him somewhat distractedly in the morning, nor does a woman mean to arouse a man's sexual interest by paying polite attention to his conversation at a cocktail party. (Wrong 1979, p. 4)

Consider the last case. Wrong's discussion is very restricted in its applicability and value as a guide to practical action in the postfeminist world in which many people, including professors of sociology, are increasingly obliged to act, perhaps including even Wrong himself. The reasons for this lack of utility are the restriction of the concept of power to a notion of intentional agency rather than to a conception of rules of the game. That the game might be patriarchally and sexistly skewed does not figure in Wrong's account: All that matters is the account of the (male) protagonist of his intentions (conceived as interior and anterior mental and causal states). The response of the (female) antagonist does not enter into analysis other than as something either confirmed or confounded by the privileged (male) discourse. The discourse is privileged because of the account of intentionality as causal and as a unique private, mental condition.

The researchers who did most to overthrow the limiting assumptions of Dahl's framework were Bachrach and Baratz (1962). "Two faces of power" were identified by these writers. One face Dahl's formal model illuminated clearly, but at the cost of casting the second face of power into the shade. Lurking in the dark was the structural face of power. Enlightenment could be cast not only by focusing the investigative gaze on concrete acts of decision making by specific agencies but also by directing it towards a phenomenon that they were to call *nondecision-making*. By only looking at things that happened, one neglected, so the critics said, that power might be manifested not only in doing things but also in ensuring that things do not get done. Whether this "ensuring" was itself a "doing" or should be considered in more structural and less agency-oriented terms was a debate that has raged intermittently ever since.

When Bachrach and Baratz published their long-awaited empirical study of Baltimore politics, as *Power and Poverty* (1970), there were significant retreats from some of the positions initially advanced in the theoretical papers that they had produced in the early 1960s. For instance, the notions of nondecision-making and mobilization of bias were diluted. The idea of *mobilization of bias* had been a key term of debate that had come into the currency of political exchange with its adoption by Bachrach and Baratz (1962). The term was originally coined by Schattschneider (1960). Reference to a mobilization of bias indicates that behind any episode of power that occurred in an organized setting there was a structure that prefigured the concrete exchange. Structure prefigured power's exercise and was itself always saturated with power. It was not something external, residual, or incidental to power. For instance, organizations that were effectively "masculine" in their power structures would be hardly likely to mobilize a bias proactively toward feminist issues. The theory suggests that, first, one can effectively categorize issues in terms of their interests and saliency, and second, that organizations that have an effective bias toward a male-dominated agenda rather than one more alert to feminist issues will systematically and routinely work against the interests and agenda that feminists might otherwise bring to the agenda.

The concept of mobilization of bias was later to be given a novel twist by Newton (1975), who seized and turned it into a weapon aimed straight at the core of the empirical test on which Dahl (1961) rested his case. It proved to be a case of being hoisted with one's own petard. The study of New Haven came under renewed scrutiny, not so much in terms of what it included but in terms of what it did not include. Yet, the notion of inclusion was specified in such literal terms that no empiricist objections could be raised. A tacit assumption of the study of New Haven, or any other community, was that the formal area of local authority governance coincided with the boundaries of some real community. Newton made a simple but potent observation. The boundaries of administrative entities in the United States are constructed in specific and restricted ways. New Haven was no exception to this. Many of the notable members of the New Haven community were not residents of the New Haven political arena as identified by the local authority. Consequently they had little interest in what went on with the taxpayers' money within this area of governance. Nor was it an accident that this was so, he suggested. The drawing of political boundaries in the formal sense is itself always an act of politics, representing a mobilization of bias, particularly where a desirable suburban space can be isolated from an adjacent and problematic urban space. The costs and blight of the latter can be isolated; the charm and serenity of the former maintained. Why would issues of housing or schooling in the urban arena concern notable citizens of the community who neither lived in nor were taxed by that urban area local authority? The narrative limits of accepting that assumption of a political community of interest that Hobbes implied at the beginning of the modernist project of power become evident in a strikingly empirical manner. The "Community Power Debate" was premised on questionable assumptions not only about what constituted power but also what constituted a community.

The critique that Bachrach and Baratz offered was not universally accepted. Some doubted that any hidden or obscured phenomena lurked in the dark, outside the empiricist gaze. If something such as the second face of power could not be seen, they argued, what proof could there possibly be that it existed? Writers such as Wolfinger (1971a, 1971b) accorded the idea that there was something unobservable called nondecision-making about as much credence as they might have done to the notion that there were fairies at the bottom of their garden. Nor were the mediations of diplomatists such as Frey (1971) given much shrift by skeptics such as this. Either things were real and could be clearly seen or they were not real at all, except in what was taken to be the hothouse imagination of left-wing zealots. Such people's political preoccupations clearly seemed to indicate a disturbed mind, in Wolfinger's view. Although this was a representative judgment by a leading member of the United States' political science community it was not one unanimously shared in British sociological circles where Bachrach and Baratz's critiques were to be well received by writers such as Lukes (1974), Clegg (1975), and Saunders (1979, p. 29). Lukes's response was not only the earliest, it was also the most decisive.

POWER AND THREE DIMENSIONS:
A RADICAL VIEW

In 1974, the debate received a major new contribution with the extension of Bachrach and Baratz's two faces of power to one of three dimensions, as a result of the publication of Lukes's (1974) *Power: A Radical View*. Although the main focus of research and conceptualization of power had until now occurred within the context of the "Community Power Debate," the analytic center of gravity changed to a concern with power per se. Lukes (1974) introduced the nomenclature of *dimensions* into power analysis in a move that successfully usurped discussion of the "two faces" of power. From now on, debate focused on three dimensions rather than two faces as the latter perspective declined.

Lukes's analysis sought to make a full break with earlier critical accounts by writers such as Bachrach and Baratz (1962). It did this by rejecting their conception that in the analysis of power, intentions can function as causes, as merely "qualified behaviourism." Surprisingly, he did not seek to replace this with a more sociological account of intention. Such an analysis (e.g., Blum & McHugh, 1972; Mills, 1940) is absent in Lukes, despite his linking of power and responsibility using other aspects of Mills's work.

Where intention was addressed, in Bachrach and Baratz (1962), instead of an analysis of the situational logic of motive and intention statements, there is an assumption that these terms somehow describe inner, psychological causes of action. Bachrach and Baratz (1962) sought to extend causal argument by admitting that things other than merely observable events might have the status of causes. What people thought and intended to happen, usually expressed in terms of "reasons" people might give for their actions, could be causes. Such reasons, motives, intentions, conceptualized as prior and antecedent to social action, had an explanatory and causal role to play in the analysis of power.

Certain problems are associated with accessing just what the internal mental and intentional wellsprings of another's causal actions might be. These will necessarily present themselves to any analyst who wants to argue that intentions can function as causes. Other people may well have minds but how on earth can we know what is in them other than by asking them to report on their "state of mind"? The first problem is evident. People may well lie about their intentions: This phenomenon, for instance, seems to explain some, at least, of the stunning disparities between the predicted result, based on polls, and the actual result of the British General Election of 1992. Given the narrative practice of the debate about power there are some evident problems with asking people what their intentions are. Not only may they be untruthful—this much is somewhat unproblematic—but more difficult is the argument that they may be mistaken. This problem arises from a discourse whose most pervasive assumption about the nature of subjectivity and consciousness is that it is somehow mistaken, occluded, concealed, false, and unreal. For instance, Lukes's "three dimensional" and "hegemonic" approach to power argues that it is "the supreme exercise of power to get another or others to have the desires you want them to have . . . to secure their compliance by controlling their thoughts and desires" (Lukes, 1974, p. 23). If this argument is correct, then when people say what their consciousness of something is, these accounts can neither be taken at face value nor can they function as explanations. So, any recourse to the actors own account as an explanation will be flawed. From this perspective, it may be said that people do not know their minds. It is precisely the false belief that they think that they do that is the locus of the problem of hegemony.

This conception of power bears the traces of an older conception of *sovereignty*. In this conception, power is a locus of will, a supreme agency to which other wills would bend, as prohibitive. In short, this is the classic conception of power as zero-sum, as the negation of the power of others. At its most subtle, with the hegemonic and three-dimensional approaches, this unravels into conceptions of power that penetrate into the very thoughts and consciousness of others. A form of supremely sovereign will is constituted from which there seems no escape. Those subject to power's sovereignty are literally unable to recognize their will, captured as it is by the sovereign power of another. Models of ideology and hegemony present such conceptions of power as "false" consciousness. Thus, one can see how Lukes's (1974) "third dimensional" conception of power as something unknowably lodged in one's subjectivity and consciousness against one's "real interests" was only a further stretching of the extant terms of power's causal, sovereign domain.

The central problem with Lukes's (1974) model for the analysis of power results from his attachment to a vocabulary of *real interests,* a term that he takes directly from Marxian debate. Lukes's conception uneasily ties what he sees as the necessarily morally irreducible nature of any idea of interests with the claim that some interests are more real than others. Interests can be conceived from one or other of a liberal, a reformist, or a radical perspective in any analysis of power, Lukes suggested. Some people will be liberals, others reformists, some radicals. From the three moral positions flow three distinct dimensional approaches to the analysis of power. The radical conception of real interests, especially where it does not coincide with the claim to interests that subjects would themselves make, is the litmus test of what interests really are. The model sits uneasily between a conventionalist epistemological position and one closer to a realist position. Conventionalism proposes that knowledge is wholly socially constructed; realism accepts this, but would also add that social constructs change as real structures become better appropriated through knowledge constructs. Lukes's model refracts some elements of a Marxist analysis, such as the concern with real interests, through a humanistic and morally relativistic (rather than theoretically absolutist) lens (Clegg, 1989).

DOMINANT IDEOLOGY AND
DISCIPLINARY POWER

Lukes (1977, p. 29) defines the key problem in terms generally accepted as the definitive specification of the issues involved: "No social theory merits serious attention that fails to retain an ever present sense of the dialectics of power and structure." What links power and structure according to Lukes's model are the practices of "hegemony." Much of the recent debate about power has focused on the ways in which ideology operates through conceptions of hegemony. The concern with the concept of ideology has focused on one or other of two things. First, there has been a suggestion that much of both Marxism and sociology is flawed by the *dominant ideology thesis* (Abercrombie et al., 1980). A second emphasis proposes that instead of thinking of either ideology or hegemony as a state of mind one would better regard each as a set of practices, primarily of a discursive provenance, that seek to foreclose the indefinite possibilities of signifying elements and their relations, in determinate ways (Laclau & Mouffe, 1985). The thrust of this second emphasis derives from "post-structuralist" perspectives, particularly those that have been encouraged by Foucault's work on disciplinary power. Foucault (1977) provides a sophisticated discussion of power that explicitly breaks with any conception of ideology.

Foucault is interesting in at least two ways. First, he provides us with a critique of many conventional "views" on power. The core of this critique is that the conception of power needs to be freed from its "sovereign" auspices as a prohibitive concept. Such a concern with the facilitative and productive aspects of power relates well to the kind of arguments made most clearly by Parsons (1967). Foucault's emphasis is a useful additional contribution in this regard. Second, Foucault provides us with a detailed history of some power practices and techniques that have characterized capitalist modernity, but he does so in a way that is nonreductive. Compared with some Marxist accounts of similar events the discussion is all the better for not being reductive.[1] In comparison with such accounts the historical record that Foucault produces stands as a corrective; in addition, it complements Weber (Dandekker, 1991).

In recent years, Foucault has become one of a whole series of French intellectual fashions for many English-speaking writers. Many critics who have "taken up" Foucault have not been trained sociologically, any more than Foucault was. The absence of a sociological framework led Foucault to understate the importance of Max Weber's (1978) contribution to arguments concerning discipline. Consequently, Foucault's work is not as discontinuous with central traditions of analysis in the social sciences as it might initially appear to be. Despite Foucault's objections to both structuralist and interpretivist analysis, and his canonization as an exemplar of "poststructuralist" analysis, deep thematic roots in central concerns of a Weberian-influenced sociology are to be found in the centrality of "discipline" to "poststructuralist" analysis of "subjectless" power such as Foucault presents. Yet, it is as a "poststructuralist" that Foucault has been influential.

CIRCUITS OF POWER

Several researchers in the sociology of science have gone furthest in developing the insights that one might draw from poststructuralism into a workable approach to the sociology of power. (Interestingly, they do not themselves acknowledge that this is what they have done.) In a group that clusters around the work of Michel Callon, Bruno Latour, and their various colleagues, there has developed a highly distinctive sociology of *translation*.[2]

At the core of this way of viewing power is the insight that any generally applicable theory of power also must be a theory of organization. Indeed, more specifically, the theory of power in organizations orients towards the explanation of how organizational obedience is produced. Essential to an adequate conception of organization is an appropriate understanding of the concept of *agency*. Agency is achieved. It is a concept deliberately stretched to fit a number of different forms within its contours. Agency is something that is achieved by virtue of organization, whether of a human being's dispositional capacities or of a collective nature, in the sense usually reserved for the referent of "organizations." Organization is essential to the achievement of effective agency. It is the stabilizing and fixing factor in circuits of power. The point of using agency in this way is to avoid reductionism to either putative human agents or to certain conceptions of a structure that always determine. In the terms of organization analysis, such matters of determination are always almost contingent as an effect of organization.

A theory of power must look to the field of force in which power arrangements are fixed, coupled, and constituted so that, intentionally or not, certain 'nodal points' of practice are privileged in this unstable and shifting terrain. Better to think of power not as having two faces or three dimensions but as a process that may pass through distinct circuits of power and resistance. How these channels or circuits of power are fixed and reproduced is the crucial issue. A radical view of power thus would consist not in identifying what putative "real interests" are but in the strategies and practices by which, for instance, agents are recruited to views of their interests that align with the discursive field of force that the enrolling agency can construct. Part of this may, of course, consist precisely in claims made about the nature of interests, real or imagined. By contrast with a view of power that starts from a judgment about the adequacy of interests, the circuits framework provides a sense of a far less massive, oppressive, and prohibitive apparatus of power. Certainly, such negative effects can be secured by power, but nowhere near as easily as some "dominant ideology," "hegemonic" or "third dimensional" views would suggest.

Following Lockwood (1964), the nature of system and social integration can be conceptualized as distinct circuits of facilitative and dispositional power, respectively, to be seen in the context of their relationship to the episodic agency circuit of power (see Figure 1.1). Episodic power is the normal type of theoretical power that has captured the imagination from Hobbes to Dahl. It concerns agents getting other agents to do things that they would not otherwise do, deploying whatever resources and causal powers are available to them. Still, episodic power relations between agents are not the whole of the story. Power is also expressed through other circuits. These are circuits of facilitative and dispositional power, of social and system integration. The circuit of power passing through system integration is conceptualized in terms of techniques of discipline and production, whereas the circuit of social integration is conceptualized in terms of rules fixing relations of meaning and membership. Facilitative power, following the insights of theorists such as Parsons and Foucault, as well as the everyday insight that power can sometimes make things happen, looks at the way power is positive and can open social spaces and innovate rather than being merely the zero-sum of a set of antagonisms. Frequently, following Foucault, we would expect this to occur through new forms of disciplinary practice, often allied with new technologies, which serve to destabilize existing circuits of power, to transform existing relational fields, by empowering some and disempowering others.

To the extent that power remains purely episodic and does not enter into the other circuits of power, it can be argued that analysis does not need to be constructed in terms other than those of a modified version of the classical framework, where an A gets a B to do something that B would not otherwise have done. Contrary to Lukes (1974), it can be maintained that the unproblematic reproduction of power through a one-dimensional circuit of power does not restrict power. On the contrary, it maximizes it most effectively and economically. Power that makes only one circuit, that has no need to struggle against relations of meaning and membership or to innovate new disciplinary techniques of production or of force, is an economy of power. It is power that can efficiently deploy given capacities where resistance, if it too remains in that circuit, will be overwhelmed. Evidently, there is more at stake for resistance than for power as well as more incentive to switch out of the episodic, taken-for-granted circuit of power. Of course, incentive may provide motivation, but it will rarely be either the mother of invention or the reshaper of meaning—or reality would be far more fragile and problematic in its reproduction than it usually is.

Returning to the figure, pressures toward *institutional isomorphism* in the circuit of social integration will tend dispositionally to reproduce existing fields of force, whereas the circuit of system integration will tend to facilitate innovation in this field of force. These are only tendencies, however. Innovation and reproduction do not necessarily run only through these circuits. System integration, premised on techniques of production and discipline innovated under imperatives of competition and environmental efficiency, will tend to be a potent source of transformation and strain, opening up opportunities both for resistance under existing rules and for changes in the rules, changes that can create new agencies, new handicaps and advantages, and new pathways through existing fields of force. Before any such changes can take place, however, there has to be an effective organization on the part of any agencies that aspire to strategicality.

The notion of power being routed through distinct circuits makes one major break with the central narrative traditions of power analysis. It does not start from an assumption that what people say, say they think, or do is in some way "false" or "erroneous." Therefore, it brackets moral judgments about the adequacy of social action to live up to the moral ideas of social theory or theorists. Instead, it deals with empirical givens.

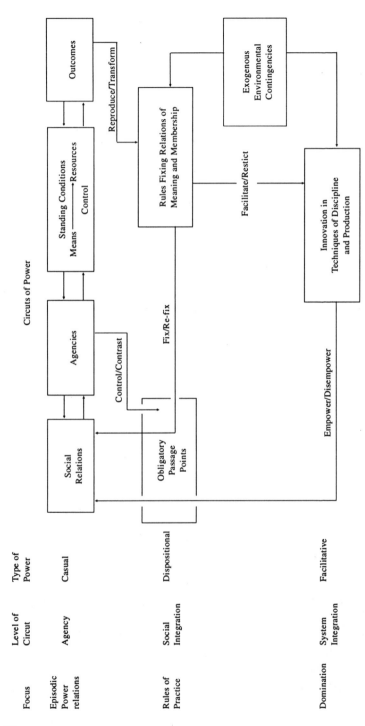

Figure 1.1. Representing the Circuts of Power

30

What does it entail, to deal with empirical givens but not simply to parrot whatever it is that those we talk to tell us? This, of course, is the great risk of all forms of ethnographic methodology: What is the status of the analyst's account of the accounts of others if it is ultimately grounded in the categories and sense-making procedures of these others? If the categories and consciousness of those in the empirical world is incorrigible then there is little to do other than to ignore them (as Dahl effectively recommends) or to base one's theoretical story on a retailing and retelling of the stories that one finds in this world, with no stable arbiter of falsehood and error, unless one adopts an arbitrary standard of what is true and false (which is the destination to which Lukes leads us).

Can the narrative of theory be brought into a dialogue with the narrative structure of everyday life, rather than working against its grain, ignoring it, or consigning it to falsehood? Can the narrative of theory take the narratives of everyday life as a serious object of analysis, and not simply treat them as the reflexes of stooges, dupes, or fools? The first step in orienting to the narratives of everyday life in this way is to listen to what people say. Not necessarily to retell it in exactly those terms but to enquire into how it would be possible for them to say that. What kinds of assumptions in what types of possible world could produce those accounts? The general thrust of the argument can be seen best when, to pardon a pun, it is at work. The context in which most work gets done is organizational; therefore, the choice of organizational work is the topic for the remainder of this chapter.

LANGUAGE IN USE: NARRATIVES AT WORK

The analysis of language in use need be neither a means for displaying a technical competence by both analyst and speaker (as Boden, 1993, does to brilliant effect) nor the authenticating frame of an ethnographic study, for which the members' own stories (usually, but not always, boys' own stories) provide "local color" and detail. Whereas the former typifies "conversational analysis" concerns in ethnomethodology, (to which Heritage, 1984, pp. 232-292, provides an excellent introduction), the latter characterizes researchers with a concern for verisimilitude, such as Nicholls and Benyon (1977). For the former, the focus on language use is frequently an end in itself in order to research those pervasive mechanisms through which much of the everyday work of conversation takes place (e.g., Sacks, 1972; Schegloff, 1968). In the ethnographic approach, language is more or less transparent; it reveals a reality outside itself to which it refers and defers. Its stories are the stories of everyday life trimmed and shaped into narrative form by the skilled ethnographer/sociologist/storyteller.

For the conversation analyst, following on from Garfinkel (1967), language primarily reveals the order contained within its use. Its narrative is one not of content but of form. Whereas the ethnographers address language use as a mirror on social reality, the conversation analysts may often be said to regard it as social reality per se. Not always, of course: It is the case that many subsequent ethnomethodologists have used strictly conversational analytical techniques to study substantive aspects of power—such as Molotch and Boden's (1986) analysis of the Watergate tapes; McHoul's analyses of how classroom authority is maintained (1978) or sexuality achieved (1987), and Zimmerman and West's (1975, 1983) analysis of gender differences, and power, in talk.

What McHoul (1987) has termed an "anti-realist approach" can be used to complement both ethnography and formal conversation analysis. It is an approach that addresses language use as an important medium and outcome of the accomplishment of both social structure and social action. McHoul (1987, p. 366) identifies the key terms thus: "Realism is the view that language means what it means by mapping on to a real state of affairs that is available to us through non-linguistic means. Our statements receive their sense, on this theory, from the conditions under which they are true."

Realist assumptions have been apparent in both the functionalist and the Marxist traditions of analysis. Correspondence is at work in both the narratives of revelation and those of concealment. In Marxist-influenced accounts, the world corresponds to its depiction in theory only through a discourse of concealment. The mechanisms of concealment reside in and are orchestrated through lay language, through the concepts of mundane consciousness and the inability of practical reason, as normally constituted, to pierce through occlusion, opacity, and false consciousness. Simultaneously, in this position, Herculean claims are made for the clarifying power of theoretical reason. By contrast, theory can be made to correspond with (a particularly truncated view of) the observable empirical world, as in Dahl's methodology, where the theory of language and the language of theory are restricted to what can be made to correspond in terms of some more or less sophisticated licensing of empiricist method with behavioral and positivist protocols.

Narrative is treated as either concealment or revelation in, respectively, Western Marxism and functionalism. By contrast, to treat narrative in terms of neither concealment nor revelation is to assume an anti-realist relation between the language of stories and the world rather than a relation that is realist. A realist relationship between these terms is invariably based on the assumption that some correspondence principle governs their inter-relation. Analysis constructed on the lines of an anti-realist, anti-correspondence principle begins to take a distinct approach to the stories of everyday life and the stories of theory. Both are to be interrogated for the "impersonality" of their discourses and their operation, for the specifics or "local particulars" of their operation. In terms of language that is not formally produced as social theory, as a specialist gloss on ordinary sayings and doings, one can be said to address the "material word" in the "material world" where it is put to work. Much of this work is done in and through the organization-specific production of language. And this language is a language of power, in which, according to anti-realism, language means what it means by virtue of conventions concerning its use. Our statements receive their sense from the conditions under which they can be properly uttered. Although this rules out an appeal to a determining link between language and "reality," it nevertheless, and importantly, employs a weak kind of verification, for it appeals instead to the practical and technical accomplishment by which the sense of specific relations gets to be fixed, maintained, and changed. It is not just the formal skills of the hearers and speakers that produce social sense; although it is a technical accomplishment, it is not only that. On the contrary, one must listen to what people say and the terms in which they say it.

Conceived in this way, the analysis of language use in organizations can address the major analytical problem in the study of power. After Dahl's (1968) definition of power as an A getting a B to do something that they would not otherwise have done, this became centered on the debate initiated by Bachrach and Baratz (1962, 1970) on the questions of nondecision making and non-issues. At its core was the concern to distinguish a "false" consensus on, for instance, goals or values from one that was "genuine." Power is frequently, but not necessarily always, a discursive phenomenon. When it is a discursive phenomenon, it can be as neither transparency nor veil but as a materially structured reality. Language and its socially available categories of rational action pre-structure the field of power while not determining its outcomes.

LANGUAGE ANALYSIS AND POWER: AN EXEMPLAR

Irrespective of the approach, if power is to be conceived discursively, in and through language, for organization analysis, then some limitations of its specifically organizational location, in naturally occurring conversations, must be noted.

First, there must be some story that is interesting enough to bear retelling. This is the fundamental ground rule of ethnography: That the stuff of everyday life can be made as rivetingly narrative as the plots and scripts of the dramatic arts. Second, particularly where one attends to the "naturally occurring" conversations of everyday life, there are some practical organization problems attendant on its recording. These are particularly acute on construction sites, the research setting that these data report. Construction sites are very noisy, very dangerous, very mobile settings in which people are rarely stationary. It is physically very difficult, without extremely sophisticated bugging equipment (which is not to be recommended on ethical grounds), to tape-record naturally occurring conversations in work settings such as construction sites, at least out on the site itself. In addition, in almost every significant-sized organization, it will often prove difficult to gain access to its inner sanctums and circles. As is well known, it is far easier to access, relatively, the less powerful than those who are more powerful. Constraints that developed from these factors meant that the data collection had to occur in an office rather than on site, and in the site organization rather than elsewhere—in the borough corporation or the contractor's head office. I did not notice these constraints much at the time.

When I started to do empirical research on construction sites in the early 1970s I had a small portable tape recorder that had a built-in microphone. I had permission to use the machine but I did not want to make it too conspicuous that I was doing so. I sat in the corner of a room measuring about 8 m long by 4 m wide (26 ft by 13 ft) at a desk with building materials and documents piled up on it. I looked much like any other building worker around the office. My garb and appearance was appropriate to the site conditions: blue jeans, black donkey-jacket, black Wellington boots, and modishly long hair for the times. Much of the time I appeared to be almost "part of the furniture," just another young man on site. There was one difference. I had the tape recorder going.

Why did I choose the office setting from all the possibilities on the busy site? Well, partially because the actual immobility of a room as a locale enabled taping. Once I had made the decision to tape data then I had to find a locale in which the technology would function efficiently. The room was the project manager's office, one in which there was considerable traffic. It was also the locale for site meetings. Site meetings held in this office became the major source of data—not entirely, because other kinds of data were used as well. Site meetings were particularly important, however.

Much more important than the practical problems encountered in data collection are some analytical aspects of interpretation. To what extent is access to the reality of power and organizations possible through the analysis of language. Conversational analysis would suggest that one could make access through studying phenomena such as turn-taking, closures, and interruptions, formulating the various kinds of rules that structure the form of the content (Schegloff, 1968; Sacks, 1972, would be some key references here). Take, for instance, these data in which there is a discussion between two people, PW and Ray:

PW: I'm going to write a letter, you know, item by item, what I've got Ken [Assistant Measurement Engineer] doing at the moment, I roughed it out on there, an enlarged vertical scale, so you can see what you're talking about, a section through the site of each grid line/
Ray: Yeah/
PW: with the basements plotted in, and the ground levels as known/
Ray: Yeah/
PW: and then plot in our bases, and soon as you do that you start seeing that, we haven't gone down deep as they're saying, eh, if you look at the picture I drew yesterday, said he, said he [searching] . . . this hole here, this inspector's office base, that they looked at the clay, we took a check all around it yesterday, and in fact, just around the one hole,
Ray: Yeah
PW: that sandy clay was up and down anything/
Ray: Yeah/
PW: up to/
Ray: Yeah/
PW: six hundred mills around it, so we take the average, ninety eight one five-O.
Ray: Yeah/
PW: take the six hundred and ten that we've got to go into it, gives us an average level of ninety seven five forty/
Ray: Yeah.

So far, Ray's contribution to the conversation has been "Yeah." He does improvise further on in the conversation, he says "Aye" and toward the end of the conversation he makes one or two interlocutions. Who is exercising power here? Once we know that PW is the project manager and that Ray is the site foreman, do we really need to make reference to a linguistic text that tells us, in a circumlocutive way, what should be already evident and apparent from the organization chart? Of course, if the real world of organizations looked just like the organization chart, we would never need to do fieldwork, so it is as well to have empirical data that can, in principle, disconfirm what other texts might suggest. In this instance, it is relatively unproblematic to see it as an occasion in which Ray is offering narrative prompts to the continuity of what is effectively a monologue by PW. It turned out to be a significant aspect of everyday politics on the site, however (see Clegg, 1975).

POWER AND PRACTICAL REASONING: THE INCLEMENCY RULE

On construction sites, at least in the United Kingdom, joiners have as part of their contract the statement that they shall not work in "inclement weather." Now, that sounds fine, of course, but clearly there is no operational definition that constitutes inclemency—something I learned in an interesting and roundabout way when I was working as a laborer on site. Normally, it is obvious; where it is not, "managerial prerogative" ordinarily prevails. One day we were out on site and the ganger (the man nominated as the work unit's "leader") said, "Ay up lads, 'appen it's coming on a bit inclement," holding up his finger to the wind as he said so. We looked up and stopped and looked around and some said, "Aye 'appen it is." We downed tools and went back to the hut where we started a game of cards and brewed up some tea. After about 10 minutes or so the site foreman came down and said, "What you buggers doing, you should be out on site." The gangerman responded, "Joiners don't work in inclement weather hey, it's come on inclement." The foreman went away and got the project manager who came down about 10 or 15 minutes later. A verbal altercation followed, there was some degree of negotiation, and eventually sheepishly we went out on site. It was drizzling slightly on site. Now the first time this happened I did not think much of it; I did not ask anything about it; I just thought, "OK, I know joiners don't like getting wet and they don't work when its raining." It happened again 2 or 3 days later. I began to wonder what was going on because this time it was hardly raining at all. With a wink and a sly look the gangerman said, "Hey up, seems like it's a bit inclement lads" and we trooped off. This went on several times over a period of 2 or 3 weeks.

What I believe was happening was the following: The job was organized so that the joiners were making a very poor bonus. A joiner's wage packet comprises several aspects: an attendance allowance, money for being there that includes a cost for traveling to work and also a standard flat rate wage, but the bulk of the increment is a piece-rate group bonus that depends on the amount of shutterage (the amount of framework constructed for concrete to be poured into) that the joiners can make per meter over a period of time.

What the joiners were doing was to use the inclemency rule in an ironical but quasi-legitimate way. The pressure was on an incompetent management to organize the job more efficiently so that materials and supplies would come on site on time. If this had been the case, they could have worked harder so that they would have earned more bonus.

In power terms, the "inclemency rule" is of considerable interest. Marxist writers such as Burawoy (1979) have talked about the games that workers play in organizations as a way of making out and creating space outside managerial surveillance. The joiners, although playing similar kinds of games, were doing so not to make out and create space outside managerial control but to put pressure on the management to increase control and thus more efficiently exploit them. That is a very strong kind of power. It is one in which subjects happily collude in intensifying their subjection. What it points to is that this power is not simply discursive although approached through a discursive analysis. Consequently, the text of the everyday-life world does not stand in some necessary relationship to truth and falsehood, to revelation and concealment. Instead, questions of power in that situation are tied up with systems of wage relations, of social relations of production (cf. Abercrombie et al., 1980). The discipline of power there is not purely a discursive phenomenon but resides in the normalization of those circuits of power through which power ordinarily proceeds. Wage-payment systems thus have a key role to play in this.

One can point to discursive instances of power on the site such as a foreman issuing orders (in a more developed version of Wittgenstein's, 1968, example of the laborer and builder at the beginning of *The Blue and Brown Books*). Although these are a form of power, they are not the most significant. It is not how power is normally done. It gets to be done rather more through the structuration of things such as wage payment systems, which are nondiscursive phenomena, and through traditional occupational practices.

POWER AND ISSUES

Site meetings represent an excellent opportunity for one interested in power and organizations, because their point is to discuss issues raised in terms of the ongoing nature of the project. In particular, they are oriented to negotiating and resolving the frequently conflicting interpretations of contractual documents associated with the site. The contract, the bill of works, concerned the design statement and its accomplishment. What interested me in these meetings were the opportunities for studying power as it is "normally" constituted in the routine processes of the site organization. That was an example of the Dahlian "A getting B to do something that they wouldn't otherwise do" model. It became apparent not only from theory but also from simple observation in the construction site setting that one really did not get much purchase on the reality of power and organization by just going and watching people doing things. Theoretically, the most important kinds of power were already constituted in those occasions when A's didn't have to get B's to do things because B's would do those sorts of things anyway. Simple empiricism would not be sufficient.

With respect to the empirical setting, what became clear over a period of some weeks was the way in which the issues that were occurring for contestation and conflict, the issues over which the A-B type power plays occurred, were not wholly random, unrelated, independent, or contingent phenomena. They had a narrative rationality that inhered within the basic framework of the construction site.

A construction site is not a single organization but a complex play of interorganizational relations. There is the contractor's organization; the client organization that in this case was the borough corporation of a northern town; the suppliers; the subcontractors; the tradesmen; the local police (who would be there to handle disruptions to traffic flow, for example); demolition firms; and very many more. It was important in understanding this very complex pattern of interorganizational relationships to appreciate how a single discourse, a single set of texts, constituted it. The constitutive texts of the construction site were the contractual documents, the bill of works, the documents that were the legal bidding basis for the competitive tender.

The formal literature of architectural practice contains many injunctions. For instance, in the Royal Institute of British Architects (RIBA) *Handbook* can be found the injunction: "The system requires that before bills of quantities are prepared full working drawings shall be completed." According to the RIBA *Handbook,* these drawings "will embody final decisions upon every matter related to design specification, construction and cost and full design of every part and component of the building." After this instruction, in heavy type comes the warning "that any future change in location, size, shape or cost after this time will result in abortive work."

In practice, the principles of the RIBA account seemed inapplicable in the letter of the text. Such a formal representation did not account for the documents' inherent indexicality. Documents must be read and interpreted to be used as documents. To say that they are indexical simply means that their sense is not evident, there is no notional meaning, no one correct sense that inheres in them. The sense of the contractual documents can only be read in terms of the constitution of the meaning of those documents in particular situated actions in particular contexts.

From the limited degree of observation of construction sites that organization researchers have made, an important finding is the high degrees of conflict and high degrees of ambiguity, often concerning the contract itself, that characterize them. In the organization theory literature this is often expressed in terms of notions of uncertainty, where the uncertainty is treated as a contingency, sometimes even one that is climatically based. For instance, rain or snow may be seen as a climatic variation that introduces uncertainty. This is a comparatively insular view of the world given the range of climatic variations within which construction sites routinely occur. A more sophisticated view of contingency is required.

Where the contractual documents specify every variable in the building process, then the normal mode of rationality, particularly for the contracting company, is to try to negotiate or renegotiate the contract. The contract is the only variable not specified by the contract. The kinds of issues that were emerging for the exercise of power in particular pieces of power play had an underlying mode of rationality.

Very often construction companies will tender for a contract in order to keep plant, machinery, and employees who were a stable part of the core labor force employed. Often they would do so where the contribution to profit might be very low, or where it might even be negative, on a job that was losing money. One reason for doing this is because there is always the possibility of exploiting the indexicality of the contractual documents to renegotiate them on any occasion that occurred. The construction site materials display an exquisite temporality on site; one constituted in terms of events "before" and "after" normal clay. Normal clay became a benchmark issue around which all the other issues were collected.

I had better explain what normal clay was. The documents contained instructions to excavate 3 m (almost 10 ft) into clay; they also contained, elsewhere, instructions to excavate into sandy stony clay. The possibility, of course, is that 3 m into clay and into sandy stony clay do not coincide. The construction company's argument was that they did not. Regrettably, when the clerk of works was not present, they had to excavate extra soil for which they expected a substantial payment for the extra work involved. That became the issue around which all the subsequent issues began to emerge. The issues were, on the one side, the construction company attempting to exploit systematically any forms of equivocality that they could indexically constitute out of the documents. On the other side the architect, representing the corporation, was attempting to preserve the integrity of the design and of the contractual relationships at all costs. The participants in this were the project manager of the construction company, the client organization, and various subcontractors.

NARRATIVES: TOWARD A STORY

One thing that became apparent from this empirical work was that if power involves concrete decision making, then one problem with the social world is that it is rather like Jean-Luc Godard's view of cinema, a subversion of the classical Aristotelian form of narrative. Films may have beginnings, middles, and ends but they are not necessarily nor recognizably found in that order. Most of the time one only sees middles, one rarely sees beginnings, and ends are not always what they seem. It is quite difficult to constitute actual beginnings and very difficult to achieve closure, because episodes often move out of one arena and into another. Rather than located in decision making, power was found in the play of the discourse, in the way in which the available categories for talk in particular contexts lodged within a mode of rationality.

Analytically, one needs to move in a full circle in analyzing power and language to focus on not only the language of power but also the power of the language of power. Part of the problem with power resides in the "problem of power" itself, elaborated from a certain view of power as foundational, as a premise from which subsequent debate developed. One might want to suggest that it is not really possible to take the simple A-B notion of power as a foundation on which to build a second and a third dimension (in which the latter usually ended up being an analysis in terms of ideological illusion, implicit or explicit to notions of hegemony in a more or less Gramscian mode). Such an argument, in Lukes (1974) for instance, seeks analytically to build "structure" out of the foundations of "action."

The initial and problematic narrative framing the theory of power constrained the way in which its subsequent debate could develop. Only a certain kind of space, only a certain kind of play for innovation, became available in that debate. What Bachrach and Baratz (1962), Lukes (1974), and others did was to run up against the limits of the language that formulated that conceptualization of power. The injunction of Wittgenstein (1968) to study the meaning in use has been understood cross-sectionally, because of the influence of ordinary language philosophy. Another way might be to think of it as a historical injunction. Consequently, one can look at the development of an intellectual discourse about power as something that has developed, perhaps rather like a Foucauldian genealogy, from a causal, mechanistic, and individualistic conceptualization in its genesis from Hobbes to the present day. The problem of "the problem of power" could then be related to that initial conceptualization of power as if it were something that was wholly causal, mechanistic, and individualistic. The language game extending this discourse of power, one could argue, has thus become condemned to tracing the limits and frame of an originating discourse of sovereign assumptions (Clegg, 1989).

The root of this modern analysis of power began with Hobbes. Hobbes attempted to justify a narrative in which order articulated around the architectonic powers of the sovereign. At first, this was literally in and through the body of the monarch as the sovereign subject ensuring the maintenance of a discursive community of subjects. The original frontispiece of *Leviathan* (Hobbes, 1962) even represented this emblematically: the huge figure of the monarch constituted by the tiny figures of his subjects was ordered into an overwhelming representation of corporeal awesomeness. Such a representation was a striking example of a pure symbolic logic given to a largely illiterate population.

In the 20th century Hobbes's metaphorical complexity was reduced to the wholly unironical impulses of a behaviorally rationalized concept of causality. Transparent empiricism, allied to the protocols of behavioral science, had triumphed. It was only with the critique of Bachrach and Baratz, founded in "intentionality," that the modern narrative of concealment began to unravel toward its hegemonic end in a conception of "real interests." Had one wanted to address the narrative of everyday life on the building site in terms of this narrative trajectory, one would have been practicing a way of not listening to what people said. Behind the expression of the inclemency rule lay an interest in work. Was this interest in some way false, untrue, unreal? Only if one approached the articulation of language from preestablished positions designed neither to listen to those stories that people themselves have to say nor to be reflexively aware of the narratives through which one makes one's address.

In social research, a suspicion toward narrative is necessary. However, the narratives that one should suspect are not so much those of everyday life, which, although clearly not irremediable, do work in context. It is this work in context to which one should attend in analysis. Moreover, ideally, one should seek to engage this work in context, to engage with the accounts of everyday life. Mundane social practices warrant less suspicion of their narrative practices whereas more circumspection is required of those theories that would demean, ironicize, or mock the stories by which people ordinarily live their lives. To repeat the central message: These do work in context. If one is to be suspicious, perhaps it should be of those social theories that seek to subsume everyday accounts to their overwhelming narrative. In contemporary power analysis this has been a narrative of concealment, as a refraction of orthodox functionalism with its narrative of revelation. Neither revelation nor concealment is a necessary narrative practice. Neither recommend themselves for social analysis that seeks to engage with the empirical world.

If one is to make a practice of suspicion, I would recommend a wariness with respect to the grand narrative themes that have organized the modern experience. This suspicion, born of the postmodern condition, might usefully be coupled with a respect for the stories that one finds in the mundane sites of the social world. Yet, respect does not mean surrendering to their narrative any more than to those of grand theory. These mundane sites should no more be taken at face value than should the meta-narratives of modernity. Instead, in both instances, one should look to an analysis of the way in which the language game and its moves serve to secure and stabilize circuits of power: circuits both of power in theory "proper" and of power in the practice of everyday life "outside theory." Of course, for some, theory is the mundane practice of everyday life. Here, then, it is even more important that the dialogue between theory per se and other practices of life occur. Otherwise, one claims a position of privilege from which only ex cathedra judgments of revelation or concealment could be anticipated. By contrast, this chapter recommends that one might seek to address how such judgments are possible in theory and how, in practice, one can attend seriously to what it is people say they are doing in the business of everyday life.

NOTES

1. Lentricchia (1988, p. 60) has suggested that, in some respects, the Foucauldian account of "discipline" is not incompatible with a theory of "practical capitalism," particularly in its

implications for an understanding of Taylorism and its practices of "drill." Under "scientific management," surveillance comes to be based less on a knowledge of preexisting rationalities and more on the imposition of new rationalities based on a knowledge abstracted from the contexts in which its effects are held accountable, in the separation of "conception" and "execution." However, it might be more appropriate to regard this less as a theory of "practical capitalism," as Lentricchia suggests, than as a theory of practical managerial control, control that can be relatively indifferent to the economic system within which it occurs. It is doubtful if Marxist bridges would remain useful conduits if the specifically "capitalist" nature of the terrain were challenged and found wanting.

2. For a good example of the genre see Callon (1986).

REFERENCES

Abercrombie, N., Hill, S., & Turner, B. (1980). *The dominant ideology thesis*. London: Allen & Unwin.

Anderson, P. (1976). *Considerations on Western Marxism*. London: New Left Books.

Bachrach, P., & Baratz, M. (1962). Two faces of power. *American Political Science Review*, *56*, 947-952.

Bachrach, P., & Baratz, M. (1963). Decisions and nondecisions: An analytical framework. *American Political Science Review*, *57*, 641-651.

Bachrach, P., & Baratz, M. (1970). *Power and poverty: Theory and practice*. Oxford, UK: Oxford University Press.

Ball, T. (1978). Two concepts of coercion. *Theory and Society*, *5*(1): 97-112.

Bauman, Z. (1977). *Sociam: The active Utopia*. London: Allen & Unwin.

Blum, A. F., & McHugh, P. (1971). The social ascription of motive. *American Sociological Review*, *35*, 98-109.

Boden, D. (1993). *The business of talk*. Cambridge: Polity.

Burawoy, M. (1979). *Manufacturing consent: Changes in the labor process under monopoly capitalism*. Chicago: University of Chicago Press.

Callon, M. (1986). Some elements of a sociology of translation: Domestication of the scallops and the fishermen of St. Briene Bay. In J. Law (Ed.), *Power, action and belief: A new sociology of knowledge?* London: Routledge and Kegan Paul.

Clegg, S. R. (1975). *Power, rule and domination: A critical and empirical understanding of power in sociological theory and organization life*. London: Routledge and Kegan Paul.

Clegg, S. R. (1979). *The theory of power and organization*. London: Routledge & Kegan Paul.

Clegg, S. R. (1989). *Frameworks of power*. London: Sage.

Clegg, S. R., Boreham, P., & Dow, G. (1986). *Class, politics and the economy*. London: Routledge & Kegan Paul.

Clegg, S. R., Dow, G., & Boreham, P. (Eds.). (1983). *The state, class and the recession*. London: Croom Helm.

Dahl, R. A. (1957). The concept of power. *Behavioural Science*, *2*, 201-5.

Dahl, R. A. (1958). Critique of the ruling elite model. *American Political Science Review*, *52*, 463-469.

Dahl, R. A. (1961). *Who governs? Democracy and power in an American city*. New Haven: Yale University Press.

Dahl, R. A. (1968). Power. In *International Encyclopedia of the Social Sciences* (pp. 405-415). New York: Macmillan.

Dandekker, C. (1991). *Surveillance, power and modernity.* Cambridge: Polity.

Durkheim, E. (1964). *The division of labour.* New York: Free Press.

Feher, F., Heller, A., & Markus, G. (1983). *Dictatorship over needs.* Oxford: Blackwell.

Foucault, M. (1977). *Discipline and punish: The birth of the prison* (Trans. Alan Sheridan). Harmondsworth, UK: Penguin.

Frey, F. W. (1971). Comment: "On issues and non-issues in the study of power." *American Political Science Review, 65,* 1081-1101.

Garfinkel, H. (1967). *Studies in ethnomethodology.* Englewood Cliffs, NJ: Prentice Hall.

Heritage, J. (1984). *Garfinkel and ethnomethodology.* Cambridge: Polity.

Hobbes, T. (1962). *Leviathan* (Ed. M. Oateshott). Originally published 1651. London: Collier-Macmillan.

Horton, J. (1966). Order and conflict theories of social problems as competing ideologies. *American Journal of Sociology, 71,* 701-13.

Hume, D. (1902). *An enquiry concerning human understanding.* Originally published 1777. Oxford, UK: Clarendon Press.

Hunter, F. (1953). *Community power structure.* Chapel Hill: University of North Carolina Press.

Laclau, E., & Mouffe, C. (1985). *Hegemony and socialist strategy.* London: Verso.

Lentricchia, F. (1988). *Ariel and the police.* Madison, WI: University of Wisconsin Press.

Lockwood, D. (1964). Social integration and system integration. In G. K. Zollschan & W. Hirsch (Eds.), *Explorations in social change* (pp. 244-257). London: Routledge and Kegan Paul.

Lukes, S. (1974). *Power: A radical view.* London: Macmillan.

Lukes, S. (1977). *Essays in social theory.* London: Macmillan.

Marx, K. (1976). *Capital* (vol. 1). Original English edition published 1887. Harmondsworth, UK: Penguin.

McHoul, A. (1978). The organization of turns at formal talk in the classroom. *Language in Society, 7,* 183-213.

McHoul, A. (1987). Discussion note: Language and institutional reality: Reply and response. *Organization Studies, 8,* 363-374.

Merton, R. K. (1940). Bureaucratic structure and personality. *Social Forces, 18,* 560-568.

Merton, R. K. (1968). *Social theory and social structure.* New York: Free Press.

Mills, C. W. (1940). Situated actions and vocabularies of motive. *American Sociological Review, 5,* 904-13.

Mills, C. W. (1956). *The power elite.* Oxford, UK: Oxford University Press.

Molotch, H., & Boden, D. (1986). Talking social structure: Discourse domination and the Watergate hearings. *American Sociological Review, 50,* 237-286.

Newton, K. (1975). Community politics and decision making: The American experience and its lessons. In K. Newton (Ed.), *Essays on the study of urban politics* (pp. 1-24). London: Croom Helm.

Nicholls, T., & Benyon, H. (1977). *Living with capitalism: Class relations and the modern factory.* London: Routledge and Kegan Paul.

O'Connor, J. (1973). *The fiscal crisis of the state.* New York: St. Martins Press.

Parsons, T. (1937). *The structure of social action.* New York: McGraw-Hill.

Parsons, T. (1967). *Sociological theory and modern society.* New York: Free Press.

Presthus, R. E. (1964). *Men at the top.* Oxford, UK: Oxford University Press.

Russel, B. (1938). *Power: A new social analysis.* London: Allen & Unwin.

Sacks, H. (1972). An initial investigation of the usability of conversational data for doing sociology. In D. Sudnow (Ed.), *Studies in social interaction* (pp. 31-74). New York: Free Press.

Saunders, P. (1979). *Urban politics*. Harmondsworth, UK: Penguin.

Schattschneider, E. E. (1960). *The semi-sovereign people: A realist's view of democracy in America*. New York: Holt, Rinehart & Winston.

Schegloff, E. A. (1968). Sequencing in conversational openings. *American Anthropologist, 70*, 1075-1095.

Simmel, G. (1900). *The philosophy of money*. London: Routledge and Kegan Paul.

Stouffer, S. et al. (1949). *The American soldier* (Vol. 1). Princeton, NJ: Princeton University Press.

Weber, M. (1976). *The Protestant ethic and the spirit of capitalism*. London: Allen & Unwin.

Weber, M. (1978). *Economy and society: An outline of interpretive sociology* (Ed. G. Roth & C. Wittich). 2 Volumes. Berkeley, CA: University of California Press.

Whyte, W. F. (1943). *Street corner society*. Chicago, IL: University of Chicago Press.

Wittgenstein, L. (1968). *Philosophical investigations* (Trans. G. E. M. Anscombe). Oxford, UK: Blackwell.

Willis, P. (1977). *Learning to labour: How working class kids get working class jobs*. Farnborough, UK: Saxon House.

Wolfinger, R. E. (1971a). Nondecisions and the study of local politics. *American Political Science Review, 65*, 1063-1080.

Wolfinger, R. E. (1971b). Rejoinder to Frey's "Comment." *American Political Science Review, 66*, 1102-1104.

Wrong, D. H. (1961). The oversocialized conception of man in modern sociology. *American Sociological Review, 26*, 183-193.

Wrong, D. (1979). *Power: Its forms, bases and uses*. Oxford, UK: Blackwell.

Zimmerman, D., & West, C. (1975). Sex roles, interruptions and silences in conversations. In B. Thorne & N. Henley (Eds.), *Language and sex: Difference and dominance* (pp. 105-129). Rowley, MA: Newbury House.

Zimmerman, D., & West, C. (1983). Small insults: A study of interruptions and cross-sex conversations between unacquainted persons. In B. Thorne, C. Kramarae, & N. Henley (Eds.), *Language, gender and society* (pp. 102-117). Rowley, MA: Newbury House.

PART II

NARRATIVE AND CONTROL IN
DIVERSE SOCIAL CONTEXTS

Chapter 2

FAMILY STORYTELLING AS A STRATEGY OF SOCIAL CONTROL

Kristin M. Langellier and Eric E. Peterson

FAMILIES TELL STORIES: about the time Lee's smiling sister caught his line-drive whiffle ball in her new braces, or the day Debbie and her brother started a lunch counter on the lawn when their parents were gone and sold all the food in the refrigerator to the neighborhood children at bargain prices; about how Michael Jordan sticks out his tongue when he concentrates—just like his father; about Aunt Helen's near miscarriage of twins in a taxi cab; and about the loss of relatives in the Holocaust. Families tell stories of ancestors and the antics of childhood, of courtships and childbirths and deaths, of family characters and family characteristics, of lineage and legacies and losses, of skeletons and scapegoats.

Family stories may emerge in bits and pieces or in lengthy genealogies. They may be recounted casually and unreflectively over household chores; sorted through passionately and thoughtfully over long nights of kitchen talk; performed ritually and repeatedly at funerals, weddings, birthday parties, and family reunions; and confided secretly, one-on-one, never to be retold. Not confined to family storytelling rituals, they may also emerge in conversations with friends; in therapists' offices and self-help groups; in letters to Dear Abby; in celebrity interviews and political speeches; in organizational networks, classrooms, and courtrooms; and in nonfiction, novels, and plays. Whether dimly remembered and mute, told aloud with pleasure and show, confided discreetly, or kept secret, Elizabeth Stone (1988, pp. 6-7) asserts that all people carry family stories "under their skin" borne variously as weightless pleasures or painful tattoos. These family stories last not because they are well-formed stories, although they may be artful constructions, nor because they are well-performed, although they may be very entertaining; they last because "in ways large and small they matter" (Stone, 1988, p. 5).

In this chapter we explore "the ways large and small" that telling family stories matters. To date, family storytelling has received little attention from communication scholars, although researchers have investigated family communication (as reviewed in Bochner, 1976, and Bochner & Eisenberg, 1987), and researchers have also investigated storytelling in numerous contexts (as reviewed in Langellier, 1989). The phenomenon of family storytelling challenges the disciplinary fragmentation of communication studies into groups concerned with specialized bodies of knowledge. The family involved in storytelling exemplifies the process and structure of interpersonal and small-group communication, the information exchange and network of organizational communication, the generation and evolution of intercultural communication, the creativity and force of poetic and rhetorical communication, and so on. Family storytelling transects the disciplinary structure of academic knowledge because it cannot be subsumed as an object of analysis under any one group. Nor can we bifurcate family storytelling by allocating the study of family to one group of scholars and the study of storytelling to another group of scholars. For storytelling is a primary way that families are produced, maintained, and perhaps transformed. As Stone notes, "the family is always jerry-built and has to be reconstituted and reimagined every generation" (1988, p. 40) and "what blood does not provide, narrative can" (1988, p. 70).

Our approach to family storytelling views storytelling as a discursive practice that produces familial culture. Family stories are strategies carried out in diverse situations and circumstances by a multiplicity of participants. Thus, what we commonly call "the family" is not a naturally-occurring biological phenomenon but one type of small-group culture strategically produced in discourse such as family stories. Such family stories are not simple representations of preexisting family history; nor is family storytelling mere aesthetic performance or socio-emotional release by family members. Rather, family storytelling names practices of social control. Stories and storytelling both generate and reproduce "the family" by legitimating meanings and power relations that privilege, for example, parents over children, males over females, and the white, middle-class family over alternative family structures. At the same time that family storytelling participates in the social control of the family, it also can foster resistance and tactics that contest dominant meanings and power relations.

Only by considering its situated performance, that is, family storytelling as a strategic practice rather than family stories as artifacts or texts,
can the nature and function of family storytelling be specified. Our argument
proceeds in two parts. First, we develop the constructs of family and storytelling within a critical theory of discourse. Next, we elaborate a multileveled strategic model of storytelling, illustrating the model with storytelling examples.

THE FAMILY

Conceptualizing "the family" presents particular difficulties because as
a concept it has no common empirical referent (Settles, 1987). To most
people "the family" is represented either by their own real family or by
that stereotypic ideal—both theological and romantic—articulated everywhere in the media, politics and government policies, law, religion, medicine,
therapy, and the social sciences. Feminist and critical theorists (Barrett &
McIntosh, 1982; Osmond, 1987; Thorne & Yalom, 1981) note repeatedly
the strategic use of "the family" to promote political positions, illustrated
most readily by conservatives' pro-family rhetoric. Thus, to conceptualize
the family involves at the outset ideological critique as well as analysis
of the family as an economic institution, a social arrangement of gender
and generation, and the lived experiences of *doing family*. Because we
cannot assume the family "as it is," that is, uncritically, we begin this section
by delineating the assumptions of the normative family and its critiques
according to five interrelated concerns.

THE MONOLITHIC FAMILY

The assumption of the monolithic family privileges the contemporary
nuclear family united by bonds of love, sheltered in a private home, and
organized by the sexual division of labor with a breadwinner husband and
full-time wife and mother. The monolithic family projects a singular,
unchanging, homogeneous, and pervasive norm despite the fact that few
U.S. households actually resemble this form. Feminist scholars in particular (Thorne, 1981) critique the monolithic family as a natural phenomenon,
biologically determined, and ordered according to the immutable family
and sex roles of structural-functionalism. In contrast to the monolithic
family as a universal and timeless given, feminist critiques emphasize the

family as a particular social and political organization of sexuality, reproduction, motherhood, the sexual division of labor, and the gender system
itself. The ideology of The Family reproduces the asymmetrical division
of labor in the workplace and within the home that necessitates the oppression of women.

GENDER AND THE FAMILY

The monolithic family structures the subordination of women within a
sex/gender system and children within a generation system. It ignores
cultural and historical variations in the organization of families by sex and
age as they derive from particular kinship relations and economic factors.
Again it is feminist critics who have engaged in the structural analysis of
the sex/gender system whereby culture maps distinct ideological constructs
of family and sex roles onto biological raw material of sex and procrea-
tion. Feminist analyses specify how various sex/gender systems socially
create sexual identity (Coward, 1983), allocate the sexual division of labor
in the family (Eichler, 1981), regulate sexuality into "compulsory heterosexuality" and marriage (Rich, 1980), organize such things as the "maternal instinct" and pronatalism (Trebilcot, 1983), and reproduce mothering
(Chodorow, 1978). Thus, the family is exposed as a social and political
organization of sex and gender that varies cross-culturally and historically.

GENERATION AND THE AHISTORICAL FAMILY

The monolithic family is ahistorical and noncomparative because it
takes the contemporary nuclear middle class family as its norm. By placing
the family in history, critics deconstruct the mythic family of the past—the
rural, extended, three-generation family, fabled to be more stable, adapt-
able, and strong—against which the current family is judged to be in
decline and in the throes of death (Rossi, 1978). Acceptance of such myths
of the past by social scientists interferes with contemporary analysis of
the strengths of the family in its class, racial, and ethnic varieties. Other
critics (Hareven, 1978, 1987; Poster, 1978) question family history as the
linear, continuous evolution of a single structure posited by modernization
theory. Focusing on the radical discontinuities among different family
structures in European history, Poster (1978) analyzes how one model, the
bourgeois model of the mid-19th century, is privileged over other alternate
models. Significantly, the bourgeois model relies on an ideology of domi-

nance wherein parents, apart from other domestic, village, and community figures, are invested with authority over children and wherein parental love is exchanged for bodily gratification.

THE UNDIFFERENTIATED FAMILY EXPERIENCE

Conceived as the bastion of traditional social order, the monolithic family as a social regulator is static and conservative, portraying a consensual and homogeneous family. "The family" is a code word for mother, "the family decision" harmonizes both gender and generation, and "family violence" masks the crucial fact that violence runs along power lines to victimize adult women and children (Thorne, 1981, pp. 10-11). Feminist critics in particular expose the ways in which women's experiences are buried or distorted under the homogenizing and male hegemonic unit of "the family." Against this undifferentiated family experience, feminist critics expose the dynamic contradictions and power relations that glorify motherhood in the face of women's experiences of mothering (Rich, 1976), that emphasize love and consensus as the basis of marriage and family relations in the face of sexual inequality and conflict in the family (Eichler, 1981; Williams, 1980), and that promote the notion of home as a "haven in a heartless world" (Lasch, 1977) for men in the face of the organization of housework (Hartmann, 1981) and the "double shift" (Hochschild, 1989) for women. Thus, critical views of the family reveal not undifferentiated experiences but the family as a site of contradictory forces and power relations that combine to oppress women and mask that oppression.

THE PRIVATIZED FAMILY

Family theory based on the monolithic family defines the family sphere as separate from and qualitatively different from the public sphere. A "haven in the heartless world" and the place of last resort ("home is where when you go there, they have to take you in"), the privatized family of husband and children's nurturance provides psychological refuge and relief from the ruthless stress and alienation or failed social institutions of the public sphere. Likewise, the privatized family obscures the mutual legitimation of domestic violence by public and state policies. The assumption that the family can be studied in isolation from other social institutions also ignores the social-class variations illustrated by working-class and poor families. Critics of family theory vigorously challenge the private-public dichotomy by exposing the ways in which the family mirrors other social institutions, such as the economy, and is, in turn, supported by other social institutions (Zaretsky, 1981).

The critiques of The Family as ideology and institution emphasize the domination of women and children. Yet, contrary to some popular commentary, feminist critique cannot be reduced to an anti-family, anti-motherhood position, even among feminists who identify the family as the primary institution of women's oppression. Feminist criticism about the family reveals a profound ambivalence about its values, and, having elaborated its oppressive structures, we must specify its appeals. For the family also affords satisfactions not available in other social institutions. Among these appeals Barrett and McIntosh (1982) identify emotional security, the pleasure of the familiar, the supportive intimacy of marriage, the emotional rewards of having and raising children, and the appeal of the natural. Other feminists explore alternatives to patriarchal and capitalist relations, for example, the special qualities of "maternal thinking" (Ruddick, 1981) and the home economy (Brown, 1981). The ambivalence between family and society and between individualism and nurturance has historically challenged and continues to challenge feminist critics, often dividing women against each other (e.g., the "Mommy wars," issues of class, race, sexual preferences).

Family theory generated by social scientists has, to a great extent, uncritically assumed the ideology of the monolithic family as a natural, biologically given, and functionally determined unit, static and homogeneous, ahistorical, and set apart in a private sphere. The nostalgia for the mythical family of the past, the emphasis on the social regulation of women and children, the neglect of social differences among families, and the strict private-public dichotomy paint the family as both conservative and fixed. Osmond (1987) concludes that the monolithic family results in a *social psychology* of family and relationships within families that ignores the family as a social product mutually interpenetrated by other social structures, the historical setting, and political economy. The pervasive psychologism of the family locates problems in the individualized family or in the individualized family member. Methodologically, the individual family or the individual within the family is the unit of analysis, or alternately in family therapy, the unit of treatment. Peterson (1987) adds that the monolithic, neo-bourgeois family may also be preferred by social scientists because of the methodological ease with which the researcher/parent may observe the family/child as a discrete unit.

Bochner's (1976) definition of family for communication, which persists today in communication studies, likewise perpetuates the ideology of the monolithic family: "an organized, naturally occurring relational interaction system, usually occupying a common living space over an extended period of time and possessing a confluence of interpersonal images which evolve through the exchange of messages over time" (p. 382). If the family is a *naturally occurring* phenomenon characterized by *interpersonal* communication, then researchers need not interrogate the generation and reproduction of the family as a social and historical arrangement, in particular as a social organization constructed through differences in gender and generation. The removal of the family from its relations to other social and economic institutions allows researchers to uncritically emphasize its internal, companionate qualities. With the assumption of the monolithic family, communication becomes something that happens *in* families and the family becomes a "container" for communication as family process (Bochner & Eisenberg, 1987) accessible by studying individuals, dyads, or triads (Fitzpatrick, 1987). The effect of defining family communication as interpersonal or small-group communication and focusing solely on relationships within the family is to ignore the family as a social and cultural product, a dynamic site of interactions and asymmetrical power relations that are historical, gendered, and generational.

FAMILY STORYTELLING

The critique of The Family is a necessary but not a sufficient grounding for the analysis of family storytelling. As Barrett and McIntosh (1982, p. 21) assert, "Familism is not a ruling-class or patriarchal ideology repressively foisted on an unwilling population." But even as we actively participate in the family because of its many appeals, the family cannot be reduced to the romanticized companionate institution characterized by the internal relations of intimacy, emotional security, and the nurturance of children. For the family is first of all a phenomenon we live through in all its contradictions, a unique and irreducible reality constituted by a plurality of participants and practices. The family-as-lived grounds equally the meanings of love, safety, and euphoria and of alienation, violence, and despair.

The family-as-lived, replete with its multiple and contradictory meanings, is organized and maintained daily and over generations through a variety of discursive practices by which we "do family." Doing family embraces practices that present the family as legitimate and interpretable. One important strategy for doing family is storytelling—both stories to tell and secrets to keep. Davis (1978, p. 96) identifies family history as "the most important cultural source for a wholehearted sense of family identity and aspiration," Stone (1988, p. 17) calls family stories "the corner-stones of family culture," and McLain and Weigert (1979) advance biography as thematic to the family. Family stories are the basic way in which the lived-experience of doing family is organized and legitimized; they merit particular research attention because they problematize the meanings, processes, and power relations involved in doing family. In this section, we define and describe family storytelling as a prelude to the final section in which we present a model of how family storytelling strategically produces families as small-group cultures.

Genealogy, family history, and biography all name forms of family narrative, but we prefer the terms *family stories* and *family storytelling* for three reasons. First, families do not mundanely "do" or perform their genealogies, family histories, and biographies. Family narratives emerge more fragmentarily, circumstantially, and promiscuously than is suggested by the deliberate, continuous, and complete flavors of these terms. More to the point, genealogies, family histories, and biographies are constituted by the phenomena of family stories. Second, the term *family story* captures both the referential function of family events and the evaluative functions of their meanings and significance (Labov & Waletsky, 1967). As Stone writes, "Family stories are revealing in ways genealogies can never be" (1988, p. 9). And third, *family storytelling* calls attention to the performative nature of family culture as a strategic process that constitutes family.

In *Black Sheep and Kissing Cousins: How Our Family Stories Shape Us*, Elizabeth Stone (1988) assembles a lively and evocative analysis of family stories collected in interviews with over 100 people of diverse ages and regional, racial, and ethnic backgrounds. Using Stone, we describe family stories and how they embody the contradictions of The Family. On the basis of this description, we then critique the limitations of a family stories approach that does not problematize family storytelling as a strategic process.

Stone defines family stories generously: "almost any bit of lore about a family member, living or dead, qualifies as a family story—as long as it's significant, as long as it has worked its way into the family canon to be told and retold" (p. 5). For Stone, the emphasis is not on the *form* of the story, defined a priori as a "good story," nor on its *performance* as a "well-told" aesthetic display but on its meanings for the family. Moreover, she states that "attention to the stories' truth is never the family's most compelling consideration. Encouraging belief is" (p. 7). The family story, is, in short, a form of social control rather than a preexisting genealogy or an expressive family tradition. Understood as a form of social control, family stories legitimate dominant forms of reality and lead to discursive closure (Mumby, 1987) that restricts the interpretations and meanings of family stories.

FAMILY DEFINITIONS

The family's first concern is itself and its own survival. As Stone states it: "The family, as an inherent partisan of the good-of-the-many, mostly offers stories in support of its own interest, though paradoxically these stories are told by the very individuals who may have to subordinate themselves to it" (p. 34). Family definitions, for example, establish family identity as what it means to be a "so-and-so." Family definition includes stories about who X takes after, how Y was as an infant, and what Z did and why. These stories define a particular family as positive and special, and they function to include and exclude—as black sheep—individual members. Stories about ancestors, family "blood," names, and physical or temperamental traits naturalize the present by linking it to a seemingly immutable past, however that past may have actually been, and, in addition, project an apparently inevitable future along the lines of the family definition. Family definitions thus mask the contradictions of a particular family history as well as the family *in* history (Hareven, 1978), where definitions of sex roles, the meanings of age, status, and the nature of family obligations undergo transformation. As a form of social control, family definitions naturalize the present as "the way the so-and-so's are."

FAMILY MONUMENTS

Any family that has a stake in perpetuating itself "must relentlessly push the institutions that preserve it" (Stone, 1988, p. 50)—heterosexual love, marriage, and childbearing especially. Family monuments are stories that mark these institutions: courtship stories of love and marriage, pregnancy and childbirth stories, family moves, and deaths in the family. Family monuments embody particular experiences of "family time" and "family space." *Family time* refers to the timing of marriage and children over the life span and generations (Hareven, 1978). Courtship stories, for example, establish "How This Family Began," and Stone describes the "enormous imaginative undertaking" in which founding stories figure so largely. Stories about *family space* chronicle "Where We Have Lived." As McLain and Weigert (1979, p. 176) summarize, "Domesticity defines family space; house concretizes it; and home symbolizes it as a metaphor." Thus, stories marking family time and family space simultaneously represent a particular family as unique (*"our* family album") and as the embodiment of The Family. In this way, family monuments promote the interests of particular historical institutions, especially marriage, and represent them as universal. At the same time, family monuments mute and marginalize stories and meanings not serving family institutions, such as divorce, homosexuality, and remaining single or childless.

FAMILY RULES

Stories about family rules—ground rules and underground rules—instruct, warn, and regulate family members. "The first and cardinal rule of family life, as embodied in family stories, is that when people are really suffering, you can count on family" (Stone, 1988, p. 18). Families come through, indeed, *must* come through, in hard times. Stone reports stories of self-sacrifice, of family loyalty, of almost telepathic powers between family members separated in crisis. Family stories also regulate proximity, protocol, and decorum. Underground rules, often tersely coded as myths, point to the "dark side" of families: alcoholism, mental illness, suicide, violence, sickness, incest, and criminality. Family rules address the reciprocity of perspectives that ground the norms and forms of family culture. McLain and Weigert (1979) suggest two directions of rule formation, each with its own tensions and contradictions: "biographical fusion" between spouses, wherein more or less biographical differences are actively modified to produce a common family biography, and "biographical fission" in parent-child relationships, where the unity initially taken for granted becomes increasingly possible developmentally (pp. 176-77). Rules that privilege a collective family biography over individual biographical differences establish the potential for both physical and mental violence in the family, particularly for women and children. The emphasis on collectivity and consensus works to deny the contradictions and defines conflict over family rules as interpersonal—between spouses or between parents and children—rather than serving institutional interests of gender and generational politics.

Stone is also aware that the family must be legitimized in the social world, too. The particular family as a finite province of meaning transects with other social institutions, such as law, religion, medicine, and the social orders of racism, classism, sexism, heterosexism, and so on. Stone's interviewees include stories about the social pecking order but especially money stories of family fortune and misfortune. She argues, for example, that immigrant families tell assimilation stories in pursuit of the American Dream. Significantly, there are few stories of racial relations and working class and the poor; such worldly concerns as politics, religious affiliation, and educational values are also muted; and there are no stories reported on homosexuality. Family stories about the social order suggest two conclusions. First, subordinate groups actively self-identify with dominant interests. Second, the sparsity of these stories reinforces the privatization of the family. As a result, the particular economic and historical contradictions that legitimate social differences of race, class, ethnicity, religion, and sexual preference remain obscured and intact.

We have emphasized thus far the way family stories evolve from and reproduce interests, power structures, and meanings of the family. As narrative, family definitions naturalize the vagaries and contradictions of family histories; family monuments represent particular social institutions as universal; and family rules define conflict as interpersonal rather than serving the interests of gender (i.e., patriarchal) politics, generational (i.e., parental) authority, and the social oppression of differences. But family stories can also delegitimate or contest dominant meaning systems. Rossi (1978) suggests that family stories, forged by families themselves rather than imposed externally, may reveal family strengths less visible in other types of family analyses. Stone presents individual storytellers who refashion family stories and reappropriate meanings by adopting "fairy godmothers" and "patron saints" from their ancestral past.

Here, gender becomes thematic as Stone uncovers a legacy of sexist identities for sons and daughters. Contemplating infant stories in which daughters are forgotten or left behind in carriages or car seats, Stone writes that whether or not this happens more often to girls is both impossible to answer and irrelevant: "The fact is that girls, more often than boys, are told that they were forgotten or left behind. And so the telling itself is a transaction between mother and daughter" (p. 183). In contrast to a legacy of feminine identity, she offers, a "subversive legacy" of stories of strong and rebellious women. Thus, family stories offer the potential to delegitimate dominant meanings for gender identities.

We can now summarize the contributions and the limitations of Stone's approach to family stories. Stone's analysis successfully unveils the use of family narrative as social control at the same time that it locates the family as a site of contradictions and potential resistance to dominant meanings. The analysis of family stories reveals that the family is not simply a ruling-class ideology nor a socioeconomic institution but a discursive practice with the potential to oppose as well as oppress. As bell hooks (1989, p. 21) comments, "Even though family relations may be, and most often are, informed by acceptance of a politic of domination, they are simultaneously relations of care and connection."

But the family stories approach also has limitations. Despite the effort after diversity among interviewees and the concern with gender, Stone's analysis still assumes the monolithic, neo-bourgeois, homogeneous, and privatized family as its norm. We have already suggested above that social differences among families, such as race, class, and religion, receive too little attention and thereby reinforce both the monolithic and privatized family. Stone's analysis overestimates the consensus on the meanings of family stories, assuming a more homogeneous experience of the family than is warranted. The assumption of homogeneous family experience masks both differences *among* families (social and historical) and differences *within* family experiences that emerge from the arrangements of sex and age. Whereas the analysis of family stories opens the possibility of individual resistance, alternatives to normative family arrangements—for example, same-sex households, single-parent households, cultural variations such as the kibbutz and Native-American kinship systems, and contemporary communal families (Swerdlow, Bridenthal, Kelly, & Vine, 1989)—are not conceived.

Finally, Stone's analysis of the immigrant experience also participates in the myth of the past family as more extended and strong than contemporary family arrangements. Rossi (1978, p. 250) insightfully suggests that family theorists "mistook the close ties of first-generation immigrants to distant kin (aunts, uncles, cousins) to represent kin relations in peasant communities in Europe, rather than adaptations to the stress of settling in an alien society by substituting less closely related kin for parents and siblings they left in their country of origin." In the assumption of an ahistorical, neo-bourgeois family Stone likewise mistakes narrative *strategies* for a normative reality.

One way to problematize the analysis of family culture through story-texts is to consider Stone's assertion that family stories are a women's genre: "Through the universe of family stories, we glimpse a world in which women play a more substantial role than men and come through far more untarnished. Thus family stories are the obverse of more public and codified cultural genres in which men invariably play the more dominant and flattering roles" (1988, p. 20). Our point is not to dismiss this claim but to stress that such a claim must depend on the analysis of storytelling *performances* not story-texts—performances that are unavoidably gendered, generational, and historical. To reiterate Stone herself, "the telling itself is a transaction" (p. 183). Following Maclean (1987), we argue that the politics of family storytelling cannot be determined on the basis of story-texts alone because all stories are performed—by a particular speaker with a particular audience in a particular situation. A story about a forgotten daughter may be oppressive or it may be resisting depending on who tells it to whom and under what conditions. Narrative performance—family storytelling—is the basis for the multileveled strategic model we develop in the final section.

FAMILY STORYTELLING AS PERFORMANCE

Maclean (1988) grounds her view of narrative as performance in speech act theory.[1] Speech act theory defines language as action—words do things as well as have meaning. Speech acts depend on context for their effects, that is, the shared conventions and obligations between partners in the narrative contract as well as between the collective social and cultural forces controlling language and the individuals putting it into practice. Maclean (1988) notes the special characteristics of the narrative performative frame "I will tell," I will relate," and "I will recount" within speech act theory: "This illocutionary act is, as I have said, a sort of performative, since it not only sets up a two-way contract between addresser and addressee, as all true speech acts do, but it also promises a performance and constitutes the hearers as audience. Implicit in every narrative performative is the double contract, '*Listen*, and I will tell you *a* story' " (p. 25). We argue that the narrative performative frame can more effectively account for family storytelling for three reasons.

First, keying the narrative performative frame indicates a change in the status of the discourse. The teller and listeners accept a new frame of reference implied by "Listen, and I will tell you a story." Maclean posits two speech acts, the first of which operates in natural discourse and direct speech (Austin's "serious" performatives) and the second of which operates in fictional discourse and everyday narratives ("nonserious" speech acts). Family storytelling is both "serious" and "nonserious." A family story purports to recount lived reality while, at the same time, the effect of the family story is to enhance experience by exceeding referentiality and to create within the two-way narrator-audience contract another possible world in performance. Telling a family story is always a mediation and construction of reality rather than simply its representation. Family stories are constrained by the forces of narrative as well as a narrator's strategies of telling.[2]

Second, the key factor in the narrative performative frame is the creation and maintenance of an audience. Analytic attention must focus both on the labor performed in the speaker's communicative display and the audience's participation, for example, the refusal to listen, challenges to the speaker, supportive responses, or deferential listening. Performance is seen as a site of strategic interaction, sometimes competitive, sometimes cooperative. We are reminded that all family storytelling and story listening are gendered and generational. For example, Hall and Langellier (1988) explore the cooperative and collaborative strategies of mother-daughter storytelling about food as they negotiate different generational storytelling roles. Baldwin (1985) distinguishes women's and men's roles in family storytelling as they compete to get in the last word.

Third, when we look at the creation and maintenance of an audience in family storytelling, we encounter not just interactional dynamics but also the constraints of discourse that ground power relations in culture and society. And here we are compelled to consider questions about the distribution of narrative authority and storytelling rights and about excluded audiences and enforced listeners. The teller of a family story may be vulnerable as an individual, because as Labov (1972) has shown, the listener may always stop listening or challenge the speaker with the "So what?" question. But the teller of a family story may be a member of a privileged social group or a representative of hegemonic discourse—in the family, a father. As Maclean (1987) notes, it is not just that a speaker may assume the narrative authority that comes with performance but may also wield actual authority within the family culture. And many listeners—women and children particularly—are not in the position to say "So what?" because they have to go on listening. In this context, we can interrogate Stone's thesis that family stories are a women's genre. We can ask, for example, about the politics of family storytelling: Is it a women's genre because it is associated with the private sphere and women's role in family maintenance—and thereby trivial under traditional definitions of story-telling? Under what conditions do women, men, and children tell stories and with what effects?

Against the assumption of particular genres such as family stories as male or female, or particular stories as sexist or feminist, Maclean (1987) focuses on practices of gendered telling and listening, to which we would add generational telling and listening. Approaching family stories as gendered and generational performances views them as potential strategies of the powerful and tactics of the weak. But such determinations can be made only on the basis of a multileveled analysis that neither denies contradictions nor collapses them to a simple opposition.

A STRATEGIC MODEL OF FAMILY STORYTELLING

In approaching family storytelling as situated performances, we adopt a strategic model based on McFeat's (1974) analysis of small-group cultures and Wilden's (1987a, 1987b) "context theory" of communication.[3] McFeat analyzes the ordering of information that constitutes and maintains a small-group over generations thereby becoming a small-group culture. Thus, a family is both the communication medium of "material expression" as well as the ordering of information and meanings inscribed in that medium.

McFeat articulates three levels or orders of information that concern a group-culture: content-ordering, task-ordering, and group-ordering. Each level of information ordering can be distinguished by its generality, or logical type, and complexity. *Content-ordering* is the most general level of information ordering and concerns the basic information or content that group-cultures store, retrieve, and transmit. Task and group-ordering are dependent on content-ordering, for if a group-culture fails to manage the ordering of content over time it will cease to exist. *Task-ordering* is more complex than content-ordering because it focuses on maintaining a productive climate for content-ordering. In order to generate a productive link with the environment, a group takes on structure and specialized task definitions. *Group-ordering* is the most complex level of information ordering in that it depends on successful content- and task-ordering. As a group-culture stores, retrieves, and transmits information across time by a structured adaptation to the environment, it also differentiates internal boundaries through self-interpretation. A group innovates identities, as

McFeat points out, "only after all the 'serious stuff' of culture has been looked after, such as adapting to the environment (i.e., task-ordering) and 'passing on the culture' to a new generation (i.e., content-ordering)" (1974, p. 170). Content-ordering, task-ordering, and group-ordering constitute what Wilden (1987a) calls a semi-dependent hierarchy (see Figure 2.1). In a semi-dependent hierarchy, the lower orders (such as group- and task-ordering) normally depend on or exist within the environment of the higher order (such as content-ordering). Wilden notes that while the generality of constraint increases as one moves upward in the hierarchy, complexity increases as one moves downward. In the previous description of small-group cultures, we have taken care to indicate both complexity and how each level depends on the previous level. Group-ordering depends on task-ordering, which in turn depends on content-ordering. For as McFeat points out, a small group that fails to order content over time ceases to exist. This comment illustrates what Wilden (1987a, p. 74) calls the "extinction rule": a test to determine which order contextualizes the others. It is important to note that relationships between orders in a semi-dependent hierarchy are boundaries in an open system, not relations of opposition or exclusion. In fact, Wilden (1987b) points out that innovation in a lower level of the hierarchy may condition changes in a higher level. "The innovation breaks through the constraints of the existing code (or codes) and restructures it, making radically new messages possible. The hierarchy then re-assumes its normally dependent character" (1987b, p. 235). But before we examine relations between orders of the hierarchy, let us examine each order in greater detail.

CONTENT-ORDERING

In order to persist through succeeding generations, a small-group culture orders information so that it can be stored, retrieved, and transmitted over time. Thus, *doing family* involves not only ways of creating, defining, and sharing meanings and sensibilities but ways of maintaining and perpetuating those meanings and sensibilities as well. McFeat identifies two means of ensuring the perpetuation of a small-group culture: generality of knowledge and timing of transmission. The generality of knowledge is perhaps most readily demonstrated by the wide circulation of selected stories at family gatherings and holidays. These stories are told and retold to the point they become "family classics" (e.g., "The time Tom

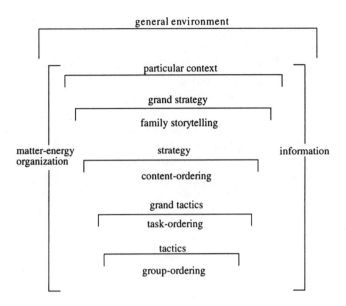

general environment

particular context

grand strategy

family storytelling

matter-energy   strategy   information
organization

content-ordering

grand tactics

task-ordering

tactics

group-ordering

Figure 2.1. A Strategic Model of Family Storytelling (see Wilden, 1987b, p. 234; used by permission)

nearly burned down the house"). Content-ordering, however, is not limited to the family by itself. Indeed, much of the shared meanings and sensibilities for family are widely circulated in communities, public culture, and mass media. This generality of knowledge about family provides an important resource for ensuring the storage of information in a small-group culture.

At the same time the wide circulation of knowledge ensures orderly perpetuation of a small-group culture, it provides a form of over-determination and social control for the kinds of content ordered by families. The "information rich" environment of society may overwhelm the storage of alternative types of knowledge preferred by a particular small-group culture. One way of countering this form of social control can be seen in the ways a family includes and excludes information. For example, a family may counter "external" information about The Family by restricting the circulation of certain information to family members. Secrecy and silence are a way of ordering content that is "too important" to share "outside" the culture (Hall & Langellier, 1988). As bell hooks (1989) recalls from her own experience, "Secrecy about family, about what went on in the domestic household was a bond between us—was part of what made us a family" (p. 156). This type of content-ordering may help to explain how secrecy and silence about alcoholism and domestic violence become a resource that ensures their perpetuation.

A second way to order content concerns the timing of information transmission. Peterson (1987) describes how stories of pregnancy and birth are told *after* a pregnancy is announced. In this case, information is withheld until it becomes salient, thus ensuring its orderly transmission. The timing of pregnancy stories is hardly neutral, however. This silence works to mystify pregnancy and motherhood before giving way to access to information. In a similar manner, the timing of information affects stories of courtship or family "beginnings" as well as stories of divorce and family continuity, to take two examples.

TASK-ORDERING

Timing and the generality of knowledge work to maintain a boundary between the small group and its environment. Thus, content-ordering entails the ordering of tasks to survive in a larger environment. At the minimum, family storytelling involves tasks of telling and audiencing, of retrieving, transmitting, and storing information. Family stories cannot be passed to succeeding generations without being told; nor can information be exchanged or stored without being retrieved. In the groups McFeat studied, task-ordering involved a three-generational structure where the middle generation transmitted basic information, subject to correction by the senior generation, to the junior generation (1974, p. 154). Senior members utilized their knowledge of basic information to maintain control of group activities. Yet, at the same time, they could not refuse information retrieval without endangering the group's continuity. This tension between access and manipulation of information is most clearly evident in the previous examples of storytelling: for example, pregnancy stories that are told only on a daughter's pregnancy, stories of sexuality and sexual behavior that are told only on the onset of puberty, and so on. What is important here is not the timing but the question of who controls what is told to whom and when.

The three-generational structure identified by McFeat appears particularly suited to the organization of the "nuclear family," where the primary unit of parents and children typically has only intermittent contact with grandparents and other relatives. We should expect to find alternate task structures for other forms of family. For example, Tafoya (1989) describes how the transmission of information differs for many Native Americans because of a different type of family organization. In the family system described by Tafoya, siblings (which includes cousins) form the inner-most of three concentric circles of relations. The next circle includes grandparents (and may include "great aunts or uncles") as caregivers providing training and discipline. The outer circle includes biological parents as well as their siblings. The resulting structure of task-ordering differs from the structure identified by McFeat. In this case, the senior generation ("grandparents") are responsible for storytelling and guiding the education of the junior generation ("all siblings").

Task-ordering distributes storytelling rights and audience responsibilities according to gender and generational differences. This distribution of rights and responsibilities may lead to enforced listening or excluded audiences identified by Maclean (1988). Or, it may involve different ways of negotiating the meanings of family storytelling. For example, in the family system Tafoya describes, the elders do not "transmit" information by direct teaching. Instead, they "guide" or educate by creating a situation where a youth comes to " 're-cognize' what they [the elders] already knew" (1989, p. 40). This process contrasts with the group production and interpretation of stories displayed by the African-American families studied by Heath (1983). Heath describes how such stories may be "coopera-tive" in that they are "told with the help of the audience or with two or more participants in an event sharing the recounting" (1983, p. 183). These differences in task-ordering have significant consequences for small-group cultures: Both Tafoya and Heath describe how individuals from "outside" the culture may not understand such events as storytelling or even recognize that a story has been told.

GROUP-ORDERING

A family works to interpret the meanings of storytelling through task-ordering. Task-ordering makes possible the next level of the hierarchy—group-ordering. In group-ordering, a culture innovates information as a way to differentiate internal boundaries and a group identity. For this reason, McFeat argues that small-group cultures produce local models. As McFeat writes, groups "appear to require regulatory mechanisms which accom-modate sets of contrary facts: what brings uniqueness and adaptation is opposed to that which brings disturbing features from the outside that will not go away" (1974, p. 167). In the family, group-ordering works to regulate the tensions between group interests and individual interests. As Stone's example of infant stories about daughters forgotten or left behind in carriages and car seats illustrates, group definitions of family identity may be contested or delegitimated by individuals (Stone's example) or by alliances within the small-group (such as mothers and daughters in examples by Bell, 1988, and Steinem, 1989).

The "truth" of these stories, bell hooks (1989) points out, lies not in their correspondence to some previous reality (also, see Bradley, 1989). For these stories are personal narratives: "a unique recounting of events not so much as they have happened but as we remember and invent them" (hooks, 1989, p. 157). Thus, bell hooks locates family history (and the "self-regulation" of group-ordering) as a primary constraint shaping personal autobiography. At the same time, it is important to recall that the family can function also as a resource for individuals within it. For example, the junior generation may look to a senior generation member rather than the middle generation (or "parents") for models of identity. Or, a family member may adopt versions of family history told by aunts and uncles that contradict versions preferred by other factions within the family. Writers Sara Paretsky (1989) and Clyde Edgerton (1989), for example, describe how they look to Cousin Agnes and Uncle Bob, respectively, for guidance in innovating personal identity. In these cases, children utilize the "accommodation of contrary facts" within the family to circumvent a generational structure of power and control of knowledge.

In sum, storytelling provides one way for small-group cultures to organize as families. In terms of a strategic model (see Figure 2.1), storytelling is one strategy by which a small-group culture persists through succeeding generations. The strategic model is based on Wilden's (1987b) distinction between strategy and tactics. "In the simplest sense, strategy is what we want to do and tactics are how we go about it" (p. 233). Wilden further distinguishes *grand strategy* as the setting of general goals, *strategy* as the orientation of means to reach those goals, *grand tactics* as the framing of operations within those means, and *tactics* as the punctuation of action within the framing of operations (p. 233). To illustrate the relations between these orders in the hierarchy, we turn to two examples of family storytelling. The first example, taken from Riessman's (1988) analysis of narratives on marital conflict, illustrates the strategic operation of gendered family storytelling within one generation. The second example, taken from Silberstein's (1988) analysis of courtship narratives, illustrates the strategic operation of family storytelling over three generations.

NARRATIVES OF MARITAL CONFLICT

Riessman (1988) contrasts two stories of "marital difficulties" as a way of illustrating how differences in women's experience of marriage is reflected in the mode of discourse. Riessman examines the narratives of "Susan," an Anglo, and "Marta," a Puerto Rican. She articulates the *particular context* of marital conflict over gender roles within the "constraints of class, ethnicity, and family history and structure" that distinguishes each woman's "perceptions and experiences" (1988, p. 170). The process of telling a marital history, therefore, acts as a *grand strategy* to reconstruct the experience of marriage.

Within this particular context, each woman adopts a specific narrative *strategy* to order the content of her narrative. Susan adopts the sequential structure of a habitual narrative where events are remembered and recapitulated in a linear temporal sequence. Susan describes how she married, had children, lost intimacy with her husband, then moved to separate sleeping quarters. Marta, in contrast, adopts an episodically structured narrative where a series of topics are loosely connected by theme rather than time. Marta describes how the conflict of leisure time relates to doing things as a family, which in turn relates to differences in acculturation and socializing, which relates to Marta's husband's dislike of her employment and, finally, to cultural conflict between her husband's family (island-oriented) and her family (city-oriented). Riessman argues that the choice of narrative structure in each case does not illustrate a stereotyped distinction between Anglo and Puerto Rican cultures (indeed, in later research Riessman, 1990, locates four narrative possibilities). Rather, the narrative—in both topic and structure—embodies each woman's meanings and understandings for marital events. In terms of the model, Marta and Susan are not limited to one type of narrative because of their different cultural backgrounds or their shared gender. Both types of narrative are possible choices for each woman. Thus, the choice of narrative structure is *strategic* in how it functions to articulate meanings for gender conflict in marriage.

The choice of different narrative structures contextualizes the ordering of tasks that forms the focal point for the marital conflict. The division of tasks according to gender ("the sexual division of labor") comprises the *grand tactic* by which each woman frames the operations of "mulling over and evaluating" her marriage. For Susan, the linear temporal organization marks out the increasing disintegration of her marriage. She characterizes this disintegration by depicting her husband's increasing lack of participation in marital "labor": intimacy, help with childcare, and communication. For Marta, the episodic frame marks the complex development of a theme by which she contrasts her aspirations for achievement with traditional Puerto Rican expectations for a woman (taking care of children, husband, and home). Marta "constructs her point" by presenting scenes of conflict over the division of labor that overlap in terms of their theme rather than chronology.

Conflict over the division of labor in marriage articulates specific gender roles or identities for individuals and specific forms of the ideal family. Thus, each narrative produces identities as a particular *tactic* of group ordering and a fulcrum for marital conflict. Susan, for example, adopts the "companionate ideal" of Western, middle-class culture. When her expectations for emotional sharing and reciprocity are increasingly dislodged, she finds that her identity ("all of what I needed for myself") is submerged ("buried") in the marriage. Marta, however, situates her identity and that of her marriage by locating it within the larger history of both her and her husband's families. Instead of the conjugal conflict of Susan's narrative, Marta describes her marital conflict as the failure of marriage to reconcile the differing values of two families: old-fashioned and modern, island-oriented and city-oriented, less acculturated and more acculturated, and so on. These examples illustrate how individual and family identity are tactics of group-ordering within family storytelling. Riessman (1990) concludes, on the basis of empirical evidence collected in a larger study of 52 women and 52 men, that although women and men use different types of narratives depending on context and strategic aims, these differences do not constitute a distinct "women's genre" or "men's genre" of family storytelling (pp. 243-244).

COURTSHIP NARRATIVES

Narratives of marital conflict illustrate the strategic function of storytelling within one generation of a family. In order to understand how such storytelling functions in a small-group *culture*, we must situate family storytelling as a specific social and historical practice. An example of such a social and historical analysis comes from Silberstein's (1988) study of heterosexual courtship stories told by three generations of two white middle-class families. Silberstein argues that courtship storytelling embodies the "ideological process which creates and maintains gender as a social category" (p. 126). Courtship storytelling, therefore, acts as a *grand strategy* by which small-group cultures work at "renewing, recreating, defining, and modifying" dominant meanings and values.

Within courtship stories, Silberstein focuses on the ideological evolution of how shared "vocabularies of motive" are conventionalized. She describes how courtship stories told by women change over three generations to accommodate alternative or oppositional meanings for gender suggested by the second wave of the Women's Movement. First-generation women do not include justifications for life choices in their narratives, whereas second-generation women tell of conflict between public and private sphere participation and third-generation women tell how "choosing a partner" is consistent with one's "public-sphere identity." In contrast, the courtship stories told by men remain unchanged across generations. Men's stories do not display any conflict between marriage and personal needs, nor do they display any recognition of the changing discourse on gender demonstrated in the women's stories. These examples illustrate how courtship narratives order different content for women and men, or, in this case, "vocabularies of motive" as a *strategy* in storytelling.

The primary *grand tactics* used to enact this strategy are "narrative devices" that order the task of storytelling. Whereas women articulate the task of courtship as "deciding" on their relationship with men and the degree of their commitment, men articulate the task of courtship as "orchestrating" the competition and conquest of women. Two additional narrative devices concern how the stories are told—the task of performance. Both women and men incorporate forms of "impression management" into their storytelling. In Silberstein's study, the men speak more slowly than do women (words per minute) even though they produce a similar number of "fillers" (e. g., "ah," "um," and "oh"). Silberstein argues that the men's storytelling creates the "assurance of audience"—the prerogative to speak slower on the assumption that they will not be interrupted—an assurance that women storytellers do not share. The women, in contrast, utilize forms of impression management that seek assurance from their audience. The women will cite the opinions of others in support of their motivation and refer to moral obligations. The men, however, can speak with irony and disapproval about the women.

The difference between these two approaches to storytelling is supported further by the next pair of grand tactics as to the amount of detail included in courtship stories. Silberstein notes that whereas the women recall such details as the "opinions of others" during the courtship, the men work at "reconstruction" of the courtship and display uncertainty as to details. Furthermore, the men are far less certain of their parents' and grandparents' courtships. Indeed, the men constantly make statements that place the responsibility for remembering such stories on the women: "Now Kay would be able to remember, I can't" (1988, p. 144). On this basis, Silberstein argues that the task of courtship storytelling is not a male domain.

The final pair of narrative devices more accurately describe *tactics* employed in courtship storytelling. This pair of devices concerns the articulation of gender identity. For women, the question of what kind of person they are cannot be left to the audience. The women make explicit statements as to the kind of people they are, such as, "I was a very conscientious person." The men, however, create an identity as "gentlemen" by not mentioning what might be embarrassing moments for women. They tell of their own rejections, for example, but do not describe women's rejections by men. In addition, they use hedges (such as "I think," and "I suspect") when speaking for their partners—something the women never did. Silberstein argues that the "same gallantry by which men omit mentioning women's defeats and hedge when speaking for women is simultaneously a mark of male stature and assurance" (1988, p. 146). Thus, men's silence has the double advantage of both supporting their image as "gentlemen" and justifying their privilege in avoiding the tasks of remembering and retelling courtship stories.

The strategic model takes the analysis of courtship storytelling beyond articulating narrative devices. Locating these devices as specific orders of information has the advantage of indicating how they work together in a semi-dependent hierarchy. For example, following the strategic model we would not expect a change in meanings for gender identity experienced by women to affect the tasks of courtship storytelling. The specific punctuation of gender roles in group-ordering depends on the higher order of storytelling practices allocated in task-ordering. For men, women's attempts to change the punctuation of gender roles remains a minor tactic as long as they fail to alter the grand tactics by which courtship narratives are told. Nor should we expect the framing of storytelling tasks to change without a shift in the strategic level of content-ordering. The overall ideological production of gendered individuals through courtship stories can easily accommodate changes in minor tactics. Silberstein makes this point by emphasizing social and historical circumstances—the sexual division of labor that frames courtship storytelling. "These circumstances remind us that the process of learning to mark on[e]self narratively as male or female is not an isolated cultural artifact" (1988, p. 147). Thus, a strategic model has the advantage of emphasizing the very processes by which family storytelling works to produce the gendered and generational structures of small-group cultures.

CONCLUSION

Family storytelling involves much more than recalling and recounting anecdotes about ancestors and offspring. Nor is family storytelling the mere representation of reality or truth, an entertaining or expressive tradition, or even a rhetorical appeal for consensus on shared meanings and beliefs. Rather, family storytelling describes a multileveled strategic process constrained by social and historical conditions, oriented by a variety of narrative means and structures, framed by the interactional dynamics of telling and audiencing, and punctuated by particular choices and actions. This multileveled strategic process functions to produce "family" as a small-group culture.

A strategic model accounts for *family formation* as well as the ordering of basic information in narrative, the organization of storytelling and listening tasks, and the innovation of group and individual identity. Thus, family storytelling constitutes the family as one site of struggle for both control and opposition, for both the restriction and facilitation of possibilities for small-group cultures. Family stories are not merely "under our skin," as Stone suggests, they are out in the world as discursive practices and ways of doing family. The challenge for communication research lies in exploring family storytelling in all its complexities, probing the ambivalences and multiple meanings, interrogating the workings of gender and generation, and nurturing possibilities for growth and diversity.

NOTES

1. The conceptualization of performance within speech act theory differs from the folkloristic definition of performance as a verbal art (see Bauman, 1986). In the following description, we follow Lanigan's (1977) articulation of a speech act phenomenology for communication.

2. For example, family stories are constrained by conventions of oral narratives. Furthermore, the ways in which such stories are collected—whether in an individual or group interview or in observational research—constrain and shape what is told and how it is told.

74 *Family Storytelling as a Strategy*

3. Although Wilden describes this approach as a context *theory*, we adopt Lanigan's (1988) argument that Wilden's proposal is an "eco-system" *model* of human communication. The following strategic model is guided by the meta-theoretical constraints identified by Lanigan.

REFERENCES

Baldwin, K. (1985). "Woof!" A word on women's roles in family storytelling. In R. A. Jordan & S. J. Kalcik (Eds.), *Women's folklore, women's culture* (pp. 149-162). Philadelphia, PA: University of Pennsylvania.
Barrett, M., & McIntosh, M. (1982). *The anti-social family.* London: Verso.
Bauman, R. (1986). *Story, performance, and event: Contextual studies of oral narrative.* Cambridge, UK: Cambridge University Press.
Bell, S. E. (1988). Becoming a political woman: The reconstruction and interpretation of experience through stories. In A. D. Todd & S. Fisher (Eds.), *Gender and discourse: The power of talk* (pp. 97-123). Norwood, NJ: Ablex.
Bochner, A. P. (1976). Conceptual frontiers in the study of communication in families: An introduction to the literature. *Human Communication Research, 2,* 381-397.
Bochner, A. P., & Eisenberg, E. M. (1987). Family process: System perspectives. In C. R. Berger & S. H. Chaffee (Eds.), *Handbook of communication science* (pp. 540-563). Newbury Park, CA: Sage.
Bradley, D. (1989). Harvest home. In C. Anthony (Ed.), *Family portraits: Remembrances by twenty distinguished writers* (pp. 47-66). New York: Doubleday.
Brown, C. (1981). Home production for use in a market economy. In B. Thorne & M. Yalom (Eds.), *Rethinking the family: Some feminist questions* (pp. 151-167). New York: Longman.
Chodorow, N. (1978). *The reproduction of mothering: Psychoanalysis and the sociology of gender.* Berkeley, CA: University of California Press.
Coward, R. (1983). *Patriarchal precedents: Sexuality and social relations.* London: Routledge and Kegan Paul.
Davis, N. Z. (1978). Ghosts, kin, and progeny: Some features of family life in early modern France. In A. S. Rossi, J. Kagan, & T. H. Hareven (Eds.), *The family* (pp. 87-114). New York: Norton.
Edgerton, C. (1989). A four-blade case. In C. Anthony (Ed.), *Family portraits: Remembrances by twenty distinguished writers* (pp. 79-92). New York: Doubleday.
Eichler, M. (1981). Power, dependence, love and the sexual division of labor. *Women's Studies International Quarterly, 4,* 201-291.
Fitzpatrick, M. A. (1987). Marital interaction. In C. R. Berger & S. H. Chaffee (Eds.), *Handbook of communication science* (pp. 564-618). Newbury Park, CA: Sage.
Hall, D. L., & Langellier, K. M. (1988). Storytelling strategies in mother-daughter communication. In A. Taylor & B. Bate (Eds.), *Women communicating* (pp. 107-126). New York: Ablex.
Hareven, T. K. (1978). Family time and historical time. In A. S. Rossi, J. Kagan, & T. K. Hareven (Eds.), *The family* (pp. 57-70). New York: Norton.
Hareven, T. K. (1987). Historical analysis of the family. In M. B. Sussman & S. K. Steinmetz (Eds.), *Handbook of marriage and the family* (pp. 37-57). New York: Plenum.

Hartmann, H. I. (1981). Family as the locus of gender, class, and political struggle. *Signs, 6,* 366-394.

Heath, S. B. (1983). *Ways with words: Language, life, and work in communities and classrooms.* Cambridge, UK: Cambridge University Press.

Hochschild, A. (1989). *The second shift: Working parents and the revolution at home.* New York: Viking.

hooks, b. (1989). *Talking back: Thinking feminist, thinking black.* Boston: South End.

Labov, W. (1972). *Language in the inner city.* Philadelphia, PA: University of Pennsylvania.

Labov, W., & Waletsky, J. (1967). Narrative analysis: Oral versions of personal experience. In J. Helms (Ed.), *Essays in the verbal and visual arts* (pp. 12-44). Seattle, WA: University of Washington.

Langellier, K. M. (1989). Personal narratives: Perspectives on theory and research. *Text and Performance Quarterly, 9,* 243-276.

Lanigan, R. L. (1977). *Speech act phenomenology.* The Hague: Martinus Nijhoff.

Lanigan, R. L. (1988). Semiotic phenomenology as a metatheory of human communication. In *Phenomenology of communication: Merleau-Ponty's thematics in communicology and semiology* (pp. 184-193). Pittsburgh, PA: Duquesne University.

Lasch, C. (1977). *Haven in a heartless world.* New York: Basic.

Maclean, M. (1987) Oppositional practices in women's traditional narrative. *New Literary History, 5,* 37-50.

Maclean, M. (1988). *Narrative as performance: The Baudelairean experiment.* London: Routledge and Kegan Paul.

McFeat, T. (1974). *Small-group cultures.* New York: Pergamon.

McLain, R., & Weigert, A. (1979). Toward a phenomenological sociology of family: A programmatic essay. In W. R. Burr, R. Hill, F. I. Nye, & I. L. Reiss (Eds.), *Contemporary theories about the family* (pp. 160-205). New York: Free Press.

Mumby, D. K. (1987). The political function of narrative in organizations. *Communication Monographs, 54,* 113-127.

Osmond, M. W. (1987). Radical-critical theories. In M. B. Sussman & S. K. Steinmetz (Eds.), *Handbook of marriage and the family* (pp. 103-124). New York: Plenum.

Paretsky, S. (1989). Wild woman out of control. In C. Anthony (Ed.), *Family portraits: Remembrances by twenty distinguished writers* (pp. 165-179). New York: Doubleday.

Peterson, E. E. (1987). The stories of pregnancy: On interpretation of small-group cultures. *Communication Quarterly, 35,* 39-47.

Poster, M. (1978). *Critical theory of the family.* New York: Seabury.

Rich, A. (1976). *Of woman born: Motherhood as experience and institution.* New York: Norton.

Rich, A. (1980). Compulsory heterosexuality and lesbian existence. *Signs, 5,* 631-660.

Riessman, C. K. (1988). Worlds of difference: Contrasting experience in marriage and narrative style. In A. D. Todd & S. Fisher (Eds.), *Gender and discourse: The power of talk* (pp. 151-173). Norwood, NJ: Ablex.

Riessman, C. K. (1990). *Divorce talk: Women and men make sense of personal relationships.* New Brunswick, NJ: Rutgers University.

Rossi, A. S. (1978). Epilogue. In A. S. Rossi, J. Kagan, & T. K. Hareven (Eds.), *The family* (pp. 237-259). New York: Norton.

Ruddick, S. (1981). Maternal thinking. In B. Thorne & M. Yalom (Eds.), *Rethinking the family: Some feminist questions* (pp. 76-94). New York: Longman.

Settles, B. H. (1987). A perspective on tomorrow's families. In M. B. Sussman & S. K. Steinmetz (Eds.), *Handbook of marriage and the family* (pp. 157-180). New York: Plenum.

Silberstein, S. (1988). Ideology as process: Gender ideology in courtship narratives. In A. D. Todd & S. Fisher (Eds.), *Gender and discourse: The power of talk* (pp. 125-149). Norwood, NJ: Ablex.

Steinem, G. (1989). Ruth's song (because she could not sing it). In C. Anthony (Ed.), *Family portraits: Remembrances by twenty distinguished writers* (pp. 251-274). New York: Doubleday.

Stone, E. (1988). *Black sheep and kissing cousins: How our family stories shape us.* New York: Time Books.

Swerdlow, A., Bridenthal, R., Kelly, J., & Vine, P. (1989). *Families in flux.* New York: Feminist Press.

Tafoya, T. (1989, August). Coyote's eyes: Native cognition styles. *Journal of American Indian Education* (Special Issue), 29-42. [Reprinted from (1982) *21*(No. 2), 21-33.]

Thorne, B. (1981). Feminist rethinking of the family: An overview. In B. Thorne & M. Yalom (Eds.), *Rethinking the family: Some feminist questions* (pp. 1-24). New York: Longman.

Thorne, B., & Yalom, M. (1981). *Rethinking the family: Some feminist questions.* New York: Longman.

Trebilcot, J. (Ed.). (1983). *Mothering: Essays in feminist theory.* Totowa, NJ: Rowman & Allanheld.

Wilden, A. (1987a). *The rules are no game: The strategy of communication.* London: Routledge and Kegan Paul.

Wilden, A. (1987b). *Man and woman, war and peace: The strategist's companion.* London: Routledge and Kegan Paul.

Williams, J. H. (1980). Equality and the family. *International Journal of Women's Studies, 3,* 131-142.

Zaretsky, E. (1981). The place of the family in the origins of the welfare state. In B. Thorne & M. Yalom (Eds.), *Rethinking the family: Some feminist questions* (pp. 188-224). New York: Longman.

Chapter 3

CULTURAL NARRATIVES AND THE THERAPEUTIC MOTIF: THE POLITICAL CONTAINMENT OF VIETNAM VETERANS

Peter Ehrenhaus

NOT SINCE the Civil War had the fabric of American society been so tested. Passionate support was equaled by opposition. And while foreign policy and national morality were debated and protested, the death toll mounted inexorably. Vietnam was the nation's most divisive war in a century; with the fall of South Vietnam in 1975, America turned its attention inward, repressing memory of that lost war. And as the personification of that war, America's Vietnam veterans were shunned and forgotten, relegated to the corners of society. But one veteran, unexceptional by all appearances, became consumed with the idea that those who sacrificed must be remembered. With assistance and perseverance, and against political opposition and overwhelming odds, his dream became a reality, and on Veterans Day 1982, the Vietnam Veterans Memorial was dedicated.

It was a catalyst for the nation. Americans returned their attention to the unfinished business of Vietnam—honoring those who served. Throughout the nation, the need to remember supplanted the need to forget. State and local memorials were erected; parades were held belatedly to celebrate and welcome home the Vietnam veteran. Finally, America could face its past, embrace its warriors, and make amends for having turned its back on its own sons. More important, veterans could begin to face openly both the traumatizing effects of that war and the social stigma of their service, which had forced them to endure their psychic scars in silence for a decade or more. The time for reconciliation and reintegration, both personal and national, had arrived. And more than any other site, the Vietnam Veterans Memorial in Washington, DC, has become the preeminent symbol of that healing process.

This brief story displays the essential elements of the dominant cultural narrative regarding the meaning of the Vietnam veteran in American society: service in the context of controversy; symbol of a nation's failure and humiliation; object of derision, sympathy, and pity, transformed from pariah to patriot. It is a familiar story to most Americans, poignant and reassuring in the closure it provides. Yet the very fact of its widespread acceptance is the impetus for this essay. Linked in narratives to the Vietnam Veterans Memorial, stories about the Vietnam veteran are sites of ideological struggle over national consciousness—struggle over the meaning of that war and the lessons to be drawn from it (see Ehrenhaus, 1990; Haines, 1986). I shall argue that the framework on which this narrative rests—the therapeutic motif—contains and co-opts the Vietnam veteran as a voice of political opposition; it renders veterans harmless by casting them in terms of metaphors of psychological dysfunction, emotional fragility, healing, and personal redemption; it effectively silences the voice of the veteran as a source of legitimate knowledge about the nature of contemporary warfare, thus subverting a potentially effective challenge to discourses advocating the use of "legitimate," state-sanctioned violence as a tool of national policy.

FRAGMENTATION AND AMERICA'S VIETNAM EXPERIENCE

Despite its likely familiarity to the reader, in no one place is this chapter's opening narrative located. Rather, it is constituted from fragments of public discourse; from print news and feature stories in the press; from popularized feature and documentary accounts of the war and its human consequences in books, television, and film; and from specialized and scholarly treatments of the cultural legacies of Vietnam for American society and its Vietnam veterans.

It is altogether fitting that a "coherent" narrative be created from discrete, tangentially related, rhetorical fragments. Vietnam was America's first postmodern war. That experience was (and remains) an essentially fragmented one: no clear military or political objectives; no recognizable enemy; engagement more by chance than design; objectives fought for, abandoned, then retaken, all the while the cost in human lives mounting;

disillusionment with political institutions; a loss of faith in "truth," much less a knowable "reality"; and no social consensus even today about how Vietnam should be incorporated within national memory.

American culture and public consciousness have fragmented. As McGee (1990) argues, this fragmentation has resulted in a transformation of the critic's role. Texts no longer exist, in the modernist sense of stable, self-contained objects-within-contexts for analysis. As a result, the task of critical analysis is no longer to elucidate their "meaning" or "worth." McGee states (1990, pp. 287-288):

> I would want to explore the sense in which "texts" have disappeared altogether, leaving us with nothing but *discursive fragments of context*. If by "text" we mean the sort of finished discourse anticipated in consequence of an essentially homogeneous culture, no texts exist today. We have instead fragments of "information" that constitute our context. The unity and structural integrity we used to put in our texts as they faithfully represented nature is now presumed to be *in us ourselves*.

Because of this transformation, therefore, we should

> look for *formations of texts* rather than "*the* text" as a place to begin analysis. . . . [W]e are dealing with *fragments*, not texts, and . . . we mean to treat a "formation" as if it were a singular text. . . .
>   I would want to explore the sense in which we are constantly harassed by the necessity of understanding an "invisible text" which is never quite finished but constantly in front of us. . . . The only way to "say it all" in our fractured culture is to provide readers/audiences with dense, truncated fragments which cue *them* to produce a finished discourse in their minds.

In sum, the responsibility of critical analysis in a postmodern world is to construct texts from diverse fragments and then explain how interpretive communities are able to imbue those fragments with coherence. In so doing, the critic can begin to shed light on the processes of social signification by which symbolic, social formations emerge and shape public consciousness and social arrangements.

Postmodernist positions such as McGee's have significant implications for the study of narrative. As Hayden White (1987) explains, this owes much to contemporary challenges to conventional views of text, context, and the relationship of language to consciousness and the material world. From a postmodern perspective, critique of an "authored" text centers on the analysis of its ideological codes and the manner in which the text further legitimates, and furthers the positional interests of, its author—the one authorized to explain the meaning of the past and impose moral order on it (see White, 1980).

But if, as McGee suggests, we subscribe to the premise of cultural fragmentation, and no longer presume the integrity of the autonomous, authored text as a "natural" unit of analysis, then the responsibilities of critical analysis shift further. Once we commit to construct our own "narrative" from fragments, we dispense with the autonomy and authority of one legitimated, clear voice in expressing a coherent and morally positioned storyline. Hence, our conception of narrative itself becomes fractured. Voices of discourse compete, intersect, and contextualize each other. Authority no longer resides in individual authorship but in the dominance of a particular symbolic, social formation that enables members of the interpretive community to create coherence from many voices. And because of their ability to impose coherence in terms of that social formation, members of the interpretive community can make (i.e., create, construct) sense. As White (1987) observes, this capacity has implications for determining one's placement in social hierarchy—one's "rightful" and "natural" place in the broader constellation of social relations.

> [N]arrative is revealed to be a particularly effective system of discursive meaning production by which individuals can be taught to live a distinctively "imaginary relation to the real conditions of existence," that is to say, an unreal but meaningful relation to the social formations in which they are indentured to live out their lives and realize their destinies as social subjects. To conceive of narrative discourse in this way permits us to account for its universality as a cultural fact and for the interest that dominant social groups have not only in controlling what will pass for the authoritative myths of a given cultural formation but also in assuring the belief that social reality itself can be both lived and realistically comprehended as a story. Myths and the ideologies based on them presuppose the adequacy of stories to the representation of reality whose meaning they purport to reveal. When belief in this adequacy begins to wane, the entire cultural edifice of a society enters into crisis, because not only is a specific system of beliefs undermined but the very condition of possibility of socially significant belief is eroded. (p. x)

The value of the concept *narrative* is therefore its convenience as a shorthand notation for the multiplicity of intersecting fragments that the critic circumscribes in constituting a working text—a story grounded in the social formations through which individuals, as members of an interpretive community, understand the world they inhabit and reproduce that world through their discursive participation and actions.

Consider again the narrative with which I began this essay. Some of its detail may have been new to the reader; yet its gist and tone, in all likelihood, are quite recognizable. The reason? Its storyline is organized in terms of a *therapeutic motif*, the dominant framework for public discourse about the aftermath of America's Vietnam experience. This motif casts all issues and questions of relationship in matters related to Vietnam—be they personal, cultural, or political—in terms of healing and recovery. The body is ravaged by war; the wounded must make peace with what remains. The mind is haunted by images, aromas, and sounds; veterans must learn to face their demons. Identity is fractured by the contradictory injunctions of survival in a war zone and those of civilized conduct back in "the world" (the latter of which requires the warrior persona to be concealed); the veteran must build a new sense of self. And a political community must contend with the culture's greatest indignity imaginable—failure; it must reconstitute its conviction in its nobility, strength, and moral purpose.

Clearly, the therapeutic motif draws its potency from the genuine human need to contend with the often brutalizing and devastating consequences of warfare on the body and the mind (Egendorf, 1986; Fussell, 1975, 1989; Lifton, 1973). It is now widely accepted, for example, that Vietnam veterans—combat veterans, in particular—often suffer effects known as post traumatic stress disorder (PTSD) syndrome; and those whose lives are bound up with theirs often become afflicted with the same disorder. Yet even more broadly, all whose lives were touched or shaped by the Vietnam War are its veterans, and as such, we all must make peace with the scars of war we bear in memory and in our relations with each other as members of a national community.

And it is here that the problem begins. Once healing is reified to the national level, then we tend to view all variety of issues pertaining to Vietnam in terms of the therapeutic motif. Once healing becomes a societal imperative, then the Vietnam veteran, as but one element within that broader construct, becomes subsumed by it. The veteran is reduced to a clinical challenge; rendered dysfunctional by the war, the motif takes the veteran's personal healing and reintegration as its locus. On the level of the national community, the narrative draws attention to the recognition of collective wrongdoing and the guilt due to responsibilities unmet; national cleansing is accomplished by facing up to old accounts and settling them—making amends for past wrongs by public celebration and commemoration of those wronged, setting aside old antagonisms, asking for and granting forgiveness. National healing can only be accomplished by enabling the veteran to heal; and the veteran can heal only if the national community undertakes its own redemption. By recognizing the mutual interdependence of the veteran and the broader community, full social reintegration and national reconciliation can be achieved. In these ways can the ledger on Vietnam be closed.

The tyrannizing power of the therapeutic motif is recognizable in any number of public characterizations of the Vietnam veteran and post-Vietnam America (see, for example, Edelman, 1985; Lopes, 1987). It predominates to such an extent that it precludes alternative interpretive frameworks from emerging to contextualize mainstream public discourse about America's Vietnam experience. Some years ago, Philip Wander examined the assumptive grounds of United States foreign policy rhetoric. He wrote that "the 'ground' on which foreign policy is debated in this country" is "so pervasive, so obvious, so free of challenge that, once articulated, one can but say that such is the nature of foreign policy rhetoric" (Wander, 1984, p. 353). The same can be said of discourse where the meaning of the Vietnam veteran is concerned. Precisely because the therapeutic motif is so pervasively used in framing discourse about the veteran, it seems to vanish. The motif becomes naturalized in national consciousness.

The central icon of the therapeutic motif is the Vietnam Veterans Memorial. As Egendorf (1986) argues in *Healing From the War*, "The Vietnam Veterans Memorial has become the focus for national mourning because the Vietnam veteran has become a popular metaphor for the nation's postwar conflicts" (p. 32). A cursory review of recent books, periodicals, films, and television programming bears this out.[1] The prominence of the Memorial as cultural icon draws our attention to the sacrifices of individuals. It also distracts us from what are, arguably, greater concerns—the nature of war, the use of war as an instrument of national policy, and the mythic obligations that link individuals to the state. The therapeutic motif decontextualizes the warrior, and by separating the warrior from the war, we attend to one at the expense of the other. Consequently, although discourses of healing are sanctified —linked, as they are, to patriotism, service, and honor—it is the very enormity of warfare's obscenity that is barred from acceptable public dialogue. The ideological crisis that the Vietnam War precipitated for American cultural and political institutions is transformed into a transitory, yet painful, disruption of personal well-being and interpersonal relations. In sum, the exclusion of the warrior's knowledge of the nature of contemporary warfare (beyond the hackneyed platitude of "War is hell") contributes by its absence to perpetuating the intricate web of social and discursive practices that keep warfare a viable option of national policy. Thus, those who experience and endure warfare are objectified and prevented from having an impact of any consequence on the social formations through which we live out our lives. In the therapeutic motif, "healing" is privileged over "purpose"; the rhetoric of recovery and reintegration subverts the emergence of rhetoric that seeks to examine the reasons that recovery is even necessary.

In making this claim, I do not wish to belittle the human consequences of warfare. Its impact on individuals is traumatizing, and the need to heal and recover is genuine. Yet the very fact that I *must* acknowledge the legitimacy of healing (and thus, the legitimacy of the therapeutic motif) is testament to its privileged position in sanctioned American discourse practices about Vietnam, specifically, and warfare, more generally. (Moreover, I am compelled to offer a personal disclaimer, lest I be perceived as callous and inhumane.) In sum, the "problem" is not that the therapeutic motif contributes to shaping public consciousness about Vietnam but that it mitigates against the emergence of alternative interpretive frameworks and oppositional readings of the discourse of Vietnam veterans.[2] A motif that celebrates unity (personal, relational, national) cannot abide discourse that engenders division. This is the tyrannizing power of the therapeutic motif.

NARRATIVE AND POWER

The capacity of narratives based in the therapeutic motif to shape public consciousness and silence the voices of veterans in matters of public deliberation raises the general question of the relationship between power and communication practices. The work of Stephen Lukes (1974) is instructive in this regard. Lukes proposes three models of power, which he discusses in terms of "dimensions" of power. Each model can be located along a continuum, with its poles defined by the extent to which power is conceived as transparent or opaque. More recently, Leslie Good (1989) has explored the implications of these models' assumptions for the study of communication. Two of the models approach communication as a means of social integration; the other views it as a vehicle of social control. Together, all three models contribute to understanding the potency of the therapeutic motif. As entailed by Lukes's one-dimensional model, communication is viewed as a means of social integration. Here, power is a manifest and transparent instrumentality; it emerges in the healthy, open conflict of deliberative decision making by which consensus is reached in the ideal of a pluralistic society. The model takes as its starting point a disagreement between parties; this disrupts the harmony of extant social arrangements. Diverse (read: competing) viewpoints, all with equal access to the public forum, are joined in rational discourse; the result is an informed public that weighs the relative merits of the positions and then renders a wise decision (i.e., the greatest good), thus enabling a return to harmony. As conflict is resolved and stability returns, power ceases to be an issue.

The two-dimensional model focuses our attention on the failure of discursive practices to operate integratively. Here, the genuine consensus that can result from open exchanges in the public space is distorted and supplanted by apparent consensus. Conflict ceases to be overt and becomes covert when those in positions of privilege block potential issues from the public space or when they disparage those whom they have marginalized; in this model, power is viewed as the capacity of one interest to suppress or undermine voices whose positions challenge it. Good (1989) notes that when issues are denied access to the public agenda, "When marginal social groups are prevented from gaining access . . . the process of agenda-building, rather than the agenda itself, becomes relevant" (p. 57).

Despite appearances, this model does not endorse a foundational critique of pluralism. First, it assumes that we can freely select our own relations of power, our own systems of social relationship. Moreover, this view of power and communication functions as an apology for the "common good" conception advanced in the first model. What we find here, then, is a qualified critique of the covert social processes that distort the creation of genuine consensus (which would result if all viewpoints are voiced fairly). Here we find a fundamental commitment to the ideal expressed in the one-dimensional model, along with a recognition that specific social practices are distortive of that ideal. In its implications for communication, Good refers to this two-dimensional model as "apologetically integrative." By revealing the flaws of communicative practice, it seeks to rescue the ideal of the pluralistic model.

Only with Lukes's three-dimensional model do we encounter a challenge to the view of communication as socially integrative. Here, power ceases to be examined as a vehicle of social integration to effect stability; nor is it any longer viewed as an instrument wielded by individuals. Rather, communicative practices ostensibly concerned with social integration are recast as means of social control. In contrast to the second view of power, which leads us to focus on how power *prevents the expression of grievances* in the public space, this third view leads us to examine how power, through its sanctioned communicative practices, *subverts the formation of potential grievances* in the first place.

When we conceive of communicative practices as social control, all cultural narratives, and the social arrangements from which they arise (and with which they are linked), reveal relations of power. These relations reveal the structure of ideological domination, whether embedded within the informal fabric of everyday life or within more formal, institutional practices at the intersection of the public and the private. In this model, power is latent, since it infuses the character of all social arrangements. In direct contrast to the first model, which conceives of power arising manifestly in the disruption of those arrangements, here power resides in the smoothly functioning, unproblematic conventions of social practices. Thus, from this perspective, power infuses all cultural narratives precisely because they organize and coordinate social and institutional arrangements and imbue them with meaning. Reiterating White's (1987) assertion, narrative is "a particularly effective system of discursive meaning production by which individuals can be taught to live . . . an unreal but meaningful relation to the social formations in which they are indentured" (p. x).

The dominant cultural narrative about the meaning of the Vietnam veteran in American society asks us, its readers, to take it as a fair and neutral representation of a series of historically related events. The story reveals a self-referential commitment to the ideals of the pluralistic view of power: Renewed, open, and reasoned interaction between once estranged citizens is cast as a means of achieving social reintegration in the wake of that divisive war. The voice of the narrative is that of a removed, yet compassionate, observer—undefined, yet credible. The subject matter is the sociocultural landscape of America following war. Within that context, the storyline describes obstacles to the establishment of harmony following that war and explains how those obstacles were overcome. However, although the narrative is committed to the ideals of the pluralistic model, it tells us of the nation's failure to live up to those ideals. Because of the traumatizing effect of America's Vietnam experience, veterans' legitimate voices were suppressed, as the nation coped with its own trauma through the unhealthy repression of all things related to Vietnam.

Drawing on Turner (1982), Haines (1990) observes that the Vietnam narrative is structured as a social drama, enacted through four phases: social breach; crisis; redressive; and reintegrative. "The concept of social drama provides a way of thinking about and describing how societies represent their ideological struggles within the rituals enacted by cultural forms" (Haines, 1990, p. 102). Social dramas begin with a social breach, a tear in the social fabric that interrupts smoothly functioning social life. Crisis follows when the community fractures into opposing coalitions and factions. Redress, the third phase, begins only when past wrongs against members of the community are acted on. And reintegration is achieved by the healing of old wounds, accomplished in part by assigning meaning to the troubled past in such a manner that it fits within the community's mythic narratives. Haines's astute assessment of the Vietnam War as a social drama is germane to appreciating the structural development of this chapter's opening narrative:

> The Vietnam War rendered problematic an array of interrelated salient relationships. Both the nature of the breach and the ensuing crisis developed as matters of vitriolic dispute. . . . Nothing less than our sense of national identity—how, and in whose interest, to define "America"—emerged as the objective of ideological struggle. . . . As the oral histories now suggest, many combat soldiers experienced the crisis phase in the "lie" of Vietnam. . . .
>
> Vietnam's redressive phase developed as an extraordinarily painful social experience, profoundly influencing the postwar position of combat veterans. . . . In the redressive phase, the soldier's lived ideological crisis recedes into the background like a fade-out in a silent movie. American cultural forms, unaccustomed to a rhetoric of defeat, employed a rhetoric of avoidance that associated further explanation of the war with unnecessary debate. Adjustive mechanisms mystify the war, strategically forgetting or, at best, *psychologizing the men who fought and sacrificed*. It is here in the redressive phase . . . that American society "abandons" the combat veteran, demonstrated by the failure to process his lived social experience of ideological crisis adequately.
>
> The Vietnam Veterans Memorial . . . signifies a return of the repressed to discursive practice and the movement of the social drama into its final, so-called "reintegrative" phase in which the wounds of Vietnam are healed. The reintegrative phase originates in the attempt to assign meaning to the sacrifice of American lives in Vietnam, a process inspired in this instance by Vietnam combat veterans. (pp. 102-104, emphasis added)

"As the story goes," then, American society failed to act in ways consistent with its ideals of democratic pluralism. As Haines argues, American society adjusted to its ideological crisis by repressing memory of the war; Vietnam veterans were victimized by that repression. In practice, public discourse in the aftermath of the Vietnam War reflects the deficiencies that define Lukes's two-dimensional model of power; the legitimate interests of Vietnam veterans were suppressed and denied fair and open access to the public space in the wake of the war. But with the dedication of the Vietnam Veterans Memorial, we find a "return of the repressed to discursive practice." It is significant that in these cultural narratives not only are veterans "psychologized" but American society is portrayed in similar terms. We find here an acknowledgement of the failure of the national community to have met its postwar responsibilities. By admitting that deficiency (and defining it as a singular event rather than as an inherent defect of the system of relations), the narrative contains a limited critique of American society. On its face, it is "apologetically integrative."

In its relational implications, the Vietnam narrative functions as an apology, initiated by the national community and offered to the veteran. In essence, this apology conforms to the rules governing the class of speech acts known as *accounts*. Accounts are explanations or justifications given in response to an (in)action that has resulted in a violation of expected conduct. As I have noted, the Vietnam narrative does more than define and delimit the legitimate voice of its Vietnam veterans through the therapeutic motif. The narrative both explains American society's failure to meet its obligations to its veterans and excuses that violation in terms of that same motif of debilitation. "Forgive us for being late, but we got a flat tire on the way over" differs only in degree from "Forgive us for having ignored you, but we were traumatized and in denial." Violation is followed by explanation. But explanation is not enough. For an account to be accepted and therefore successful, it must be based in a premise deemed legitimate—and disability is such a premise. It places the cause of the violation beyond the violator's control. Thus, in this self-proclaimed, "apologetically integrative" narrative, the nation implicitly asks its veterans for forgiveness. And the veterans' implicit acceptance constitutes relational healing, a repair of the social fabric.

Clearly, then, the preferred reading of the Vietnam narrative is through its express commitments to the ideals of democratic pluralism and the goals of relational repair—national reconciliation and social reintegration. Yet, just as one may question the legitimacy of the premise on which an account is constructed, we can easily imagine the righteous indignation that would result from an oppositional reading with its suggestions that the narrative manipulates (and by implication, that power's commitment to the therapeutic motif is less than selfless). As I earlier indicated, when we examine communication as a means of social control, inquiry centers on how it subverts potential grievances and challenges extant social arrangements. Analysis centers on how communication practices operate as means of domination (see Giddens, 1979, Ch. 5; Mumby, 1987). In the case of America's preferred Vietnam narrative, we are led to inquire how the dominance of the therapeutic motif serves the interests of those persons, institutions, and industries in positions of privilege at the expense of those less well positioned.

By its own voice, the narrative concedes that the Vietnam veteran has been marginalized. It would also have us accept that, because of the community's renewed concern with healing, veterans have been fully reintegrated into society and have, once again, full and equal access to the public space. Certainly, Vietnam veterans now have a voice in the public space that they were once denied. The question, however, concerns the sanctioned nature of that voice and the circumstances of access to the public space.

Marginalized voices often can and will be heard. But these public expressions occur in ways that defuse those voices, often by integrating them into the broader system of social relations from which they have been excluded. And integration involves locating those marginalized within the symbolic, social formations by which power makes (i.e., creates, imposes) sense. I refer here to the co-optation of the margins. This is not a matter of power relegating groups to the margins or of ignoring them once they are marginalized. Rather, it is a matter of power adjusting to the disruptive potential of those who are marginalized. Through the communicative options it sanctions, power can defuse opposition before it crystallizes; it can create the illusion of opposition to demonstrate pluralism's openness and tolerance and inclusiveness; and power can dictate the conditions under which genuine opposition can and will be heard, thus rendering it ineffectual. Gitlin (1980) observes that the hegemonic ideology of contemporary American culture meets challenges to it by co-opting those who offer the challenge. "[O]nly by absorbing and domesticating conflicting values, definitions of reality, and demands on it, in fact, does it remain hegemonic" (p. 256).

Because of their lived experience as both participant in and witness to the Vietnam War, Vietnam veterans know the material obscenities of war and its human costs, stripped of all trappings of noble purpose and moral righteousness. Collectively, veterans are well-positioned to challenge those who advocate the use of state-sanctioned violence, destruction, and terror as a tool of foreign policy while silently passing over its brute realities. As such, Vietnam veterans are potentially disruptive of that ground on which foreign policy rhetoric is played out (see Wander, 1984) as well as the grounds of ancillary rhetorics such as those concerned with masculinity, patriotism, and duty. The therapeutic motif effectively contains veterans by rendering them politically impotent. By its focus on personal and collective trauma, the emotional fragility that trauma produces, and the need to recover from that debilitated state, the motif creates a context that defines the warrior as cripple and muzzles the warrior as witness. Taken in its broader cultural context, any act of "witnessing" becomes systematically distorted, cast as a matter of personal catharsis and healing, thus undermining its potency as a foundation for political challenge (see Hansen, Owen, & Madden, 1992; Terry, 1985).[3]

In sum, by viewing the Vietnam narrative as a means of social control, we find that veterans are "helped," but only in ways that protect those dominant social interests, institutions, and symbolic social formations from potential challenge. Returning, again, to White (1987): "Myths and the ideologies based on them presuppose the adequacy of stories to the representation of reality. . . . When belief in this adequacy begins to wane, the entire cultural edifice of a society enters into crisis . . . the very condition of possibility of socially significant belief is eroded" (p. x).

CO-OPTING THE VETERAN'S EXPERIENCE: FRAGMENTS OF *THE* TEXT

Through the therapeutic motif, the Vietnam narrative seeks to contain and co-opt the Vietnam veteran. However, opposition is possible, even in the face of dominant ideological interests. The tyrannizing power of the therapeutic motif is never complete; it is an ongoing accomplishment. And the same can be said of opposition. One of the most compelling examples of an oppositional voice is *Parallels*, an organized and edited collection of personal narratives about the experience of war (Hansen et al., 1992). Drawing largely, but not exclusively, on veterans of Vietnam, the collection is at its best when veterans of several wars are telling their own stories; among those whose stories are included are Soviet veterans of the war in Afghanistan, their "Vietnam." One is struck not only by the enormity of warfare-as-everyday-life but by the seeming inability of any discursive framing device to diminish the impact of these narratives *if* they were to enter fully and centrally into mainstream public discourse and consciousness.

Confronted as power is with the disruptive potential of authentic war narratives to rattle the very foundation of established political, economic, and social arrangements, it is no wonder that those whose stories hold such potential are co-opted. When viewed as social control, communication subverts the emergence of effective challenge; co-opting the margins by domesticating opposition (here, through the therapeutic motif) is one such way.[4] Controlling the circumstances in which oppositional voices may express themselves is another. One Vietnam veteran, Steve Tice, shares his hope that the wisdom of returned warriors will be widely heard at some point:

> When the messenger is bringing back a message that society doesn't want to hear, society has a way of rejecting messengers. . . . It's more like an assassination of character . . . a few people started telling their stories in the seventies and got rejected. . . . The message is finally starting to filter through, and some people are starting to hear, and the message is essentially about war. (Hansen et al., 1992, pp. 227-228)

Tice refers specifically to collections such as *Parallels*, to Ron Kovic's *Born on the Fourth of July*, and to Oliver Stone's films. An important book, *Parallels* is but one small voice. And any substantive impact on social formations of commercially successful films is likely to be ephemeral. Moreover, if postmodern scholarship teaches us anything, it is that the integrity of any self-contained text is illusory; thus, McGee (1990) argues that critical analysis must give primacy to the politics of representation and to the struggle for control of those symbolic, social formations that shape consciousness.

The critic's role, as McGee notes, is to "look for *formations of texts* rather than *the* text" (p. 287). What follows are fragments of "the text," all grounded within the therapeutic motif. All take as their topic the discourse and actions of Vietnam veterans and those who are defined through them (e.g., mothers, fathers, sisters, brothers, sweethearts, widowed spouses, children). All reveal the social definition of the veteran through the Vietnam Veterans Memorial. And, as illustrative of the therapeutic motif, all center on matters of relationship, removing that discourse and those actions from the historical, cultural, and political context of the Vietnam War.

Insofar as healing requires the recognition of illness or impairment or dysfunction, the therapeutic motif first reveals itself in characterizations of Vietnam veterans even prior to the dedication of the Memorial in November 1982. Throughout the 1970s and, although much abated, even continuing to this day, action-adventure and suspense television programming and feature films have semiotically coded the veteran as "mad" or "bad," an out-of-control character around whom the central conflict of the plot is based.[5] "Vietnam" has served as a shorthand device to denote, though never explain, psychopathic and sociopathic behavior. Essentially coincident with the years during which the traumatizing effects of Vietnam were being argued, challenged, defined, and identified (e.g., PTSD, Agent Orange; see Severo & Milford, 1989), it is not surprising either that "Vietnam" would be used as a dramatic shorthand for character mystification or that the growing recognition of the sometimes disabling effects of Vietnam would simply be acknowledged to advance the central plot and then ignored.

But all this began to change with the dedication of the Vietnam Veterans Memorial. Through association with the Memorial as a physical site, "the Vietnam veteran" was transformed from an inchoate "issue" to a tangible image, crystallized in national consciousness. By their identification through the Memorial, the "focus for national mourning" (Egendorf, 1986, p. 32), veterans came to be defined primarily in terms of all those issues that bear on mourning—in other words, the therapeutic motif.

Even before its construction was complete, veterans began to bring offerings in memory of fallen comrades. And beginning shortly after its dedication, mourners making pilgrimage to the Memorial have brought letters to the dead as acts of remembrance. Two years after its dedication, the Memorial was presented to the people of the United States by the Vietnam Veterans Memorial Fund; since that time, the National Park Service has collected for archival purposes all letters and offerings left at the Wall.

In both popular and academic treatments of the letters written in memory of those killed in Vietnam, we glimpse the subtle operation of power in public discourse, shaping the meaning of death and sacrifice and obligation in the absence of coalesced opposition. Harry Haines (1986) has argued that the meanings of the Memorial and of veterans—now defined through the Memorial—have been appropriated by vested political interests who seek to locate remembrance of the war within the mainstream of American mythic memory. "Dead glory," as Michael Madden (1988) once wrote, must be celebrated and sanctified if calls for future sacrifices to foreign policy are to be made justifiable.

And that is precisely the point. How shall we interpret these expressions of grief and remembrance? As what shall we take them? Shall we simply see grief? Or might we see grief as the result of an intricately orchestrated system of cultural signification, which exploits human beings in the name of national purpose, and which then sanctifies those sacrifices as a means of justifying that exploitation?

The tyranny of the therapeutic motif engulfs the letters left at the Wall. By relegating the recovery of hope to the realm of the private, it contains the despair of those who write the letters and renders them harmless. Most recently, the motif has been extended to the next generation, the now-adult children of those killed in the war. On Father's Day 1992, more than 300 sons and daughters gathered at the Memorial to leave offerings and to share stories of the stigmatizing effects of Vietnam on their lives. Not surprisingly, nationally syndicated news stories reported this gathering much as an outing of a clinical support group (see "Children of Vietnam War Dead," 1992; Maves, 1992).

The therapeutic motif precludes a political interpretation—of the act of writing, of the substance of the letters, of the placement of those texts in that public place. It prevents those who suffer despair from realizing that they, and those whom they mourn, have participated in their own co-optation by identifying with the interests of those who play the world "geopolitically." Absent this realization, they are denied the opportunity to act in ways that enable them to discover, and recover, their own best interests. Opposition is defused before it crystallizes.

Two texts about the letters are illustrative of this co-optation of the margins, revealing the power of the therapeutic motif. The first is a book written for a general audience, Laura Palmer's (1987) *Shrapnel in the Heart*. Its introduction conveys the poignancy of the motif:

> They were ours. In the simplicity of those three words is the power of the Vietnam Veterans Memorial and the purpose of this book. The memorial asks that you remember; here are the names. *Shrapnel in the Heart* lets you listen; here are their stories, told by the people who loved them. (p. xi)

Each "story" begins with a letter written to the dead and left by a loved one. Following each letter is a brief, personal sketch linking the author with the fallen son, or husband, or father; the substance of these sketches are recollections of their days together before Vietnam. As we are told on its jacket, this book "is not about despair. It is a book about love that bombs couldn't shatter and bullets couldn't kill."

The second fragment is scholarly, a Burkean analysis of letters left by mourners at the Memorial over the course of 17 months. Working within the therapeutic motif, Carlson and Hocking (1988) argue that the letters reveal each writer's attempt to purge guilt through strategies of scapegoating or mortification. Their analysis explores the underlying dynamics of the various strategies they identify. As the following passage indicates, they subscribe to the preferred reading of the letters: "At the Memorial, each visitor carries his or her own source of guilt: anger unresolved, responsibilities unmet, deeds unfinished or promises unkept" (p. 206).

I question neither these authors' competence nor their fundamental caring and decency. (Again, the tyrannizing power of the therapeutic motif.) As a scholarly work, the Carlson and Hocking essay is significant, but not primarily because of its efforts to explicate the rhetorical processes involved in social reintegration. Rather, the essay provides insight into how the academy participates both in the co-optation of the margins (in this case, Vietnam veterans) and in its own co-optation, by taking refuge in an analytic virtuosity. The academy has long sought—and taught—professional legitimation through a kind of remote, neutered, technical expertise. Terry Eagleton (1983) observes that academic training provides instruction in the use of the signifier; the signified is irrelevant. Professional legitimation, he writes,

> is a matter of being able to talk and write in certain ways. . . . You can think or believe what you want, as long as you can speak this particular language. Nobody is especially concerned about what you say. . . . Those employed to teach you this form of discourse will remember whether or not you were able to speak it proficiently long after they have forgotten what you said. (p. 201)

But this need not be the case. Academics can stake out a position in the world and take the world as their domain. For example, if we privilege "critical rhetoric" over "rhetorical criticism," as McKerrow (1989) advocates, then criticism becomes an active participant in a social dialectic rather than the product of interested, yet dispassionate observers, applying interpretive criteria to a world belonging to others.

In his Introduction to *The Wall*, Michael Norman, a Marine combat veteran and former correspondent for the *New York Times*, concludes: "To touch the Wall is to touch the dead, to get close to them. And as they make this crossing—as those who never knew war come close to those taken by it—they begin to understand Vietnam and thus honor the generation of veterans who survived the war" (n. p.). Even though what he means by "understand" is unclear, we have no expectation that he should be precise. The therapeutic motif functions as a strategy of containment, in part, by its reliance on strategically ambiguous discourse: It never probes too deeply; it voyeuristically dwells on intimacy and poignancy while never violating the illusion of privacy; it never dwells on expressions of anger, or betrayal, or on moments of personal insight about the naturalization of social arrangements; it gravitates, instead, to expressions of bewilderment in the absence of an understood "purpose" or "reason" for it all; it leans heavily on bromides. There is danger in detail. Once we begin to explore and articulate "understandings," "insights," or "truths," then we begin to confront directly the scope of the ideological crisis that a close analysis of America's Vietnam experience has the capacity to produce.

NOTES

1. Although I refer to the containment of Vietnam veterans by the therapeutic motif, by implication all who are in any way linked to them are similarly contained. Most apparently this includes their immediate families and friends. But to the extent that "healing" is an objective of the national community, all who identify with or are subsumed by that construct are similarly contained. Simply because "healing" may be called for, it need not render those in need of healing incapacitated or incompetent—thus, denied access from the public space, except in their personae as "recovering from the war." The tyrannizing power of the therapeutic motif lies in the fact that it totalizes its subjects.

2. Among recent books featuring the Vietnam Veterans Memorial on their covers are Egendorf (1986), Morris and Ehrenhaus (1990), Palmer (1987), and Scruggs and Swerdlow (1985). Also see the special "Vietnam in America" issue of the *New York Times Magazine* (1985, March 31), McCloud's essay in *American Heritage* (1988, May/June), and the Spring 1986 issue of *Cultural Critique*, edited by Berg and Rowe, which features on its back cover the Memorial and on its front cover the statue added to the Memorial grounds of three Vietnam veterans. In commercial release film, see especially *In Country* (1989). In commercial television programming, see especially the final two-hour episode of *China Beach*, which concludes with a pilgrimage by all of the main characters to the Memorial.

3. Vietnam veterans are also positioned to shatter the myth that the obligation to serve the United States in its military ventures is compensated honorably. Although this betrayal has been the norm in all U.S. wars, with the singular exception of the Second World War, the scope of the betrayal is greatest in the case of Vietnam, encompassing matters of widespread drug addiction, the summary termination of benefits programs, post traumatic stress disorder, and the known, but officially denied, medical effects of exposure to Agent Orange. See Severo and Milford (1989) for an extensive treatment of this topic.

4. It is not my intent to develop the argument in this essay, but I do wish to note that the therapeutic motif "feminizes" the voice of the veteran through its metaphoric entailments of emotionality (vs. analytic rationality), fragility (vs. strength), and person-centeredness (vs. issue-centeredness). This feminization of the Vietnam veteran (and thus, of all who are defined through the veteran) contributes to their co-optation. Consequently, whereas any true story of war is inherently obscene and jarring in what it reveals, the story is, itself, defused by the social characterization of the veteran as emotionally unstable and defective. Thus, as I have noted, the political implication of acts of witnessing are systematically distorted into acts of personal recovery.

5. Astute viewers of *Silence of the Lambs,* which was voted the best picture of 1991, may have noticed that in the film's climactic rescue and shoot-out, the psychopathic killer-kid-napper had in his basement a map of Vietnam, an Army helmet, and an American flag.

REFERENCES

Berg, R., & Rowe, J. C. (Eds.). (1986, Spring). American representations of Vietnam. *Cultural Critique.*
Carlson, A. C., & Hocking, J. E. (1988). Strategies of redemption at the Vietnam Veterans Memorial. *Western Journal of Speech Communication, 52,* 203-215.
Children of Vietnam War dead honor Father's Day together. (1992, June 22) *Oregonian,* pp. A1, A8.
Eagleton, T. (1983). *Literary theory.* Oxford, UK: Basil Blackwell.
Edelman, B. (Ed.). (1985). *Dear America: Letters home from Vietnam.* New York: Pocket Books.
Egendorf, A. (1986). *Healing from the war.* Boston: Shambhala.
Ehrenhaus, P. (1990). On Americans held prisoner in Southeast Asia: The P.O.W. issue as "lesson" of Vietnam. In R. Morris & P. Ehrenhaus (Eds.), *Cultural legacies of Vietnam: Uses of the past in the present* (pp. 9-26). Norwood, NJ: Ablex.
Fussell, P. (1975). *The great war and modern memory.* London: Oxford University Press.
Fussell, P. (1989). *Wartime.* New York: Oxford University Press.
Giddens, A. (1979). *Central problems in social theory: Action, structure, and contradiction in social analysis.* Berkeley, CA: University of California Press.
Gitlin, T. (1980). *The whole world is watching.* Berkeley, CA: University of California Press.
Good, L. (1989). Power, hegemony, and communication theory. In I. Angus & S. Jhally (Eds.), *Cultural politics in contemporary America (pp. 51-64, 363-365).* New York: Routledge.
Haines, H. W. (1986). "What kind of war?": An analysis of the Vietnam Veterans Memorial. *Critical Studies in Mass Communication, 3,* 1-20.
Haines, H. W. (1990). The pride is back: "Rambo," "Magnum, P.I.," and the return trip to Vietnam. In R. Morris & P. Ehrenhaus (Eds.), *Cultural legacies of Vietnam: Uses of the past in the present* (pp. 99-123). Norwood, NJ: Ablex.
Hansen, J. T., Owen, A. S., & Madden, M. P. (1992). *Parallels: The soldiers' knowledge and the oral history of contemporary warfare.* New York: Aldine de Gruyter.
In country (film). (1989). Warner Brothers.
Lifton, R. J. (1973). *Home from the war: Vietnam veterans: Neither victims nor executioners.* New York: Simon & Schuster.
Lopes, S. (1987). *The wall: Images and offerings from the Vietnam Veterans Memorial.* New York: Collins.
Lukes, S. (1974). *Power: A radical view.* London: Macmillan.
Madden, M. P. (1988). *"A covenant with death": The President's epideictic message of legitimation and national sacrifice.* Unpublished doctoral dissertation, University of Iowa.
Maves, Jr., N. (1992, June 21). Daddy, I hardly knew you. *Oregonian,* pp. L1, L4.
McCloud, B. (1988, May/June). What should we tell our children about Vietnam? *American Heritage,* pp. 55-77.
McGee, M. C. (1990). Text, context, and the fragmentation of contemporary culture. *Western Journal of Speech Communication, 54,* 274-289.

McKerrow, R. E. (1989). Critical rhetoric: Theory and praxis. *Communication Monographs, 56*, 91-111.

Morris, R., & Ehrenhaus, P. (Eds.) (1990). *Cultural legacies of Vietnam: Uses of the past in the present.* Norwood, NJ: Ablex.

Mumby, D. K. (1987). The political function of narrative in organizations. *Communication Monographs, 54*, 113-127.

Palmer, L. (1987). *Shrapnel in the heart: Letters and remembrances from the Vietnam Veterans Memorial.* New York: Random House.

Scruggs, J. C., & Swerdlow, J. L. (1985). *To heal a nation.* New York: Harper & Row.

Severo, R., & Milford, L. (1989). *The wages of war: When America's soldiers came home—From Valley Forge to Vietnam.* New York: Simon & Schuster.

Terry, W. (1985). *Bloods: An oral history of the Vietnam War by Black veterans.* New York: Ballantine.

Turner V. (1982). *From ritual to theatre: The human seriousness of play.* New York: Performing Arts Journal Publications.

Vietnam in America (1985, March 31). *New York Times Magazine*, pp. 28-71.

Wander, P. (1984). The third persona: An ideological turn in rhetorical theory. *Central States Speech Journal, 35*, 197-216.

White, H. (1980). The value of narrativity in the representation of reality. In W. J. T. Mitchell (Ed.), *On narrative* (pp. 1-23). Chicago: University of Chicago Press.

White, H. (1987). The context in the text: Method and ideology in intellectual history. In *The content of the form: Narrative discourse and historical representation* (pp. 185-213). Baltimore, MD: Johns Hopkins University Press.

Chapter 4

NARRATIVE AND THE CULTURE OF OBEDIENCE AT THE WORKPLACE

Marsha Witten

A FEW YEARS AGO, a new consultant joining the firm of Mitchell, Hall and Josephs (a pseudonym for a leading management consulting firm in New York City) would probably have heard a story about a senior partner, Steve, and a junior consultant, Dave, that went more or less like this:

> Steve and Dave are en route to a hospital at the tip of Manhattan for an appointment with the chief executive officer, who has engaged the consulting firm to work through a merger application with another hospital. Unlike most New Yorkers who hail taxis when they need to get around, Steve is famous for driving his Mercedes everywhere. Steve and Dave have just picked up Steve's car from his garage on First Avenue. It's about a five-mile drive downtown to the hospital, but the men have plenty of time; the appointment's at 2:00, it's now 1:30.
>
> As the pair are just in sight of the Brooklyn Bridge, about a mile from the hospital, the Mercedes becomes stuck in a traffic jam; nothing is moving for miles. Steve grows increasingly agitated; honking the car's horn, he leans out of the window and finally gets out of the car and paces the roadway. Not knowing what to do, Dave tries to calm Steve down by assuring him the jam will soon give way, but Steve ignores him. Nothing budges, and the clock is ticking away; it's 5 minutes to 2.
>
> Suddenly, wordlessly, Steve gets back into the car and moves the shift into reverse. He backs the car up enough to turn its wheels to the right and

AUTHOR'S NOTE: Thanks to Eric Eisenberg, Dennis Mumby, Charles Slater, John Sutton, and Barbie Zelizer for comments on this or an earlier draft. All errors are mine alone. A much earlier version of this chapter was presented at the annual meeting of the International Communication Association, May 1986.

propels the Mercedes up onto the sidewalk of a lower-income housing project that faces the roadway. Ramming down a chicken wire fence that separates the project from the road, he slaloms the car through the complex's courtyard, where children are playing stickball and women are hanging up laundry. Dave covers his face with his hands, but then, unable to stand it any longer, screams, "Sir, what are you doing? We'll only be a few minutes late." Steve ignores the protest, careers through the sidewalks of the project to its other entrance, steers the car along some back streets, and finally pulls up at the hospital.

The two consultants arrive at the appointment precisely on time. Their meeting with the CEO goes smoothly; the officer is pleased with the work Dave has done on the case and comments to Steve about his luck in recruiting such an able young man. When the appointment is over, Steve and Dave head back uptown, chatting pleasantly about the assignment.

Back at corporate headquarters, Steve and Dave walk to their own offices. Five minutes later, Steve's secretary summons Dave to Steve's office, telling him to bring the project's working papers along. Dave takes a quick look at the papers to be certain he can efficiently discuss his next task on the project and knocks on Steve's door. Steve greets him amiably and says, "Dave, you're fired. Clean out your desk and be out of here by 5 o'clock."

As experienced consultants at Mitchell, Hall related this tale, and as new consultants listened to it, they were most likely engaged and amused. A well-constructed narrative is especially suited among communicative forms for emotionally involving both teller and listener, provoking attention, interest, and absorption (Bormann, 1983; Wilkins, 1978). As teller and listeners co-orient around a narrative's central characters and events, they achieve a sense of collective participation, shared experience, and psychological investment (Bormann, 1983; Fisher, 1984, Martin, 1982).

But at the same time as they entertain and absorb, narratives are also powerful forms of talk for the exercise of covert control at the workplace. It is in part through the recounting of narratives—such as the one presented above—that hierarchical relationships in organizations are imaged, workers are taught the parameters and obligations of their roles, and behavioral norms in service of the organization's ends are conveyed.

In this chapter, I explore some of the processes by which narrative discourse may aid in creating a culture of obedience at the workplace and exemplify these processes through an analysis of the texts of selected organizational stories.[1] This project supplements sociological studies of covert control at the workplace that suggest that the dominant workplace culture can have a forceful effect on the thoughts and behavior of employees (Burawoy, 1979; Edwards & Scullion, 1982; Jackall, 1978). However, this work neglects to specify the communicative mechanisms through which control is dramatized and reproduced. In these approaches, culture remains an amorphous, shady force whose connection to the concrete realm of workers' action is left unexplained. For example, in his study of shopfloor control, Burawoy (1979) attributes the "manufacturing of consent" to the embedding of workers in a pervasive culture of "making out," in which meeting production goals and hence producing surplus value for bosses is constituted as a game. Workers play the game both for the sake of challenging their capacities and because "making out" is a way to earn respect of other workers. In the account of Edwards and Scullion (1982), workplace cultures encouraging "chiseling"—worker pilferage of excess manufactured goods—are said to diffuse discontent that would otherwise be channeled into protest by supplying some of the benefits lost through bosses' appropriation of surplus value. For Jackall (1978), workers remain quiescent on the job despite lack of rewards because of "psychological inertia" that is produced and reproduced by a culture of "defeasibility"— beliefs that efforts to change the situation will fail because there is no notion of who is to blame.

These case studies demonstrate that the covert operations of culture can supplement more explicit means of control such as supervisory roles, rules and policies, and the structure of the workflow (Edwards, 1979). But they leave unexplained the mechanisms that mediate culture and the obedient behavior of the worker, neglecting to theorize about how workers realize the culture or how certain aspects of culture become pervasive guides for thought, feeling, and action. Further, they do not account for the mechanisms through which the culture is reproduced to continue its effects.

Consonant with recent views of some researchers in organizational communication (Clegg, 1975; Clegg & Dunkerley, 1980; Deetz & Mumby, 1990; Mumby, 1987, 1988), these issues may be resolved through a more careful formulation of the notion of culture and its functions. Culture is seen here as a set of capacities for thought and behavior—patterns of interpretation and "strategies of action" (Swidler, 1986)—available to organizational members. Control is effected through culture when capacities that benefit those who run the organization are "organized in" while alternatives are "organized out" (Bachrach & Baratz, 1970). This is accomplished as certain interpretive patterns and strategies of action are made to seem more salient, appropriate, natural, useful, and legitimate than others (Thompson, 1984). Through these means, workers may be influenced to accept a limited set of tools for interpretation at the workplace and instructions for their application.

These tools and instructions are powerfully imparted through people's symbolic behavior, of which talk is a paramount form (Berger & Luckmann, 1966). In particular, the narrative form of talk is potentially instrumental in the creation and maintenance of an obedience culture at the workplace. As I will argue, narrative is a singularly potent discursive form through which control can be dramatized, because it compels belief while at the same time it shields truth claims from testing and debate. As a result, narrative is capable of commanding attention, belief, and memory with minimal risk of the argumentative challenges that can validly be made of powerful assertions set forth in other forms of talk. And as symbolic resources that serve the ends of control are realized through practices of storytelling and listening, they are renewed to continue their effects.

Before turning to an examination of the functions of narrative in helping to enact an obedience culture at the workplace, it will be useful to situate this work within the context of related social scientific research programs.

RELATED RESEARCH

There has been a growing interest in the last decade among sociologists and scholars of communication in cultural analysis. Although these studies have represented varying definitions of the objects of concern (Wuthnow & Witten, 1988), many have focused on the role of symbolism and language in producing a shared version of reality and moral order in specific social groups. Studies of culture have provided a new set of paradigms useful in organizational analysis, alternatives to prevailing functional perspectives.

In contrast to traditional assumptions of organizational research, which have treated communication as a "conduit" for the transmission of information useful in efficient decision making, the newer cultural approaches emphasize the role of language in producing the very sense of organizational reality inhabited by participants (Smircich, 1983). These views posit that through ongoing symbolic interaction, people constitute, maintain, and change their organizational environment (Pacanowsky & O'Donnell-Trujillo, 1983). Through their talk and other symbolic behaviors, people in organizations produce a shared, intersubjective understanding of the nature of their reality; provide themselves with a scheme for making sense of that reality; and, importantly, objectify these understandings so that the nature of their constructed environment appears as "real" to them. The everyday, ordinary order of organizational reality is thus both produced by ongoing symbolic interaction and objectified into structures of meaning that take on the aura of facticity (Berger & Luckmann, 1966, p. 38). Scholars working within this interpretive understanding of organizational reality thus have focused on symbolic systems and sense-making procedures in organizations. Many of these studies have taken a descriptive focus on organizational culture, examining, for example, key organizational metaphors (e.g., Smith & Eisenberg, 1987; Smith & Simmons, 1983), accounts (Cheney, 1983; Tompkins & Cheney, 1983), linguistic constitution of subcultures (Gregory, 1983; Martin et al., 1985), and similar issues.

Recently, though, these approaches have been criticized for ignoring the power dimensions of symbolic processes within organizations. Scholars from a variety of perspectives have argued that one cannot adequately examine the social construction of organizational reality without attention to the differential ability of groups within organizations to "make their meanings count." In these views, establishing the nature of the "shared meanings" and sense-making procedures of organizational participants is only part of the researcher's task; one must further investigate the mechanisms of power and control through which apparent consensus over meanings has been created.

The theoretical impetus for these examinations of the role of power and control in organizational cultures has come from three strands of social scientific thinking. The first, spawned by the institutional school of organizational sociology, has linked Weberian notions of legitimate power (i.e., authority) with investigations of the symbolic mechanisms of power in contemporary organizations. The second two, deeply intertwined, have been concerned with examining the operations of power through ideology, as it is realized in speech and other organizational practices. Although the research agendas that these theoretical directions have inspired have taken different routes, the strands of theory are united in their critiques of the adequacy of functional approaches to studying power; in an insistence that power is a more complex phenomenon than superficial descriptions allow; and, concomitantly, in a concern with the ways in which communication practices aid in instantiating power and control in organizational life.

NEO-WEBERIAN PERSPECTIVES ON ORGANIZATIONAL SOCIOLOGY

When Max Weber produced his monumental work on legitimate domination (complete English translation, 1978), his concern was to present an overarching historical, developmental model of authority systems. Differentiating the nature of bureaucratic authority from that dependent on tradition or the charisma of the leader, Weber posited that authority in bureaucracy depends on subordinates' perceptions of the legitimacy of powerholders, based on the structural positions that powerholders inhabit. Subordinates thus obey superiors in bureaucratic organizations because of a "normative commitment" to bureaucratic structure: the right of power-holders to command and to enforce the rational, legally sanctioned, impersonal rules that govern organizational functioning.

Although useful for its intended purposes—marking distinctions among three historically dominant authority systems—contemporary critics have noted that in taking for granted subordinates' "normative commitments" to their superiors' power, Weber's scheme fails to examine the social processes generating these commitments on the part of subordinates. Among other concerns, then, recent research has attempted to enrich the understanding of the processes through which perceptions of legitimacy—and thus legitimate power, or authority—are created in bureaucratic organizations, focusing attention on the communicative work both of social structures and of individual actors. Like parallel work in communication, these studies are based on the premise that legitimacy is not a static property of a structure or person but must be achieved ongoingly through symbolic processes.

On the macroscopic level, studies such as those of Meyer (1977), Meyer and Rowan (1977), Fennell (1980), and DiMaggio and Powell (1983) have suggested that organizations, like individual social agents, must continuously dramatize their warrants to legitimacy in order to claim authority in their fields of action. One way they do so, these researchers have argued, is through the configuration of their formal structure. Often the structure functions less to guarantee the putative concern of organizations—efficiency of operations—than to serve as a narrative that dramatizes myths of "rationality" assumed by society. In other words, the very formal structure of the organization signals the legitimacy of its power to external and internal constituencies alike, as it displays appropriateness to the norms of rationality that are assumed to be rules of organizational functioning.

On the microlevel, Biggart and Hamilton (1984) have extended these arguments to the processes of social interaction among organizational actors. In their case study of officials in the gubernatorial administration of Californian Jerry Brown, the researchers explored the ways in which superiors enacted displays of appropriateness to their offices to fit subordinates' normative expectations of powerholders' behaviors. They found that superiors signalled through their communicative behavior their "competence" to achieve the duties of their roles and their "loyalty" themselves to obey the strictures of their role prescriptions. These communicative displays, they concluded, were necessary to supplement and enable the role of structure in creating perceptions of legitimate power.

THE COMMUNITY POWER DEBATE

A second contribution to the study of the link between culture and power emerged from the community power debate that engaged the field of political science in the United States in the 1960s and 1970s. As Stewart Clegg details in his contribution to this volume, the debate challenged prevailing assumptions about the nature of power in social settings and enriched understanding of the complexities of power processes. In denying that the operations of power can be fully captured through a study of overt (observable) processes, it contributed models for studying power in organizations that have supplemented those traditionally used in organizational research. In the traditional models, still represented in mainstream management studies, power is examined through analysis of the outcomes of overt conflicts in organizations, usually manifested in important situations of decision making. The actor or group prevailing in decision making is judged to "have more power" than those whose preferences and claims are defeated. As its myriad critics have pointed out, this model assumes that power is exercised only through overt conflict that arises in decision-making situations and ignores the potential for less readily observable power practices that operate to suppress observable conflict over issues.

The critiques of Bachrach and Baratz (1962, 1970) and, later, Steven Lukes (1974) have seminally influenced the later direction of organizational studies of power, including those within organizational communication. These more complex models of power have led some scholars away from a sole focus on overt conflict into a more nuanced view of power processes in organizations. The three-dimensional model of Lukes's has been especially influential in underscoring the role of covert power as it operates through ideological manipulation. Although the community power debate has not engendered a separate research project in organizational communication, it has been influential in calling attention to power processes at work through the culture of organizational members.

CRITICAL PERSPECTIVES

Coupled with Lukes's three-dimensional model of power, recent developments in continental sociology have influenced organizational communication researchers to adopt a political perspective of the relationship between communication and organizations. Drawing on Marxian formulations, these views hold that communication is intrinsically linked with ideology; just as ideology enables organizational action, including communication, so it is through communication that ideological meaning systems are created and reproduced (Deetz & Mumby, 1990, p. 42). These systems of meaning privilege particular definitions of organizational reality, legitimating and reifying these formulations and in so doing conveying power on those whose interests they serve. In its most general sense, then, a critical perspective on organizational communication calls for analysis of ideological meaning systems operating in organizational contexts and an examination of the processes through which they are produced and reproduced.

Among other concerns, recent research from a critical perspective has been interested in the ways in which instrumental rationality dominates organizational speech and sense-making procedures. These procedures are examined to see how ideologies of technical reason consonant with managerial interests are enstructured in communicative practice and, thereby, the daily lived experience of organizational members (Alvesson & Willmott, 1992; Clegg, 1975; Deetz & Kersten, 1983; Mumby, 1988). Much of this research has been rooted in the social theory of Jurgen Habermas (1970, 1971, 1975), both in its interest in unearthing and critiquing ideologies of technical rationality and in its openly articulated concern for serving educative and "emancipatory" functions in organizational settings.[2]

COMMUNICATION AND CONTROL:
ANALYSIS OF GENRES

The cumulative contribution of all three strands of theorizing and research discussed here has been to underscore the link between communicative processes and the exercise of covert power and control at the workplace. As these lines of research are developing, interest is emerging in studying the functions of specific communication genres in these processes. For example, the role of ceremonial events in encoding and reproducing dominant managerial ideologies has been insightfully studied in

Rosen's analysis of a corporate breakfast (1985) and an organizational Christmas party (1988). In both analyses, Rosen shows how ceremony works to construct dramatizations of "community" and "moral order" that reinforce the structures of the bureaucracies in which they occur. Similarly, Conrad's (1983) exploratory discussion of rituals suggests that they allow participants to manage tensions and contradictions that arise in organizational life. In studying such rituals the researcher is granted insight into the dialectic between overt and covert levels of power in a particular social setting. And Mumby (1988) has examined narrative as a device for the legitimation of dominant power relationships in organizations, arguing that narratives, read politically, are ideological forces that privilege some interests over others. The present work continues in this fairly new research tradition.

In the remainder of this chapter, I return to a discussion of the functions of narrative in the constitution of obedience at the workplace. I argue first, on the most general level, that narrative can set forth powerful and persuasive truth claims—claims about appropriate behavior and values—that are shielded from testing or debate. Second, narrative can provide models of correct behavior and rules for the extension of the models to new situations. Third, narrative can impart values that affect problem definition. Finally, narrative can create an anticipated reaction of the failure of protest based on an "invented tradition" of the firm.

I first discuss the general role of narrative in asserting and shielding truth claims and then detail and exemplify the specific functions named above.

NARRATIVES AND TRUTH CLAIMS

Through narrative discourse, speakers can make strongly persuasive assertions that are masked from examination and challenge. This is true because of the cognitive and psychological effects of stories on listeners. First, stories are especially capable among speech acts of capturing attention through such features of their language as the use of active voice, present tense, repetition, and vivid and concrete details through which plots and episodes are unfurled (McLaughlin, 1984; Wilkins, 1983). Through these linguistic features, attention is drawn to the exploits of the story's actors, the settings in which action occurs, and the consequences of actors' behavior (Weaver & Dickinson, 1982). The salience of these story details is likely to persist over time, since concrete, immediate language is memorable (Martin, 1982; Yuille & Paivio, 1969).

In addition to their cognitive impact, narratives can have strong persuasive effects. Narratives are more effective than facts or statistics in generating belief among listeners who agree with the argument (Borgida & Nisbett, 1977; Kahnemann & Tversky, 1973; Martin, 1982; Nisbett, Borgida, Crandall, & Reed, 1976). The very linguistic features of stories that command attention and memory—concrete, vivid descriptions and active voice, present tense verbs—also compel emotional investment (Bormann, 1983; Martin, 1982) and lend the quality of persuasiveness to the speech act they constitute (Fowler, 1986; Kress & Hodge, 1979; Reyes, Thompson, & Bower, 1980). The narrative form contributes further to a narrative's credibility by imposing a sense of coherence on the disparate elements the narrative contains. This effect occurs through structuring devices of plot, which unifies episodes; narrative sequence, which unifies time; and characterization, which unifies action (Carr, 1986; Ricoeur, 1984). In addition, the narrative form typically lays out a sequence of events so as to explain the outcome in terms of the beginning, integrating each detail in an unbroken chain of causality (Reiser, Black, & Lehnert, 1985).

But the unique power of narrative talk stems from its ability to set forth truth claims that are shielded from testing or debate at the same time as it is persuasive and memorable. Truth claims are implicit assertions contained within speech acts that the propositions that are uttered are true and morally correct (Habermas, 1979). The truth claims contained within narrative are shielded both because of the psychological effects of narrative on listeners and because of the conventions of storytelling as a speech act. First, the narrative's emotionally compelling language deters listeners' critical responses (Kirkwood, 1983). Although people do evaluate the narratives they hear, judgments are usually restricted to gauging the story's internal consistency (i.e., the structural relationship among characters, events, and settings) and the relevance of the narrative to the conversation preceding it (Jefferson, 1978). Further, the rules of storytelling—the conventions of the genre—make it difficult for a listener to question the narrative's contents. Narrative discourse suspends ordinary conversation, departing from a state of turn-by-turn talk among co-participants. Thus it is inappropriate for the listener to raise a challenge to a truth claim implicit in a narrative even if the faulty claim is recognized. In its suspension of the conversation, of the dialectic between conversational partners, the story constrains the types of responses that can relevantly follow (Sanders, 1984). It can convey a "ready-made" knowledge (Crable, 1982) that takes on the status of presumption. The presumption, encased in narrative, is shielded from testing or debate; it is a claim to validity that denies the need for justification or proof. In short, the narrative is a powerfully persuasive, presumed claim to truth and correctness that is not ordinarily subjected to challenge.

In addition to masking persuasive truth claims, narrative may help create an obedience culture at the workplace by modeling desired behaviors in particular situations and rules for the extension of the models.

NARRATIVES AS EXEMPLARS
FOR PERMISSIBLE BEHAVIOR

In recounting the deeds of their characters, narratives frequently embed exemplars—concrete, situated examples of action, and the consequences of action, that model correct and successful choices about behavior. Exemplars contained in narrative give pragmatic instructions to listeners by offering them situated strategies of action (Suleiman, 1983), which listeners then can appropriate to apply to new situations by analogical extension. Thus, exemplars function as paradigm cases for behaviors, from which, by analogical extension, actors can select correct behaviors in similar circumstances. For newcomers to organizations in particular, exemplars aid selection of suitable rules to follow in specific instances of choice and provide guidance for behaviors not covered by rules.

Guiding tacit knowledge, exemplars are not generally matters of conscious attention. Instead, by operating beneath the level of discursive awareness, they help form the "deep structure" of organizational order (Deetz & Kersten, 1983)—a set of taken-for-granted, unexamined assumptions about what is appropriate behavior in the organization. It may be helpful here to borrow Bourdieu's (1977, p. 72) term *habitus*—"a system of durable . . . dispositions" which enable "regulated improvisations"— that is, unconscious analogical extension of exemplars to different areas of practice. I return to the story at the start of the paper to explore the effects of an exemplar.

The tale of the two consultants in a traffic jam was typically related to newcomers in the consulting firm. The story carries a minatory message: In order to succeed in the organization, here is what one needs to do. On a surface level, the story focuses on the outcomes to Dave, conveying the warning not to challenge or react negatively to the decisions of the boss, no matter how favored an employee one may appear to be. A further message concerns a warning to new consultants not to take their standing in the firm for granted: The diligent preparation and the praise from others do not count for much in the face of disapproval from the boss. Finally, on a very basic level, the story warns employees to watch out for Steve: He's crazy.

But on another level, the story focuses not on Dave's behavior but on Steve's. It is his actions that provide the model of appropriate conduct for those who wish to succeed in the company. The story is a paradigm case of the primacy of action over thought: a literal enactment of the "fast-track" metaphor popular in contemporary businesses. Success stems not necessarily from skill or know-how but from a willingness to take matters into one's own hands to further the firm's concerns. Further, the story suggests that it is appropriate to do absolutely anything to fulfill one's duty to a client (and thus promote the company's interests)—including acts of personal risk, endangerment of others, and petty illegality. The consultant acting appropriately according to these models must be willing to put his or her own reservations and scruples aside. By analogical extension, the exemplar proposes that consultants working for the firm are an elite, above the rule of any laws except those that govern the company's interests.

Finally, the story is a lesson in power on several levels: the power of the senior consultant to fire a junior member of the company at will, and for seemingly irrational cause; the power of the boss to break the laws of New York City and not get caught; the power to scorn the welfare of the poor in the service of one's own interests; and the brute, physical power of a corporate executive in an expensive automobile to destroy the property of others. The exemplar teaches, in short, that success in the firm is ultimately based on personal and institutional force.

Closely tied to the provision of exemplars for behavior is the third function of narrative in shaping an obedience culture at the workplace: setting core organizational values.

THE ROLE OF NARRATIVE IN IMPARTING VALUES AFFECTING PROBLEM DEFINITION

A narrative circulates at Mitchell, Hall about a naive young employee who, in his eagerness to be creative, "reinvents the wheel," devoting so many hours reformulating work that has already been done that he drives himself into a nervous breakdown. Similar tales are told about ambitious newcomers who burn themselves out trying to "improve the wheel" or "create square wheelers."

A tale is told in a music publishing company about an easygoing assistant manager whose staff misses the deadline for producing the annual promotional catalogue. The assistant manager's name drops out of the tale; instead, she's called The Floater. The label is extended to refer to any supervisor suspected of not managing his or her staff appropriately. The metaphor grows: The act of giving employees too much freedom is termed "floating"; jokes are made about supervisors whose authority is in question—they are wearing "life jackets" or need the "Coast Guard to come to the rescue."

Through key aspects of their structure and the language they contain, narrative can unobtrusively and persuasively communicate core organizational values. First, narratives have frames that channel perception; like television screens, they provide enclosures for our "pictures of the world" (Hackett, 1984). The frames focus attention on the selected set of observations, impressions, and actions falling within their parameters. By including certain details from the stream of events, by highlighting them in emphatic ways through vivid, detailed, or emotionally compelling descriptions, narratives as frames can give value to certain events; by omitting other details, stories can inhibit conceptualization of issues in alternative ways. Frames can act as potent blinders to the ways people interpret their circumstances. Writers of the Palo Alto school of communication theory (Bateson, 1972; Watzlawick, Weakland, & Fisch, 1974) have shown the necessity, and the difficulty, of reframing—that is, of changing selection and emphasis of content and detail—to alter people's interpretations of the situations in which they find themselves.

Second, the special kinds of vocabulary in which narratives tend to be told—the names ideas are given—impart values in subtle ways. The vocabulary forms a set of assumed definitions within which perceptions are ordered. Metaphors (Koch & Deetz, 1981; Smith & Eisenberg, 1987; Weick, 1979), jargon (Edelman, 1971), and slogans and ideographs (McGee, 1980) frequently incorporated in narrative become shorthand for thinking, discussion, and action. Once the language is widely communicated, it is difficult to probe beneath the surface to unseat assumptions on which the language rests. The value imparted in the story thus becomes a "group-licensed way of seeing" (Kuhn, 1970), an assertion whose presumptions are difficult to penetrate.

Through frames and names, then, narratives covertly impart values that channel attention toward certain elements in the stream of events and away from others, setting parameters around elements that are salient and meaningful (Beyer, 1981; Starbuck, 1976; Weick, 1979). Values can enable or suppress conflict by affecting the ability of people in organizations to identify what they are experiencing as a problem or grievance. For example, asymmetrical distributions of power will seem appropriate and just when core values legitimize the authority of some over others; similarly, values that ascribe blame to victims of injustice will constrain the definition of grievance by inhibiting attributions of fault to external causes instead of to one's own failings (Ferree & Miller, 1985; Ryan, 1971).

Under usual circumstances in most organizations, key values are matters of "pragmatic acceptance" (Mann, 1970) as part of the dominant modes of thought—assumed without rigorous questioning, maintained as matters of acquiescence. In these situations, failure to question or challenge dominant values can serve as unobtrusive controls by constraining the ability of people even to conceive of radically, substantively different ways of doing things. Under these conditions, serious challenges to the "rules of the game" are unlikely; no "coherent alternative" (Walsh, Hinings, Greenwood, & Ransom, 1981, p. 43) to the prevailing system can be formed. I illustrate the power of narrative to set core values through their framing and naming functions by returning to the examples.

The metaphor "reinventing the wheel" has long been in use in aggressive and successful advertising agencies, consulting firms, and other organizations performing contract work for clients. On a surface level, the metaphor suggests that employees should spend time efficiently when undertaking an assignment for a client. Used to warn consultants that it is inappropriate to redo what has already been done, it directs members of a project team to adapt or recycle previously created plans and documents when creating, for example, campaigns or programs, instead of expending efforts on replacing something that already exists. On a literal level, then, the metaphor communicates the value of efficient use of company time.

However, once the metaphor is unravelled, a series of potent, embedded assumptions about values becomes visible. The first holds that, in fact, a staff member of a business organization could single-handedly invent something as creative and revolutionary as a wheel, should he or she but choose to do so. This shrouded claim helps create and maintain an exaggerated self-image regarding the importance of the businessperson to the social community. The second assumption is that reassessing prevailing ideas is contrary to good business practices; since it is of no profit to reexamine that which already exists, the goal of business should be not to invent *de novo* but rather to build from work previously created. This assumption argues against the radical examination of routine, habit, and standard operating procedure. Finally, the metaphor embodies in a particularly compelling way the myth of progress—that is, that achievements in organizations build in ongoing series, one on top of the other, and that subsequent inventions, discoveries, and works are therefore inescapably superior to the ones they follow.

The warning against "reinventing the wheel" forcefully and covertly argues against criticism. It asserts that existing protocols and practices of the organization should not be reexamined and reformulated; that the appropriate direction for business is onward and upward, despite all contingencies; and that an organizational member who probes or considers matters too deeply, or who proceeds too thoughtfully, is suspect. In reinforcing the value of efficiency over quality, it discourages the definition of issues as concerning merit rather than speed. It reinforces the prevailing value of expediency to the exclusion of other measures of worth.

The second story includes a variation on the nautical and cybernetic metaphors that have been common for centuries in the Western world's literature about politics and government; for example, the notion of the polity as a "ship of state" and of the king or ruler as captain or statesman. Taken for granted, and therefore unchallenged, in the floater metaphor and similar phrases are the following assumptions: that the organization is adrift in a vast, uncharted sea; the voyage is dangerous for the unwary; the situation is one of constant crises, with obedience to the one man in charge, the captain, essential if the organization is to survive; floating— that is, experimenting, trying things *ad hoc*, working without an explicit plan—is dangerous because that's when the sharks (read competitors) are attracted to the kill, and so on. Organizations guided by these metaphors and the assumptions they embody would be likely to value management and control over all. The connotations of the nautical imagery discourage the perception of possible grievances concerning insufficient autonomy or the opportunity to experiment and innovate. It is no accident, I suggest, that the publishing company is governed autocratically by the president, who displays an enormous ship's wheel as the centerpiece of his office.

Finally, in the next section, I show how stories can invent a tradition of the failure of protest in the firm.

NARRATIVES AS EMBODIMENTS
OF ANTICIPATED REACTIONS

A narrative is told in a research foundation—a scholarly and slow-moving place where accurate studies had always been deemed more important than speed—about the efficiency expert newly appointed as director. A burly, brusque, and uneducated fellow, the new boss is universally disliked by the foundation's staff. The director cracks the whip to ensure that grant deadlines are met, fat is trimmed from the budget, and everyone works the right number of hours. After he fires five or six senior staff members, the remaining employees recount the latest indignities to one another and end the tale by sighing, "Guess the handwriting's on the wall." One day someone posts a sign on the central staff bulletin board: MENE, MENE, TEKEL, UPHARSIN.[3] The sign stays up for a year.

Narratives may aid in maintaining a culture of obedience at the workplace by conveying an *invented tradition* of the futility of protest. They do so by illustrating the rule of *anticipated reactions,* promoting an avoidance of tests of strength. Anticipated reactions refers to the belief of relatively powerless people in a social group that they will fail if they attempt to mount challenges to the status quo. In this situation, people are able to perceive that they are in conflict with the prevailing system of values, but they do not think they can successfully protest. It does not matter whether in fact their beliefs are correct; they have set up a self-fulfilling prophecy of failure. On the basis of these narratives, people institutionalize constraints on their behavior that, in fact, they themselves have imposed.

As the invented tradition of an organization, narratives can thus help prevent challenges to existing hierarchical relationships by promoting the rule of the past over the present (Walsh et al., 1981), maintaining the powerlessness of disadvantaged groups. The narratives people tell thus both reflect and help maintain their positions of relative disadvantage, promoting and reinforcing a culture of obedience. I turn to the story paraphrased at the beginning of this section to show how invented traditions can work in this way.

A central message conveyed by the narrative is the necessity of acceding to one's situation. The familiar proverb "The handwriting's on the wall" serves to define the problem for the foundation's staff as how to go about the task of accepting fate gracefully rather than focusing the issue on the dubious fairness or appropriateness of the managing director's judgments and methods. In this case, the narrative dramatizes the inevitability of the unexpected and seemingly unprovoked firings and bureaucratic treatment of professional staff. The passive acceptance of events as lying outside one's control encourages organizational participants to believe that the organization has a life of its own, so to speak, governed by ineluctable processes that cannot be changed. The issue then becomes how to submit with grace to the manager's goal—that of rationalizing operations of the foundation—rather than of posing a serious challenge to it by means of grievance making or other action.

The selection of the quotation from the Book of Daniel has another, subtler effect on the way in which the foundation's staff is persuaded to do nothing by the rule of anticipated reactions. By posting the literal form of the original "handwriting on the wall," an academic inside joke if there ever was one, they attempt to brandish their intellectual superiority over the poorly educated managing director, a futile show of power compared to his authority to fire staff at will. It is interesting to note how this impotent gesture might contribute to their failure to take meaningful action on their grievance. As Edelman (1964) has pointed out, attachment to symbols can replace active involvement in challenging an injustice; the symbol becomes "a substitute gratification for the pleasures of remolding the concrete environment" (Edelman, 1964, p. 9).

CONCLUSION

In this chapter, I have suggested some of the mechanisms through which workplace control may be exercised through culture, focusing on the role of narrative discourse in this process. I have argued that the narratives told in organizations may play a role in creating and maintaining a culture of obedience. Because narrative talk has strong cognitive and psychological effects at the same time as it masks its truth claims from examination or testing, it is a potent vehicle for channelling thought and action. I have suggested that narrative talk can serve purposes of control by persuasively—and unchallengeably—modeling desired behaviors; by supplying core values; and by inventing a credible history for the firm in which attempts at protest are consigned to failure. If these effects can be achieved covertly by means of narrative, important implications for studying control in organizations and for examining the ethics of communicative strategies are raised.

First, the issues developed in this chapter lend further support to the growing practice of studying organizational power and control on a variety of dimensions, examining the covert operations of culture as well as more readily observable political practices such as decision making and conflict. This chapter points to the need to supplement work on the role of symbolism in covert control with investigations of the particular genres in which symbols are contained and through which they are organized. I have suggested here that symbols embedded in narrative may have more persuasive force, by virtue of characteristics of the narrative genre, than the same symbols contained in other forms of speech. At the same time, claims conveyed through narrative are more easily masked than those in conversation or argument. A more complete understanding of the genres through which organizational communication takes place will allow research into relationships between characteristics of workplaces and the forms of talk that predominate in them. For example, if narrative is a mechanism of covert control, one would expect narrative to constitute a greater proportion of the discourse in organizations or organizational subunits with relatively high levels of covert control (e.g., organizations staffed by professionals) than in organizations in which more overt forms of control predominate (e.g., assembly-line work structures).

Continuing research into the link between narrative and power at the workplace is needed to resolve some of the issues left open by this chapter and other relevant work. First, Boje (1991) has criticized the prevailing tendency in research on organizational narrative to isolate narratives from their social and interactional contexts and treat them as reified texts. He argues that an ethnographic approach is necessary both to situate narratives in concrete local cultures and to see how organizational members collaboratively produce narratives, changing details of storylines according to the interactional context. From the perspective of the intent of this chapter, at least, clearly more empirical studies such as Boje's are needed to assess whether, and in which particular contexts, organizational narratives alter as they are retold sufficiently to affect dramatizations of power and authority.

On a related issue, in focusing on the role of narrative in constituting cultural norms that promote obedience to managerial prerogative, this chapter has given short shrift to communicative functions of resistance. Recent work has stressed the interplay among systems of signification in political fields such as organizations, insisting that the making of meaning is a site of struggle, of competing discourses in which power is diffused rather than concentrated in the hands of the few. Thus, to give a fuller picture of the role of narrative with respect to power, it would be necessary to discover whether, and in what contexts, narratives of resistance, challenge, and even subversion of dominant norms surface and engage in the dialectic of control.

As a corollary, the arguments articulated here should raise some concerns about the ethics of storytelling as a communicative strategy. Since the claims embedded in stories are both persuasive and hidden, the protection of rational challenge available when one participates in dia-

logic forms of talk is not readily available. If storytelling helps generate
an obedience culture at the workplace, the obedience of employees is thus
a product of manipulation and not genuine consensus. If the stories people
hear and tell aid them in uncritically accepting organizational values; if
they teach models of behavior whose underlying assumptions are not
questioned; if they promote acquiescence and submission to "fate," their
effect is to depoliticize incipient organizational issues, removing them from
arenas of discussion and debate.

NOTES

1. The stories analyzed in this paper were collected by the author as a participant-observer
in two organizations—a management consulting firm and a scientific research foundation in
New York City—and as an observer in a third organization, a music publishing company in
suburban Philadelphia.

2. This project is currently undergoing some changes in definition as it confronts poststructuralist critiques of foundationalism. For some, the challenge of poststructuralism suggests
that critical theory will only survive in organizational analysis in a much attenuated state, if
indeed at all. Others maintain it is still possible to retain some of the goals of critical theory,
scaled down to an appropriate scope. For a thoughtful discussion and a plea to preserve the
essence of the emancipatory project, see Alvesson and Willmott, 1992.

3. In the Bible story of Daniel (Daniel 5:25), Belshazzar the king calls on Daniel to interpret
a mysterious slogan that has appeared on his wall. The slogan predicts doom for the king.
Hence our proverb, "The handwriting's on the wall."

REFERENCES

Alvesson, M., & Willmott, H. (1992). On the idea of emancipation in management and
organization studies. *Academy of Management Review, 17,* 432-464.
Bachrach, P., & Baratz, M. (1962). Two faces of power. *American Political Science Review,
56,* 947-952.
Bachrach, P., & Baratz, M. (1970). *Power and poverty: Theory and practice.* New York:
Oxford University Press.
Bateson, G. (1972). *Steps to an ecology of mind.* New York: Ballantine.
Berger, P., & Luckmann, T. (1966). *The social construction of reality.* Garden City, NY:
Doubleday.
Beyer, J. (1981). Ideologies, values, and decision-making in organizations. In P. Nystrom &
W. Starbuck (Eds.), *Handbook of organizational design, Vol. 2* (pp. 166-202). New
York: Oxford University Press.
Biggart, N., & Hamilton, G. (1984). The power of obedience. *Administrative Science
Quarterly, 29,* 540-549.

Bormann, E. (1983). Symbolic convergence: Organizational communication and culture. In L. Putnam & M. Pacanowsky (Eds.), *Communication and organizations: An interpretive approach* (pp. 99-122). Beverly Hills, CA: Sage.

Borgida, E., & Nisbett, R. (1977). The differential impact of abstract vs. concrete information on decisions. *Journal of Applied Social Psychology, 7*, 258-271.

Boje, D. (1991). The storytelling organization: A study of story performance in an office supply firm. *Administrative Science Quarterly, 36*, 106-126.

Bourdieu, P. (1977). *Outline of a theory of practice* (Trans. Richard Nice). New York: Cambridge University Press.

Burawoy, M. (1979). *Manufacturing consent: Changes in the labor process under monopoly capitalism.* Chicago: University of Chicago Press.

Carr, D. (1986). Narrative and the real world: An argument for continuity. *History and Theory, 25.*

Cheney, G. (1983). On the various and changing meanings of organizational membership: A field study of organizational identification. *Communication Monographs, 50*, 342-362.

Clegg, S. (1975). *Power, rule and domination.* London: Routledge and Kegan Paul.

Clegg, S., & Dunkerley, D. (1980). *Organization, class and control.* London: Routledge and Kegan Paul.

Conrad, C. (1983). Organizational power: Faces and symbolic forms. In L. Putnam & M. Pacanowsky (Eds.), *Communication and organizations: An interpretive approach* (pp. 173-194). Beverly Hills, CA: Sage.

Crable, R. (1982). Knowledge-as-status: On argument and epistemology. *Communication Monographs, 49*, 249-262.

Deetz, S., & Kersten, A. (1983). Critical models of interpretive research. In L. Putnam & M. Pacanowsky (Eds.), *Communication and organizations: And interpretive approach* (pp. 147-172). Beverly Hills, CA: Sage.

Deetz, S., & Mumby, D. (1990). Power, discourse, and the workplace: Reclaiming the critical tradition. In J. Anderson (Ed.), *Communication Yearbook, Vol. 13* (pp. 18-47). Newbury Park, CA: Sage.

DiMaggio, P., & Powell, W. (1983). The iron cage revisited: Institutional isomorphism and collective rationality in organizational fields. *American Sociological Review, 48*, 147-160.

Edelman, M. (1971). *Politics as symbolic action.* Chicago: Markham Press.

Edelman, M. (1964). *The symbolic uses of politics.* Urbana, IL: University of Illinois Press.

Edwards, R. (1979). *Contested terrain.* New York: Basic Books.

Edwards, P., & Scullion, H. (1982). *The social organization of industrial conflict.* Oxford, UK: Basil Blackwell.

Ferree, M., & Miller, F. (1985). Mobilization and meaning: Toward an integration of social psychology and resource perspectives on social movements. *Sociological Inquiry, 55*, 38-61.

Fennell, M. (1980). The effects of environmental characteristics on the structure of hospital clusters. *Administrative Science Quarterly, 25*, 484-510.

Fisher, W. (1984). Narration as a human communication paradigm: The case of public moral argument. *Communication Monographs, 51*, 1-22.

Fowler, R. (1986). *Linguistic criticism.* Oxford, UK: Oxford University Press.

Gregory, K. (1983). Native view paradigms: Multiple cultures and culture conflict in organizations. *Administrative Science Quarterly, 28*, 359-376.

Habermas, J. (1970). Toward a theory of communicative competence. *Critical Inquiry, 13*, 360-375.

Habermas, J. (1971). *Knowledge and human interests* (Trans. Jeremy Shapiro). Boston: Beacon Press.

Habermas, J. (1975). *Legitimation crisis* (Trans. Thomas McCarthy). Boston: Beacon Press.

Habermas, J. (1979). *Communication and the evolution of society* (Trans. Thomas McCarthy). Boston: Beacon Press.

Hackett, R. (1984). Decline of a paradigm? Bias and objectivity in news media studies. *Critical Studies in Mass Communication, 1*, 229-260.

Jackall, R. (1978). *Workers in a labyrinth: Jobs and survival in a bank bureaucracy.* Montclair, NJ: Allanheld, Osmun.

Jefferson, G. (1978). Segmental aspects of storytelling in conversation. In J. Schenkein (Ed.), *Studies in the organization of conversational interaction.* New York: Academic Press.

Kahneman, D., & Tversky, A. (1973). On the psychology of prediction. *Psychological Review, 80*, 237-251.

Kirkwood, W. (1983). Storytelling and self-confrontation: Parables as communication strategies. *Quarterly Journal of Speech, 69*, 58-74.

Koch, S., & Deetz, S. (1981). Metaphor analysis of social reality in organizations. *Journal of Applied Communication Research, 9*, 1-15.

Kress, G., & Hodge, R. (1979). *Language as ideology.* London: Routledge and Kegan Paul.

Kuhn, T. (1970). *The structure of scientific revolutions.* Chicago: University of Chicago Press.

Lukes, S. (1974). *Power: A radical view.* London: Macmillan Press.

Mann, M. (1970). The social cohesion of liberal democracy. *American Sociological Review, 35*, 423-39.

Martin, J. (1982). Stories and scripts in organizational settings. In A. Hastorf & A. Isen (Eds.), *Cognitive social psychology.* New York: Elsevier.

Martin, J., Sitkin, S., & Boehm, M. (1985). Founders and the elusiveness of a cultural legacy. In P. Frost, L. Moore, M. Louis, C. Lundberg, & J. Martin (Eds.), *Organizational Culture* (pp. 99-124). Beverly Hills, CA: Sage.

McGee, M. (1980). The "ideograph": A link between rhetoric and ideology. *Quarterly Journal of Speech, 66*, 1-16.

McLaughlin, M. (1984). *Conversation: How talk is organized.* Beverly Hills, CA: Sage.

Meyer, J. (1977). The effects of education as an institution. *American Journal of Sociology, 83*, 55-77.

Meyer, J., & Rowan, B. (1977). Institutionalized organizations: Formal structure as myth and ceremony. *American Journal of Sociology, 83*, 340-63.

Mumby, D. (1987). The political function of narrative in organizations. *Communication Monographs, 54*, 113-127.

Mumby, D. (1988). *Communication and power in organizations: Discourse, ideology and domination.* Norwood, NJ: Ablex.

Nisbet, R., Borgida, E., Crandall, R., & Reed, H. (1976). Popular induction: Information is not always informative. In J. Carroll & J. Payne (Eds.), *Cognition and social behavior.* Hillsdale, NJ: Erlbaum.

Pacanowsky, M., & O'Donnell-Trujillo, N. (1983). Organizational communication as cultural performance. *Communication Monographs, 50*, 126-147.

Reiser, B., Black, J., & Lehnert, W. (1985). Thematic knowledge structure in the understanding and generation of narrative. *Discourse Processes, 8*, 357-369.

Reyes, R., Thompson, W., & Bower, G. (1980). Judgmental biases resulting from differing availabilities of arguments. *Journal of Personality and Social Psychology, 39*, 2-12.

Ricoeur, P. (1984). *Time and narrative* (Trans. Kathleen Blamey & David Pellauer). Chicago: University of Chicago Press.

Rosen, M. (1985). Breakfast at Spiro's: Dramaturgy and dominance. *Journal of Management, 11*(2), 31-48.

Rosen, M. (1988). You asked for it: Christmas at the bosses' expense. *Journal of Management Studies, 25,* 463-480.

Ryan, W. (1971). *Blaming the victim.* New York: Vintage.

Sanders, R. (1984). Style, meaning and message effects. *Communication Monographs, 51,* 154-167.

Smircich, L. (1983). Concepts of culture and organizational analysis. *Administrative Science Quarterly, 28,* 339-358.

Smith, R., & Eisenberg, E. (1987). Conflict at Disneyland: A root-metaphor analysis. *Communication Monographs, 54,* 367-380.

Smith, K., & Simmons, V. (1983). A Rumpelstiltskin organization: Metaphors on metaphors in field research. *Administrative Science Quarterly, 28,* 377-393.

Starbuck, W. (1976). Organizations and their environments. In M. Dunnette (Ed.), *Handbook of industrial and organizational psychology* (pp. 1069-1123). Chicago: Rand McNally.

Suleiman, S. (1983). *Authoritarian fictions.* New York: Columbia University Press.

Swidler, A. (1986). Culture in social action: Symbols and strategies. *American Sociological Review, 51,* 273-286.

Thompson, J. (1984). *Studies in the theory of ideology.* Berkeley, CA: University of California Press.

Tompkins, P., & Cheney, G. (1983). The uses of account analysis: A study of organizational decision making and identification. In L. Putnam & M. Pacanowsky (Eds.), *Communication and organizations: An interpretive approach* (pp. 123-146). Beverly Hills, CA: Sage.

Walsh, K., Hinings, B., Greenwood, R., & Ransom, S. (1981). Power and advantage in organizations. *Organization Studies, 2,* 131-152.

Watzlawick, P., Weakland, J., & Fisch, R. (1974). *Change: Principles of problem formation and problem resolution.* New York: Norton.

Weaver, P., & Dickinson, D. (1982). Scratching the surface structure: Exploring the usefulness of story grammar. *Discourse Processes, 5,* 225-243.

Weber, M. (1978). *Economy and society* (Trans. G. Roth & C. Wittich). Berkeley, CA: University of California Press.

Weick, K. (1979). *The social psychology of organizing.* 2nd. Edition. Reading, MA: Addison-Wesley.

Wilkins, A. (1978). *Organizational stories as an expression of management philosophy.* Unpublished doctoral dissertation, Stanford University School of Business.

Wilkins, A. (1983). Organizational stories as symbols which control the organization. In L. Pondy, P. Frost, G. Morgan & T. Dandridge (Eds.), *Organizational symbolism.* Greenwich, CT: JAI Press.

Wuthnow, R., & Witten, M. (1988). New directions in the study of culture. *Annual Review of Sociology, 14,* 49-67.

Yuille, J., & Paivio, A. (1969). Abstractness and recall of connected discourse. *Journal of Experimental Psychology, 82,* 467-471.

PART III

NARRATIVE, SOCIETY, AND RACE

Chapter 5

STORIES AND RACISM

Teun A. van Dijk

INTRODUCTION: RACISM AND DISCOURSE

IN THIS CHAPTER I examine the role of storytelling in the reproduction of racism. This analysis of everyday stories about ethnic or racial minorities is part of a long-term research project about the discursive reproduction of racism in white, European(ized) societies. My earlier work in this field focused on everyday conversations (van Dijk, 1984, 1987a), textbooks (van Dijk, 1987b), and news in the press (van Dijk, 1991). My present research pays special attention to the role of various (other) types of elite discourse, for example, in politics, corporations, and scholarship (van Dijk, 1993).

The research project is essentially multidisciplinary. It relates properties of text and talk with underlying social cognitions of language users as social group members, and it relates both discourse and cognitions with their context, that is, with their societal, political, and cultural conditions and consequences.

THE SYSTEM OF RACISM

The ultimate aim of this complex theoretical framework is to acquire more detailed insight into the fundamental problem of white racism. Before we start our analysis of the role of stories in the reproduction of racism, therefore, we need a few (meta-)theoretical tools (for details, see, e.g., Barker, 1981; Dovidio & Gaertner, 1986; Essed, 1991; Katz & Taylor, 1988; Miles, 1989; Omi & Winant, 1986; Solomos, 1989; Wellman, 1977).

My general approach to racism combines various elements of this earlier research with a discourse analytical study of social cognitions about ethnic minorities as an important element in processes of reproduction. Crucial in this approach is a conception of racism as a form of group dominance. Ethnic dominance is understood as power abuse by white (European) groups, that is, as self-interested control over and as a limitation of access to socially valued resources (residence, citizenship, housing, jobs, wealth, education, respect, etc.). Such dominance may be defined and described at the macro level of groups and institutions, where it contributes to social inequality, as well as the micro level of everyday (inter)actions, where it manifests itself as "everyday racism" (Essed, 1991). At both levels, such relations of dominance also involve socio-cognitive dimensions, namely, as ethnic ideologies and attitudes shared by a group, at the macro level, and specific ethnic beliefs of social group members, at the micro level. Obviously, these two levels (macro and micro) and dimensions (social action/structures and social cognitions) are multiply interrelated. Thus, storytelling about ethnic affairs is, as such, a form of (discursive) interaction presupposing knowledge and beliefs of storytellers about ethnic affairs, but at the same time these storytellers implement, enact, legitimate, or challenge group knowledge, attitudes, and ideologies and thereby contribute to the reproduction of ethnic prejudices, which in turn underlie discrimination and hence indirectly condition ethnic inequality.

STRUCTURES OF DISCOURSE

Discourse may similarly be analyzed according to this theoretical square of two levels and two dimensions. Discourse analysis usually focuses on local, micro level text, talk, or communicative interaction, including both the actual discursive practices of speaking or writing, as well their observable results ("texts"), on the one hand, and the underlying cognitions of speakers and hearers, including the meanings or interpretations of such discourse, on the other hand (see the contributions in van Dijk, 1985b).

However, at a more global level of analysis, we may also distinguish structural "orders of discourse," that is, complex, societal, political, or cultural *systems* of text and talk. These systems include, for instance, the recurrent or preferred topical or thematic structures, lexical inventories, conventional text schemata, or stylistic and rhetorical strategies of groups, organizations, or whole cultures. Also these higher level, societal orders of discursive practices are in turn complemented by a high level of socially shared social cognitions, such as the norms, values, and ideologies of these social formations. It is also in this macro level sense that we speak of "racist discourse." We see that the systems of discourse and racism can be analyzed according to the same general principles. This also allows us to effectively study racism from a discourse analytical perspective. Thus, both at the macro and at the micro level, racist discourse is of course a special case of discourse in general. Conversely, discursively enacted racism is a special case of other forms of racism.

STORIES

If racism is reproduced through discourse and communication we may expect this also to be the case for stories and storytelling—in informal everyday conversation, in institutional storytelling, in the narratives of novels and movies, as well as in the special "stories" communicated by the mass media in the form of news reports.

To understand the specific ways stories contribute to the reproduction of racism, we briefly need to explain what stories are. That is, why and how are stories about an event different from a police report, a sociological analysis, or even a news report about the "same" event? And, how are stories different from argumentations, scholarly discourse, parliamentary debates, textbooks, or advertisements?

NARRATIVE THEORY

Ignoring the details of a long tradition of narrative analysis, from Aristotelian poetics to structuralist or psychological studies of narrative structures and to conversational analysis of spontaneous storytelling, we may briefly summarize the relevant properties of stories as follows (for details, see, e.g., Chafe, 1980; Communications, 1966; Ehlich, 1980; Labov & Waletzky, 1967; Mandler, 1984; Polanyi, 1985; Quasthoff, 1980; van Dijk, 1980):

a. Stories are primarily about (past) *human actions and cognitions*, although also descriptions of other events, objects, places, or circumstances may be part of stories, for example, as conditions or consequences to human action.

b. Stories are usually about events and actions that are (made) *interesting* for the audience. This "pragmatic" interestingness is usually obtained by the account of events or actions that are unexpected, deviant, extra-ordinary, or unpredictable, given the knowledge and beliefs of the audience.

c. This also implies that stories are usually told to *entertain* the audience, for example, by influencing their esthetic, ethnical, or emotional reactions. However, as we shall see below for stories about minorities, stories may also have broader social, political, or cultural functions or play a role in an argumentative schema.

d. Stories are abstractly organized by a canonical *textual schema* or superstructure consisting of a hierarchically organized set of conventional categories, such as Summary, Orientation, Complication, Resolution, Evaluation, and Coda or Conclusion (Labov, 1972; Labov & Waletzky, 1967). In concrete stories some of these categories may remain implicit. Also their ordering may deviate from the formal schematic order, whereas some categories (such as Evaluations) may occur discontinuously, that is, its installments may appear throughout the story.

e. Stories may be told from different *perspectives* or points of view, may feature the storyteller as a participant or not, and may be realistic or fictitious.

f. Conversational stories are further organized by general properties of *conversational interaction*, such as turn taking, sequences, strategies of negotiation and impression formation, and so on. Unlike many other forms of dialogue, however, storytelling usually involves the storyteller taking the floor for a relatively long time. And unlike most written stories, such everyday conversational stories are often jointly produced by several storytellers, and interruptions by the audience may become part of the narrative communicative events (e.g., by asking questions, providing comments).

STORIES AND MENTAL MODELS

Cognitively speaking, stories are expressions of so-called (episodic) *models*, or situation models (van Dijk, 1985a; van Dijk & Kintsch, 1983). A model is a mental representation of an episode, that is, of an event or action taking place in a specific social situation. People are continuously engaged in building new (personal, subjective, ad hoc) models or in updating old models of episodes they witness, participate in, or read or hear about (Morrow, Greenspan, & Bower, 1989). Models play a role both during discourse production and in discourse comprehension. When we read the newspaper, we build new models about completely new events (such as about the "riots" in Los Angeles) or update models about episodes we have read about before (e.g., the war in the Gulf).

Models are much richer than the texts that are based on them, which in principle only need to feature the information that is relevant to express and communicate. Models embody what we usually call the *interpretation* of an event but also feature personal opinions about such an event. They are organized by an abstract schema, featuring such categories as Setting, Participants, and Actions, categories we also encounter in the semantic structures of stories expressing such models.

Whereas most everyday models are mundane and hence hardly qualify as a basis for storytelling, those models that are somehow "extra-ordinary" are typically used for storytelling. Of course, descriptions of everyday, mundane events (typically so in the Orientation category: "I was simply doing my daily . . . when suddenly . . . ") may be a strategic way to set off the narrative interestingness of less common events. Finally, there is a special type of mental model—that which represents the communicative situation (and hence the storyteller, the audience, etc.) itself. This *context model* will of course monitor what of the event model the storyteller will eventually express (e.g., because of the assumed expectations or interests of the audience).

SOCIOCULTURAL FUNCTIONS

Finally, beyond the textual and cognitive properties of stories we find the many social and cultural aspects of storytelling. Stories are not merely to entertain the listeners, they may also have persuasive functions, and more generally, they may contribute to the reproduction of knowledge, beliefs, attitudes, ideologies, norms, or values of a group or of society as a whole. Similarly, stories may be used to criticize, attack, or ridicule people. They may be one of the ways to inform people or to "tell the code" of institutions (Kelly, 1985; Mumby, 1987). Finally, stories about minorities generally function as complaints by majority group members or as expressions of negative experiences or prejudices about minorities. In sum, stories are a major discourse genre for the reproduction of culture and society. Unfortunately, for the same reasons, stories are also essential in the maintenance and legitimation of dominant power and ideologies—and hence in the reproduction of racism.

STORIES ABOUT MINORITIES

In everyday conversations about minorities, stories play an important role. They are routinely told to express and communicate personal experiences with minority group members, often of the storytellers themselves but also of family members, friends, or acquaintances. Such stories usually have an argumentative or persuasive "point" rather than an entertaining function. Whereas large parts of conversations about minorities are generalizations about ethnic minority groups or ethnic relations, personal stories provide concrete information, which is used as supporting "evidence" for a more general, argumentative conclusion. The weight of this evidence is epistemological (Danto, 1985; Dipardo, 1990). It suggests that the events told about are a reliable source of knowledge, because they represent a lived, personal experience. At the same time, it is suggested that the (negative) conclusion is not ethnically biased but supported by the facts.

In order to qualify as "narratable," however, events must satisfy a number of conditions. We have seen above that such events should somehow be "interesting," preferably both for the storyteller and the audience. Specifically, stories about minorities should tell about events that are remarkable as examples of intergroup encounters. In a predominantly white society, any encounter with a member of a minority group might in principle be qualified as remarkable in its own right simply because of the uncommon nature of such encounters. Indeed, the very appearance of a black person in a wholly white European village may be sufficient reason to tell others about "having seen" such a person. In racially or ethnically mixed cities such encounters are increasingly common and hence less interesting for storytelling. In that case, it is no longer only the very group membership of the "other" story participants but the nature of the acts and events that increasingly become relevant as conditions of narratability.

What acts or events of ethnic situations are specifically remarkable? An obvious first answer to this question is that all those properties or activities of minority group members are remarkable that are interpreted as nontrivially different from those of own group members. That is, storytellers implicitly—and sometimes explicitly—compare ethnic situations to situations and events in which only white people are involved. This comparison is essential, because those events that might not be narratable in all-white situations may well become worth telling when one of the participants is not white, if only because such "solo" situations are less common or more remarkable on purely cognitive grounds (Taylor, 1981).

However, exceptionality is not a sufficient condition of narratability. That is, typically, stories about minorities usually have an overall *negative* evaluation. Positively remarkable events involving minority groups are much less used as occasions for storytelling by prejudiced white people. Cognitively speaking, this may mean that such events are not interpreted and stored as positive events in the first place, or if they are, they may be not or less easily retrievable. This is of course specifically the case if the communicative function of the story is to support a negative conclusion about minorities. Models of positive encounters may in that case be less accessible or more readily discounted as "irrelevant" for the point to be made.

If stories about minorities are primarily told to support a more general negative conclusion, we should conversely expect them to be instantiations of ethnic or racial stereotypes and prejudices. For instance, if blacks are believed to be more criminal than whites, we may expect stories that back up such a general racist opinion. Compared to other stories about crimes, such stories thus have two independent but related conditions of narratability: For most ordinary citizens crimes of minority group members are not only forms of deviant behavior or instantiations of uncommon events but specifically interesting because they are examples of a specific category of "minority crime." Crime news and newsworthiness in the white media are also premised on this condition: Stories about crimes by minority group members tend to be paid specific attention, both by the journalists and by the readers (van Dijk, 1991).

Note though that the very participation of minority group members is not enough. That is, both in news reports and in everyday stories, they are much less told about when they are victims of crime, especially when these crimes are committed by white group members. Hence, agency and responsibility are crucial in supporting negative conclusions about minority groups, because only such stories are instantiations of white group prejudice. Whites, and especially prejudiced whites, will seldom tell stories in which blacks are the victim of discrimination or racist attacks. Crucial, then, is the further condition that the negative activity should be interpreted as a real or potential *threat* to white people, if not to the white group as a whole. In other words, stories about minorities are often stories about *whites as (self-defined) victims* of acts of minority group members or of ethnic relations in general.

The class of events that may be qualified by these conditions—negatively interpreted acts of which blacks are seen as responsible agents and of which whites are considered as (innocent) victims—is potentially very large. Crime and violence are primary topics in this case, simply because the element of intergroup threat is most concrete and consequential in this case: The very safety of white group members is compromised.

However, threats and danger may also be economic, political, social, and cultural. Hence, we may also expect stories that support general prejudices about economic competition ("They take away our jobs, houses . . . ,"

etc.), political power ("They will take over in this city"), social privileges
("They are all on welfare," "They live off our pocket," etc.), and cultural
threats ("They don't speak our language," "They have a different religion," "They have a different mentality," etc.).

In all these cases, there is a gradual transition from remarkable but
acceptable differences through unacceptable deviance to immediate threats
to the white group. The more the stories are group-threatening, the more
prototypical they are as "minority stories" and hence the more persuasive
they are in making the negative argumentative point. This may mean that
there is a general narrative strategy to move from perceptions of difference
to evaluations of negative deviance and threat.

Thus, when blacks are seen to be dressing in a remarkable (e.g.,
"flashy") way, or to be driving conspicuous cars (a point made in several
stories recorded), this would as such hardly qualify as sufficient grounds
for storytelling. Rather, it is the interpretation and explanation attached
to such an observation that may become the point of the story—that such
extravagant behavior is inconsistent with the stereotype that minorities
are poor and that (therefore) such ostentatious behavior should probably
be explained at least as a provocation, if not as the consequence of deviance
or crime, such as abusing of welfare regulations or dealing in drugs.

Not only socioeconomic or cultural differences or threats may be
involved here but also (at present often hidden or even repressed) feelings
of white superiority: The minority group members are in a subordinate
position and should act accordingly; if not, they are "out of place." In
other words, a threat may also be interpreted as a threat to our superordi-
nate position or our privileges, for instance, when blacks claim equal
rights or effective measures (e.g., affirmative action) that may bring these
about. Even slightly preferential treatment in specific situations will
immediately be rejected as "reverse discrimination," that is, as an infrac-
tion of white group rights. Again, many stories, especially in situations of
changing and more developed intergroup relations (for instance in the
USA), will focus on this form of "threat."

Note finally that conditions of narratability for minority stories seem
to be internally inconsistent. If it is the case that difference, deviance, or
threat are seen as prototypical properties of minority groups, then stories
that support such general beliefs should hardly provide new, interesting,
or unexpected information for the storyteller or the (white) audience. Indeed,
the acts of minority group members in such a case would be predictable
and hence less narratable. If this is the case, we may conclude that although
such discourses are less narratable as stories, they may well be acceptable

as premises in a different kind of discourse genre—that is, in argumentation, as we have seen above. They are, indeed, less to entertain than to complain, accuse, and argue. At the same time, because of the official norm of tolerance and the "risk" that the audience may be actively antiracist, the storyteller can not always be sure that the general prejudice is shared, so that the present story may be intended not so much to make a well-known claim but to support a controversial position (see also McGee & Nelson, 1985).

AN EXAMPLE: THE CAB ACCIDENT

Let us examine one example of such a story in some detail. The story is told by a 28-year-old male maintenance worker from San Diego, originally from Ohio, living in a mixed, lower-middle-class neighborhood. The interviewer was a 19-year-old male student, and the initial topic of the semi-directed interview was the neighborhood of the interviewee.

In order to be able to place the story against the background of other statements by the interviewee, let us first give a few brief quotes that illustrate his opinions regarding ethnic minorities and ethnic relations in his neighborhood, in San Diego, and in the USA generally. When asked whether he likes his neighborhood, he spontaneously brings up ethnic minority groups in his first conversational turn, as is the case for many other people we interviewed. We can conclude from this prominence in conversation a prominence of ethnic relations in the models the speaker has of his neighborhood. After having been away for a year, the speaker noticed the following:

1. We've got a lot more Mexicans coming up here, a lot more blacks and before it wasn't half as bad as this was, the place has really changed in about a year. (LG4, 7-9)

Note that change in ethnic composition is perceived as a change for the worse when there are less white people in the neighborhood. This observation is hardly unique. Also in most of the interviews we recorded in inner-city neighborhoods of Amsterdam, "negative change" was one of the most prominent initial topics of the speakers: The increasing presence of minority groups is interpreted as a sufficient condition for seeing the neighborhood as becoming run down or as otherwise less attractive for whites. Indeed, in order to qualify as remarkable and hence as subject for stories, minorities do not even have to do anything: Their mere presence may be sufficient to qualify as a general "complication" in the "life story" of white people.

When prompted to be more specific, the interviewee hedges a bit (not exactly this area, "but down where we used to live, on . . . ") but eventually mentions the garbage lying around everywhere ("Just like Tijuana") and tells about the experiences of others, his wife in the first place ("she was afraid to walk down these streets"). The comparison with the Mexican city at the other side of the border is sufficient for locals as a negative characterization.

Once the deterioration of the neighborhood is attributed to the arrival of Mexicans and blacks, the speaker volunteers other things he doesn't like about "them":

> 2. Especially when it happens on welfare and they're getting government and they're just, you know, it gets to be a waste. (LG4, 33-35)

The conclusion from such arguments is straightforward: "They should have a lot tougher ways of getting into the United States." Or at least, if people are coming to this country, they should not get any government money for a number of years, because "they" are coming only because it is so easy to get welfare. When asked about the blacks, who after all did not come to this country because of welfare, he remains within the same topic: They want easy help, and everybody is cheating on welfare, "especially the blacks."

Such general statements, however, may be heard as racist, so when asked about whether he has black colleagues, the interviewee backs down a little with the well-known Apparent Concession Move:

> 3. You got bad blacks, you got bad whites, you see, I don't get along with a lot of some of these white people, and I don't get along with some of these black people. So it's just, you know. (106-108)

Such comparisons are a persuasive tactical move in the overall strategy of positive self-presentation: If not only blacks but also whites may be seen as "bad," then the statement cannot, at face value, be seen as expressing a negative attitude about blacks. That such statements are a form of apparent concession may be concluded from the fact that the rest of the interview will focus on examples of bad behavior by the others—and not by white people. Thus, he immediately goes on to relate that his wife was harassed by some Mexicans, and that although she was rescued by a young girl friend, this girl also was a gang member and pulled a knife to chase away the Mexican men.

Illegal immigration, he further admits, is also stimulated by the companies that hire undocumented aliens, so he proposes more active policing of employers and concludes that the government is not serious in wanting to stop illegal immigration as long as so many companies depend on cheap "slave labor."

Since he claims to hear a "lot of stories in this town," the interviewer prompts him to tell one. He then starts to tell the story that we propose to examine in more detail. Before the factual story comes up, however, he first makes a more general statement about illegal cab drivers:

4. (. . .) like half the cab drivers here are illegal aliens. I know half the cab drivers are illegal up here. It makes pretty good money doing that. It makes 50 dollars bringing them up from the border, bucks a person. (184-187)

This brief reference to illegal aliens is consistent with the more general topic of illegal work in the area. After other personal information about his job and his family, he is invited by the interviewer to talk about the different cultures in the city. It is within this general argument that the actual cab driver's story comes up (italics express special emphasis):

5. **M:** Yeah, that's one of the things I don't like. It's just, I don't know. Before, when people came into the United States, when I read *my* history, you know, they wanted to *adapt* to the American way of life, you know, maybe keep some of their own ways, you know, just hang on to their children, but they wanted to adapt, they wanted to learn English, they wanted to get a job, they wanted to do this. And now, they come over here and it's acting like, WOW!, you know, you know the state gives them everything, on the ballots they've got their own languages so they can vote in different languages. I wouldn't be surprised if they put up street signs in Spanish and (???) and stuff like that. I just think it's really stupid. It really is.

   I: You think they shouldn't have to spend the money?

   M: No, because, you know, it's uhh, I mean I was driv I drove a cab a couple of years ago, you were talking about stories, and this poor, I was driving alongside this old guy, he was in the left hand lane, I was driving alongside. All of a sudden he was coming in my lane, and I reeled it over, went up on the side of the curb, he scraped the whole side of my cab. And he could . . . so we got over and we pulled up at the gas station, and he got out, he could not speak a word of English. His daughters—he had his granddaughters with him, they were about 10 or 11—he can't speak a word of English, so they made a phone call, so that his son's coming down; they'll get it all straightened out, and this guy was just standing there, he wouldn't even talk to me, you know, he was just standing there on, and his daughter kept saying that it was my fault that I didn't know how to drive and stuff, and I'm you know, this guy couldn't even speak a word of English. What is he doing driving a car? What happens if he kills someone in the street, ran him over or something? Could you imagine him on the phone trying to get assistance or something like that! So they come over there and uhm he tried to tell the police it was my fault, that he had wanted to turn coming into my lane, that he had put his lights on and I didn't give him access to come into my lane. I was, you know, he was halfway, you know, back up the hill, you know, I come into my lane, I mean he was way ahead of me when I turned, he was right alongside of me, you know, and the then he comes right into my lane, he's, you know, telling these people that it was my fault, and it turned out it wasn't my fault. I got it taken care of, but it was just the way he was, you know, he couldn't speak a word of English, and it was stupid, you know, at least, you know, how can you read a street sign if you can't speak English, you know, or even read it. It's just, it's just what I hate, you know. They should come here fine, but a lot came here because they knew they were getting a lot of money out of the deal, and they did. A lot of them did. (201-247)

In many ways this is a typical conversational story as well as a typical story about foreigners. That it is a story in the first place may be concluded from the fact that it is about interesting past events and actions, in which the storyteller was involved and that are out of the ordinary. Accidents and near-accidents, both in everyday stories as well as in news stories, are among the most prototypical examples of such eminently narratable events. The embedding in a conversation, the overall schematic organization as well as the local style further show that it is a story and not, for example, a police report of the same event. Finally, the speaker himself classifies and marks the beginning of his story as such: "You were talking about stories."

The overall narrative schema is as follows (note that narrative schema categories do not organize local structures directly but higher-level, macropropositions or topics, which we here provide as tentative approximations of those of the storyteller himself):

1. *Setting* (Time, Participants): I drove a cab a couple of years ago.
2. *Orientation*: I was driving alongside this old guy and his granddaughters.
3. *Complication I*: Suddenly he came into my lane and scraped the side of my cab.
4. *Complication II*: We pulled over, but he couldn't speak a word of English.

5. *Complication III*: They claimed that it had been my fault.
6. *Resolution I*: I got it taken care of.
7. *Evaluation I*: It was stupid.
8. *Evaluation II*: It is just what I hate.
9. *Coda/Conclusion I*: It is dangerous to drive a car when you don't speak the language.
10. *Coda/Conclusion II*: Most of them only come here for the easy money.

This overall story structure is rather straightforward; most canonical narrative categories appear in the story. The Setting is fairly brief and merely goes back to a situation in the past when the speaker was still a cab driver. Notice the conversational repair ("I was driv I drove a cab a couple of years ago") in which the correction to a simple past refers to a general state (a profession), which is necessary to explain why the storyteller was driving a cab in the first place.

Then in the next sentence, the actual action description is expressed by a gerund ("I was driving"), thereby introducing the Orientation category, which usually describes a mundane, everyday activity ("I was just doing X, when . . ."). The Complication is duly introduced by "All of a sudden" and controls all the propositions in the conversation that describe the way the old man was changing lanes. This part is given in two installments, of which the second is even more detailed but functional as a form of face keeping for the storyteller: It should become obvious for the hearer that it was not the storyteller himself who was to blame for the accident.

The second installment of the Complication category features another unexpected and self-threatening event: The cab driver is being accused in a situation where he perceives himself as being the victim of reckless driving. The Resolution of that strand of the story is briefly summarized by the speaker as "I got it taken care of" (He doesn't tell how, or by whom), and then followed by a well-known Evaluation example: "It was stupid."

Now, this would be one of those classical everyday accident stories were it not for a specific additional complication: The other driver didn't speak "a word of English." As part of a normal "car accident" story, it might have been a minor additional problem, for example, as a secondary complication in the resolution of the incident. This is however not the case. The very fact that the storyteller several times repeats "and he couldn't even speak a word of English," suggests that this complication is far from minor for the storyteller.

Indeed, the *point* (Polanyi, 1979) of the story is not so much the car accident at all but the fact that the other driver didn't speak English. That is, in this particular interview, which is largely about minorities and ethnic relations in southern California, and following a question and response that deals with cultural differences and the alleged reluctance of present immigrants to learn English, the story's point should be related to the implications of this statement, as is indeed the case: The storyteller's Evaluation and Conclusion categories describe in detail what the possible consequences are of lacking knowledge of English when driving a car ("What happens if . . . ").

In fact, what we witness here is what may be called a *second-order story*. That is, there is a story about a car accident, but "on top of" (or "below") that story there is another story about the disastrous consequences of being unable to read or speak English in traffic (and hence in U.S. society). It is this second-order story that is the real "foreigner story," prompted by the conversational context (they are no longer required to learn the language, etc.), and leading to its own Conclusion, which is to support the thesis of the speaker in this section of the interview.

Of course, the narrative persuasiveness of the second-order story may well be carried by the strength of the Complication category of the first story. A car accident is usually such a tragic event, and a sufficiently "strong" first-order narrative, to make the second-order "foreigner story" compelling. However, in this case, there is a hitch: The cab driver only got some scratches on his car, so the first order story may well be tellable, but it is not very compelling since nothing serious happened. The storyteller implicitly knows the weakness of his first-order (car-accident) story, and therefore emphasizes the *possible* consequences of the present Complication ("What if he kills someone . . ."). This is a well-known narrative strategy to enhance the dramatic nature of complications (e.g., "I could have been dead . . .").

An alternative way of analyzing the main Complication of this story ("He couldn't even speak a word of English") is to treat the car accident itself as the Orientation. Since it was a minor accident, which took place several years ago, there is in fact little reason to tell the story in the first place; indeed, if it were not for the presence of a foreigner, it probably would fail as a first-order story. However, as an Orientation it does fine: "Some years ago when I had a car accident, it turned out that . . ." Having minor car accidents is a rather mundane fact of automotive life and may therefore be used as an introducing Orientation. Indeed, the real Complication ("The other guy didn't speak English") changes the possible outcomes of such an everyday event as a minor car accident.

Notice finally that this story has only one Resolution category—the sentence "I got it taken care of." However, this solution merely refers to the problem of what the storyteller sees as a false accusation. What is *not* resolved is the major Complication of the story: the fact that the old man didn't "speak a word of English." This lack of a Resolution category in stories about minorities is rather typical. In 144 Dutch stories we analyzed, about 50% did not have any Resolution category (van Dijk, 1984). We explained this lack of Resolution as an expression of the lack of a solution in the underlying model: The complicating event is interpreted as an unresolved predicament, which makes the whole story take the form of a complaint-story. Had the storyteller been able to solve the problem, in this case for instance by talking to the old man in another language, then the "point" of the complaint-story would have been lost: The problem would not have been serious. Stories about minorities, therefore, are accounts of events that put minorities in a negative perspective. The lack of a Resolution emphasizes the (negative) Complication category, and thereby the problematic nature of the presence of immigrants in the country.

Although less relevant as a story per se, the first-order car accident story is nevertheless narratively needed to carry the other story, because the fact that somebody unexpectedly didn't speak English on a particular occasion is hardly sufficient as a story Complication either. Its dramatic nature only becomes prominent when placed in a situation where the inability to speak the language may have fatal consequences, for instance, when somebody needs to call for help after a serious car accident.

We have seen that at several levels this complex story is told in order to support the overall conclusion that it is necessary for immigrants to learn the language. This statement both occasions and concludes the story, and is part of a more complex argumentation, given in the beginning of the example, where the speaker makes a difference between old and new immigrants. This comparison is itself introduced by an evaluative statement in response to the interviewer's question about cross-cultural conflicts:

6. Yeah, that's one of the things I don't like.

This evaluation must itself be supported by a more general evaluative principle or norm. This norm is set by the correct, past behavior of immigrants: They adapted. Both in California and in the Netherlands, it is the norm of adaptation that is most frequently associated with immigrants in everyday conversations. One of these norms, also in California, is that the immigrants should learn the language of their new country. Following a well-known "the good old times" move, the speaker concedes that the "old" immigrants really took initiatives and went out to get a job, thereby further emphasizing the bad character of present immigrants. This statement specifies his more general, earlier opinion that immigrants are being pampered by state handouts and no longer do their best, an argumentative move that is characteristic of contemporary "no-nonsense" attitudes and policies toward minorities. The language question is then further detailed by giving the example of bilingual ballots and street signs.

These earlier evaluative statements are echoed at the end of the story by the narrative conclusion of the second-order story—"It is just what I hate"—which nicely fits the story into the argumentative schema of the conversation. The storyteller does so at two argumentative levels: First, he wraps up the complaints about the alleged lack of language ability; and second, he immediately goes on to place that conclusion within the higher-level conclusion relative to the unacceptable motivations of present-day immigrants. This explicit embedding shows again that "minority stories" are primarily not to entertain but to persuade the audience of an argumentative point that—for prejudiced storytellers—nearly always implies a negative characterization of "them" and a victim role for "us."

OTHER MINORITY STORIES

Compared to the interviews collected in the Netherlands, those recorded in California have relatively few stories. Most speakers talk about their neighborhood and city, and the relations with minorities, in rather general terms, as is also the case for most interviewees in the Netherlands who live in white neighborhoods: They have few personal experiences with minorities in the first place.

At the same time, storytelling seems to be conditioned by a mixed class and education factor: Middle-class interviewees tend to speak in a more general, descriptive or argumentative mode and less in a narrative mode. Apart from the possible lack of personal experiences, this class or education difference suggests that the issue of "ethnic relations" is defined by middle-class speakers primarily as a social issue, for which argumentative discourse is most appropriate. For lower-class speakers this is also the case, but their arguments may be less persuasive if they lack detailed general knowledge about ethnic affairs. Instead they tell personal stories to support their general point. This may explain why most Californian speakers, most of whom were rather well-educated, middle-class citizens, tell fewer stories.

Against this background, a few comments are in order about some of the other stories told in California.

The Mugging

A 30-year-old male electrician is telling about the relations with his white and black friends. He relates that there were sometimes minor conflicts, such as mutual name calling ("You know, like . . . like if they be talkin' about Honkies 'n' stuff"). Asked about a particular situation he tells, very briefly:

> 7. YEAH, I got mugged one time! At a city park . . . by a bunch of black kids and one of 'em was . . . supposedly my friend. I was with him, this black kid, and . . . he joined in with them . . . they just beat the shit out of me . . . you know(. . .). They beat the hell out of me, too, they they were real aggressive . . . not happy. (. . .) 'Cause it was, you know, it was what he was supposed to do, He didn't want have then reject HIM, I guess (. . .). Ya know, I hated him for it after that. I never talked to him again. (JK1, 4-5)

The story has the usual narrative categories, including a final Conclusion/Coda. Again, it is especially the Complication that is focused on. The first-order Complication, repeated in the next turn of the dialogical story, is that some black kids beat him up, whereas the second-order Complication is about an act of betrayal: The black kid he thought to be his friend joined the other blacks. His explanation of this betrayal shows that this is the real point of the story: Even when they say they are your friends, you can't really trust them, because they will stick together. Note that also this story has no Resolution, neither of the first-order story (the mugging) nor of the second-order story (the betrayal by his friend). Interestingly, the Conclusion/Coda only pertains to the first-order events: He never talked to that particular black guy again. He does not conclude, at the second-order level, that he never had any black friends anymore.

Affirmative Action

The second story is told by a 60-year-old elementary school teacher. Asked about affirmative action, she replies that employment should be competitive, and the best people hired. She then tells the story about a friend of hers:

> 8. Yes, well I do know that happened in W., in the school system, because a friend of mine would have gotten a position but they decided to give it to a minority. And she had been my principal and she had had some kind of position in the school system in W. and she was just a gem. Now I don't know anything about the other person, but this was my friend and I felt real bad when she didn't get it because, you know, I always just expected her to go to the top. But now the other person could have had qualifications exactly like hers. And she never felt badly about it, never complained. (LD1A, 5)

Again we find the usual narrative categories and a focus on what is seen as one of the problematic aspects of ethnic relations—that white people are sometimes denied a job because a black person gets it. Note that in this case there is some kind of Resolution to the problem described in the Complication category ("but they decided to give it to a minority"): Her friend accepted the fact that she didn't get the job.

Interestingly, the presence of a Resolution category in stories about minorities is often associated with a less negative attitude toward minorities. This also appears in the statement that maybe the minority applicant was just as good, thereby legitimating that this applicant could be chosen just as well as her friend. For her, the events were merely a personal disappointment ("this was my friend") and not an example of a more general issue, for example, of unfair competition.

We see that there are two different types of negative minority stories: those that are told merely as a personal experience of a negative event in an interethnic situation, on the one hand, and stories that in addition have a more general point, on the other hand. The latter type are more clearly group stories and tend to be told primarily to make a more general negative point in an argumentation schema about a minority group, as was the case in the cab-accident story told above.

The stories by the other interviewees are in line with the findings presented here. Thus, one other woman (unemployed, 42-year-old), who had just moved to San Diego and who had never lived in an inner city before, was surprised that her prejudices about crime and threats in the city were *not* confirmed: She had left a pair of tennis shoes and other things in the laundromat and came back hours later and still found them there. She concludes the story with the following Resolution, Evaluation, and Conclusion:

9. (. . .) and there they were sitting, all neatly stacked in a nice little row waiting for me at about nine thirty at night. So, and this is called what you'd call a mixed neighborhood, you've got a little bit of every . . . social and economic strata, I think, but I don't uhh I don't find any . . . excessive amount of of crime or any real serious feeling of being threatened, if we're out late at night coming home late at night, that sort of thing. (LG3,1)

As is the case in the Dutch interviews, spontaneous positive stories about minorities or race relations are also a rather reliable indicator of the lack of or less aggressive prejudices. Note though that this woman does know about what she is supposed to expect. The point of her story is precisely, as in most stories, that "normal expectations" are being thwarted. That is, she is aware of the socially shared belief among many white people that mixed neighborhoods, or rather, nonwhite people (at least in poor inner-city areas) tend to be threatening and to steal. At the same time, her story may be understood as an example of a *counterstory*, that is, as a story that is intended to challenge prevailing prejudices. Note that such counterstories presuppose a lack of (blatant) prejudices: In the analysis of stories by obviously prejudiced speakers, I found very few positive stories about minorities.

CONCLUSION

Racism as a system of white group dominance is reproduced at several levels. In addition to acts of individual and institutional discrimination, this system is especially reproduced through discourse and communication. White people need to know about the opinions, attitudes, and ideologies of other group members and at the same time want to communicate and legitimate their own to others. Storytelling is one of the discourse genres that allows people to express their experiences and evaluations of concrete "ethnic" events.

My study of everyday conversations in the Netherlands and California has shown that such stories are usually told as functional elements in overall argumentative strategies of negative other-presentation. That is, in order to show that African Americans, Mexicans, Turks, Moroccans, or Surinamese have the negative properties that are represented in their attitudes, prejudiced white people need to support such a claim with "evidence." If not, negative statements about minorities or immigrants may be heard as racist. Negative stories, then, are presented as stating "the facts," because they report events that people have witnessed or participated in themselves.

The analysis of some examples from the Californian interviews has shown first that we may distinguish between first- and second-order storytelling. Interesting first-order Complications, such as a car accident, may become virtually irrelevant at the second-order, ethnic or racial level and merely a context (and pretext) for relating the allegedly problematic aspects of race relations, such as immigrants' inability to speak English. Further confirmation of the hypothesis was found in stories about minorities that tend to lack a Resolution category. There are two, related, explanations for this structural property of "minority stories," which they share with other "complaint stories": (a) an interactive, persuasive function, where the focus is fully on the (negative) Complication, that is, on the negative properties ascribed to minority actors, and less on what the storyteller "did about it"; and (b) a representation in mental models of ethnic events as essentially problematic, as a predicament for which there *is* no solution for the storyteller.

It was also shown that there is a systematic difference between stories told by prejudiced people and by those people who favor equality and actively oppose racism. The first stories are mostly negative and tell about events or experiences that confirm more general, negative attitudes. Such stories are as stereotypical as the attitudes that monitor the construction and retrieval of the mental models on which they are based. White people who have no or fewer problems with minorities spontaneously tend to tell more varied and more positive stories or will occasionally even tell negative stories about racist or intolerant whites. Whereas the prejudiced people will tend to repeatedly affirm that they are of course not racist, antiracist speakers don't feel the need to present themselves in this positive light. Their very stories and arguments themselves show what their position is.

Finally, it was stressed that storytelling is not merely an expression of personal experiences and opinions. On the contrary, the very difference and variations in storytelling between more or less prejudiced speakers already suggest that social cognitions are involved that are shared by different groups of people. Stories about minorities, thus, are not so much expressions of personal experiences. Rather, they are expressions of group experiences. In the same way as prejudices operate (among other things) by categorization, generalization, and de-individuation of minority group members, white speakers tell their stories *as* dominant group members. In the same way as their personal experiences with the "others" are interpreted as experiences of the white group, their stories, and hence the models from which these derive, are heavily monitored by general beliefs, attitudes, and ideologies. Indeed, such "minority stories" are in a way similar to myths and folktales: anonymous stories of group experiences, expressing group concerns, and group beliefs. In our case, they are at the same time expressing and reproducing white group power, by persuasively making the point that "we" are better than "them," or rather that "they" fail to meet the standards that are set by "our" values and norms.

REFERENCES

Barker, M. (1981). *The new racism*. London: Junction Books.

Chafe, W. L. (Ed.) (1980). *The pear stories*. Hillsdale, NJ: Erlbaum.

Communications 8 (1966). *L'analyse structurale du recit*. Paris: Seuil.

Danto, A. C. (1985). *Narration and knowledge*. New York: Columbia University Press.

Dipardo, A. (1990). Narrative knowers, expository knowledge: Discourse as a dialectic. *Written Communication, 7*, 59-95.

Dovidio, J. F., & Gaertner, S. L. (Eds.). (1986). *Prejudice, discrimination and racism*. New York: Academic Press.

Ehlich, K. (Ed.). (1980). *Erzählen im Alltag* (Storytelling in everyday life). Frankfurt, Germany: Suhrkamp.

Essed, P.J.M. (1991). *Understanding everyday racism*. Newbury Park, CA: Sage.

Jäger, S. (1992). *Brandsätze: Rassismus im Alltag*. Duisburg, Germany: DISS.

Katz, P. A., & Taylor, D. A. (Eds.). (1988). *Eliminating racism. Profiles in controversy*. New York: Plenum Press.

Kelly, J. W. (1985). *Storytelling in high-tech organizations. A medium for sharing culture*. Paper presented at the Annual Meeting of the Western Speech Communication Association, Fresno, CA, February 16-19.

Labov, W. (1972). The transformation of experience in narrative syntax. In W. Labov, *Language in the inner city* (pp. 354-396). Philadelphia, PA: University of Pennsylvania Press.

Labov, W., & Waletzky, J. (1967). Narrative analysis. Oral versions of personal experience. In J. Helm, (Ed.), *Essays on the verbal and visual arts* (pp. 12-44). Seattle, WA: University of Washington Press.

Mandler, J. M. (1984). *Stories, scripts, and scenes: Aspects of schema theory*. Hillsdale, NJ: Erlbaum.

McGee, M. C., & Nelson, J. S. (1985). Narrative reason in public argument. *Journal of Communication, 35*, 139-155.

Miles, R. (1989). *Racism*. London: Routledge.

Morrow, D. G., Greenspan, S. L., & Bower, G. H. (1989). Updating situation models during narrative comprehension. *Journal of Memory and Language, 28*, 292-312.

Mumby, D. K. (1987). The political function of narrative in organizations. *Communication Monographs, 54*, 113-127.

Omi, M., & Winant, H. (1986). *Racial formation in the United States: From the 1960s to the 1980s*. New York: Routledge.

Polanyi, L. (1979). So what's the point? *Semiotica, 25*, 207-242.

Polanyi, L. (1985). *Telling the American story*. Norwood, NJ: Ablex.

Quasthoff, U. M. (Ed.). (1980). *Erzählen in Gesprachen* (Storytelling in conversations). Tubingen, Germany: Narr.

Solomos, J. (1989). *Race and racism in contemporary Britain*. London: MacMillan.

Taylor, S. E. (1981). The categorization approach to stereotyping. In D. L. Hamilton (Ed.), *Cognitive processes in stereotyping and intergroup behavior* (pp. 83-114). Hillsdale, NJ: Erlbaum.

van Dijk, T. A. (Ed.). (1980). Story comprehension. *Poetics 9* (1/3). Special triple issue.

van Dijk, T. A. (1984). *Prejudice in discourse*. Amsterdam: Benjamins.

van Dijk, T. A. (1985a). Cognitive situation models in discourse processing: The expression of ethnic situation models in prejudiced stories. In J. P. Forgas (Ed.), *Language and social situations* (pp. 61-79). New York : Springer.

van Dijk, T. A. (Ed.). (1985b). *Handbook of discourse analysis*. 4 vols. London: Academic Press.

van Dijk, T. A. (1987a). *Communicating racism: Ethnic prejudice in thought and talk*. Newbury Park, CA: Sage.

van Dijk, T. A. (1987b). *Schoolvoorbeelden van racisme: De reproduktie van racisme in maatschappijleerboeken* (Textbook examples of racism: The reproduction of racism in social science textbooks). Amsterdam: Socialistische Uitgeverij Amsterdam.

van Dijk, T. A. (1991). *Racism and the press*. London: Routledge.

van Dijk, T. A. (1993). *Elite discourse and racism*. Newbury Park, CA: Sage.

van Dijk, T. A., & Kintsch, W. (1983). *Strategies of discourse comprehension*. New York: Academic Press.

Wellman, D. T. (1977). *Portraits of white racism*. Cambridge, UK: Cambridge University Press.

Chapter 6

DEFORMED SUBJECTS, DOCILE BODIES: DISCIPLINARY PRACTICES AND SUBJECT-CONSTITUTION IN STORIES OF JAPANESE-AMERICAN INTERNMENT

Gordon Nakagawa

THE SECOND WORLD WAR evacuation, exclusion, and internment of 120,000 people of Japanese ancestry (including 70,000 U.S. citizens) in 10 "relocation centers," though transpiring 50 years ago, remains something more than a historical curiosity or a constitutional anomaly. A half-century after President Franklin Roosevelt issued Executive Order 9066, the edict that set the exclusion and internment into motion, the legacy of this extraordinary experience continues to be visited and revisited among the Nikkei.[1] Evidence of the ongoing salience of the internment and its aftermath can be readily found: Throughout 1992, a nationwide, yearlong series of events commemorated the 50-year anniversary of FDR's signing of EO 9066; camp reunions for former internees and their families are held yearly; annual pilgrimages to former camp sites are commonplace, attended by multigenerational contingents; the vernacular media regularly include articles, columns, and editorials that detail issues germane to the internment and its effects; and expanded coverage of the internment in school textbooks and increased scholarly attention to the internment period and to its long-term consequences are priority items in the academic agenda of many Nikkei and non-Nikkei educators and researchers.

More fundamentally, the internment experience has been and continues to be a defining moment in the community's self-understanding. In concluding its report on the West Coast exclusion and detention of ethnic Japanese, the U.S. Commission on Wartime Relocation and Internment of Civilians (CWRIC, 1982) has observed:

"Before evacuation." "After camp." Words signifying the watershed in the history of Japanese Americans in the United States. Even after four decades, it is the mournful reference point from which these Americans describe changes in their communities, their personal lives, their aspirations. It is the central experience which has shaped the way they see themselves, how they see America, and how they have raised their children. (p. 301)

Cross-generational in its effects, the exclusion and internment experience remains a residual but organic force in the ongoing self-formation of the Nikkei identity and community. By examining contemporary Japanese-American discourse about the internment experience, I hope to offer insight into the formative conditions that have structured the historical self-understanding of the Nikkei community. In specific, examining this experience through the narratives of former internees can provide us with a sense of how social control or a "disciplinary" regime (Foucault, 1979, 1980) in the camps functioned to produce particular kinds of subjects. As such, the narratives function as a kind of lens or as a form and practice of symbolic mediation, which can both reveal and conceal contradictions and the local workings of power. In short, my intent is to provide a sense of how social control through the use of specific disciplinary practices are represented in former internees' stories about their experience of the internment. In developing this perspective, this chapter offers (1) an explication of the relationship among narrative, culture, social control, and marginalized communities and (2) a critical analysis of representations of those disciplinary practices that situate the Nikkei as docile and deformed subjects in stories of Japanese-American internment.

NARRATIVE, CULTURE, SOCIAL CONTROL, AND MARGINALIZATION: STORIES OF JAPANESE-AMERICAN INTERNMENT AS EXEMPLARS

Stories and storytelling are embedded so deeply in culture and everyday life that Fredric Jameson (1975-1976) has argued that "the very structure of language itself shows a deep functional vocation for storytelling, which must then be seen, not as some secondary pastime, to be pursued around the fireside when *praxis* is over, but rather as a basic and constitutive element of human life" (p. 244). Ranging from the perennial "fish" story about the "one that got away" to the cool, dispassionate accounts of news reporters to the bedtime story with which we were raised as children and from which we seem never fully weaned, these narrative commonplaces have become so sedimented and "natural" in our daily experience that only rarely, if ever, do we consider how they construct, legitimate, and perpetuate a particular order of coherence and sense making.

Understood as discursive "artifacts," stories function as reconstructed condensations of cultural experience. As Mickunas (1973) observes, cultural artifacts "contain in a 'concentrated' form the lines of the web within which they have a significant function" (p. 180). Consequently, the artifact (narrative) "functions as a clue or a witness to the culture, reclaiming it not as an empirical fact but as a system of orientations and possibilities for interpreting the lives and world of a particular people" (p. 180).

What situates these artifacts as meaningful is a particular configuration of space and time, a "cultural morphology," which is "distinct from, and more fundamental than, either the objective or the subjective conditions within which it [the object] manifests" (Mickunas, 1973, p. 180). This cultural morphology, Mickunas continues, "provides the network of significant connections. . . . On the basis of the discovered object as 'witness' or 'clue,' [the investigator] reconstructs the cultural a priori as a web of implications which makes sense of the discovered object" (p. 180). Understood as situated accomplishments in a particular sociocultural, historical, and political context, stories both constitute and represent (instantiate) this intricate formation of representations, sense making, and communicative practices.

However, stories are enmeshed within a *particular* system of representations, meanings, and practices. And positioned as they are amid a complex of discursive and nondiscursive conditions and forces, narratives highlight certain interests while hiding or repressing others. Hence, the story's structuring of events operates simultaneously within processes of cultural formation (sense making) and *deformation*, the process by which "culture is systematically distorted such that symbolic practices maintain and reproduce certain relations of dependence and domination" (Mumby, 1988, p. 104; see also, Mumby, 1987). Thus, the story manifests assumed boundaries for what is thinkable, doable, possible, and valued, which both enable and constrain perceptions and meanings that exist as "real" for cultural members. For instance, taken-for-granted conditions that privilege particular preferences—including decisions concerning who may tell stories; what stories are available and what stories should or should not be told; and how, where, when, and by what means stories can be told (and read)—are all historically and culturally determined, conceived not in a simple causal sense but as constructed out of a sociocultural ensemble of stories, storytelling, and reading practices that are embedded in a complex formation of discourse, knowledge, and power (Foucault, 1980, 1983).

This complex relationship among stories, culture, and social control is most apparent in narratives that attempt to recount and legitimate historical events marking times of social upheaval in a community. Stories that describe or account for a social crisis, that is, when a community's fundamental beliefs and values are challenged or called into question, provide perhaps the best opportunity to examine underlying systems of coherence and sense making. For it is in these representations of and by the "exile" (or the "Other") that the workings of social control are explicitly made problematic (see Bhabha, 1990a, 1990b; Said, 1978, 1990).

Accordingly, the internment experience-as-recounted offers an exemplar of the operation of social control on and within a marginalized community. The internment episode (including its rationale, procedures, and mechanisms of implementation and its effects) has been characterized by one authoritative body as "extraordinary and unique in American history" and as being of "manifest" significance (CWRIC, 1982, p. 3). Given the anomalous nature of these events, the narrative representations of this experience of exile and Otherness constitute a complex nexus where sociocultural and personal history, ideology, power, and storytelling converge.

Constituted as "hyphenated" subjects (Japanese - Americans), the Nisei (second-generation Japanese American, U.S. citizens) internees occupied the "margin" between the two cultures in more than a merely figurative sense. Their marginal experience-as-recounted provides an exemplary case of how practices of social control constitute particular forms of human subjectivity and hence inscribe boundaries for possible and permissible perceptions, experiences, and values in a community. In this sense, contemporary internment narratives provide "clues" that instantiate features of the lived-experience (the existential "reference point") of former internees and draw attention to the more general practices of social control that situate human subjects in particular ways.

NARRATIVE REPRESENTATIONS OF DISCIPLINARY PRACTICES IN STORIES OF JAPANESE-AMERICAN INTERNMENT

From the inception through the conclusion of the internment period, internees were subjected to processes of regulation and surveillance unprecedented in U.S. history. Space, time, and movement for the Japanese-

American internee were inscribed in and by a particular system of signification, power, and discourse that was geared toward the creation of docile bodies "that may be subjected, used, transformed, and improved" (Foucault, 1979, p. 136).

This disciplinary order functioned as a guarantor of docility and "normalization," where normalization refers to "a system of finely gradated and measurable intervals in which individuals can be distributed around a norm—a norm which both organizes and is the result of this controlled distribution" (Rabinow, 1984, p. 20). For the internees, this normalizing order was realized most directly within the enclosed area of the camp compound, a space partitioned in such a way that the body was subject to close observation and regulation. However, this pervasive sense of surveillance was actualized throughout the full range of institutionalized practices that deployed power in a particular fashion from the beginning to the end of the internment period.

Narrative representations of these disciplinary procedures and "technology" are replete in contemporary stories of Japanese-American internment. Previous studies of internment narratives (Nakagawa, 1990a, 1990b) have investigated modes of discourse by which Nikkei interned subjects have been constituted, offering hints of how historical practices of ideological "interpellation" (Althusser, 1971; see also, Therborn, 1980)—a process of addressing and thus constituting forms of human subjectivity—have become sedimented in current rhetorical usage. In this section I investigate how a deformation of the Nikkei subject and a reduction of the Nikkei body politic to docility are reproduced and supported by a particular configuration of space, time, and movement, as represented and sedimented in internment narratives. Derived from the 1981 Los Angeles field hearings conducted by the federally impanelled Commission on Wartime Relocation and Internment of Civilians, stories generated from the videotaped testimonies of 114 former internees were transcribed for analysis and criticism. Additional internment narratives were gathered from supplementary sources, including personal interviews, oral histories, and collections of life-histories.

The remainder of this chapter explicates those meanings, operations, and techniques that discursively constitute deformed and docile subjects in internment narratives. Traces of these practices of social control are manifested in narrative representations that converge around the following:

1. The imposition of military "orders" (or "directives") designed to regulate everyday conduct and actions.

2. The use of the "examination" in the service of constant surveillance and observation of bodies, resulting in a greater specification of individuality and thus more highly refined methods of regulation.
3. The control of space through the ordering and distribution of bodies according to the disciplinary technology of the camps.
4. The operation of rituals of exclusion and rites of scarification on the Nikkei lived-body.

Together, this collection of internment narratives offers a partial look at those practices that have circumscribed perceptions and interpretations of internment survivors in their ongoing struggle to understand, legitimate, and articulate a 50-year legacy of repressed pain and silenced voices.

MILITARY DIRECTIVES: ORDERING SPACE, TIME, AND MOVEMENT OF THE JAPANESE-AMERICAN BODY POLITIC

During the pre-evacuation period, one of the earliest and most effective methods to carry out and implement the forging of "docile bodies" in the Nikkei community was the imposition of military orders, according to a number of internees' accounts. These directives had the effect of opening a field of disciplinary mechanisms and practices that would ultimately restrict all three dimensions (space, time, and movement) of human action:

> Prior to the actual removal, the Army issued many directives that controlled and restricted the daily lives of the Japanese Americans. The directives had [an] oppressive effect, especially on my mother. My mother was against war—any war. But somehow, she remarkably accepted my brothers' serving the U.S. Army. There was a curfew, pulling down of shades at night, many ordinary household items were considered contraband (cameras, flashlights, etc.). . . . In the frenzy, believing books were dangerous, especially if written in Japanese, she . . . burned them all. Among them was a book of Shakespeare's plays, written in Old English on one page and in Japanese on the other. I miss that book.[2]

> When Pearl Harbor was bombed, most Japanese employees, including my husband, were terminated from employment due to prevailing war hysteria. Travel restrictions allowed us to travel not more than 5 miles from home, and a 10 p.m. curfew was imposed. . . . We were allowed less than a month to prepare for evacuation, including disposing of our personal property.

The pre-evacuation and evacuation orders ensured what Foucault (1979) has called "an uninterrupted, constant coercion, supervising the processes of the activity rather than its result [a coercion which is] exercised according to a codification that partitions as closely as possible time, space, movement" (p. 137). The interconnections among time, space, and movement as visibly constraining were coded in the form of directives that imposed curfews, restricted travel, proscribed items as contraband, and truncated time for the disposal of personal property.

Although among the more patently obvious techniques for regulating human conduct, these orders nonetheless were highly significant in instigating a disciplinary regime of power/knowledge/discourse relations and practices that would later take far more covert (and thus, more insidious) forms. Moreover, these directives were instrumental in establishing conditions for a normalization of conduct that the evacuees/internees would later assume and actively appropriate as necessary, "natural," and in some cases, even desirable. In this sense, then, the military directives, consistently alluded to in internment narratives, marked the inception of disciplinary control and surveillance—and the deformation of Nikkei subjects as docile bodies.

THE EXAMINATION: THE NORMALIZING GAZE, INDIVIDUALIZATION, AND TOTALIZATION OF THE JAPANESE-AMERICAN BODY POLITIC

The internment narratives chart a "political anatomy" of the Nikkei subject, a grid of power relations whose coordinates are deployed across the body of the internee. Institutionalized practices of discipline and surveillance are realized in the bodily constitution of the Nikkei subject as both "individualized" and "totalized," both of which coalesce in the service of the normalization of a population. A singularly potent procedure of this normalizing surveillance is the "examination," which, as Foucault (1979) has noted,

combines the techniques of an observing hierarchy and those of a normalizing judgement. It is a normalizing gaze, a surveillance that makes it possible to qualify, to classify and to punish. It establishes over individuals a visibility through which one differentiates them and judges them. . . . At the heart of the procedures of discipline, [the examination] manifests the subjection of those who are perceived as objects and the objectification of those who are subjected. (pp. 184-185)

In internment narratives, the "examination," broadly considered, took a number of forms, including body searches, review and censoring of mail, inspections for contraband, and the camp "intake" interviews of newly arrived detainees:

> Before leaving Tule Lake Center, we were forced to strip naked to see whether we had any concealed weapon on us. Even our safety razors and mirrors were taken away. . . . In March, 1946, we reached Crystal City, Texas. At Crystal City all our letters were censored. I wrote numerous letters to the Justice Department but received no reply as to the reason for my detainment. Upon arriving by train with people under quarantine, we were subjected to the same routine of a military shakedown. The soldiers and civilians alike searched our luggage for contraband. Through it all our older sisters had to suffer the indignities and humiliation of having their flannel undergarments waved in front of hundreds of people. The comments and insults made by the soldiers who were conducting the inspections are still very vivid in my mind today. (Noguchi in "Rite," 1981, p. 70)

> They begin to file out of the bus, clutching tightly to children and bundles. Military Police escorts anxiously help and guides direct them in English and Japanese. They are sent into the mess halls where girls hand them ice water, salt tablets and wet towels. In the back are cots where those who faint can be stretched out, and the cots are usually occupied. At long tables sit interviewers suggesting enlistment in the War Relocation Work Corps. . . . Men and women, still sweating, holding on to children and bundles, try to think. . . . Interviewers ask some questions about former occupations so that cooks and other types of workers much needed in the camp can be quickly secured. Finally, fingerprints are made and the evacuees troop out across an open space and into another hall for housing allotment, registration and a cursory physical examination. . . . In the end, the evacuees are loaded onto trucks along with their baggage and driven to their new quarters. (Leighton, cited in CWRIC, 1982, pp. 151-152)

The effect of these disciplinary techniques is to bring the individual internee into greater visibility by marking the individual as an object of knowledge. This heightened visibility transforms the individual subject into a public "spectacle," open to inspection, observation, and interrogation. There is in the spectacle what Lanigan (1972) has called a "perception [that is] not yet an expression" (p. 127): That is, the visibility of the subject is one-sided, for the subject in this context is an object to be observed, an object of knowledge not yet brought to expression, an object not yet permitted to speak. Through a precise specification of what and who the internee is, the examination in these narratives makes of the internee an individual case, a specific object of knowledge that can be situated in "a web of objective codification. More precise and more statistically accurate knowledge of individuals leads to finer and more encompassing criteria for normalization" (Rabinow, 1984, p. 22).

This systematic ordering of knowledge drawn from individual cases increases the power of authorities to exercise more refined and subject-specific regulatory practices, once again, in the service of normalizing the subject population. As Rabinow (1984) summarizes this argument, "The power of the state to produce an increasingly totalizing web of control is intertwined with and dependent on its ability to produce an increasing specification of individuality" (p. 22). Hence, both individualization and totalization are essential moments in the narrative accounts of objectification of the Nikkei subject.

Further, the examination, Foucault (1979) continues, leaves behind material traces of this disciplinary exercise of power in the form of documents and, more so,

> a whole meticulous archive constituted in terms of bodies and days. The examination that places individuals in a field of surveillance also situates them in a network of writing; it engages them in a whole mass of documents that capture and fix them. The procedures of examination were accompanied at the same time by a system of intense registration and of documentary accumulation. (p. 189)

In the case of the Nikkei subject, the "archive" that was documented in the evacuation and internment narratives included the loyalty questionnaire ("a system of intense registration") and the FBI's detailed dossiers ("documentary accumulation") on a large number of Japanese Americans (particularly the Issei and Nisei males, the latter of whom might be eligible for voluntary enlistment or conscription into the U.S. military). The former, the "loyalty registration crisis," has been discussed elsewhere (see Nakagawa, 1990a); the latter, the compilation of files or dossiers on Nikkei subjects, is also a pervasive theme in the internment narratives. As one Nisei veteran, who served with U.S. occupation forces in the Pacific theater, recounted:

> During the nine months I spent in the Jerome Relocation Center in Arkansas, the FBI conducted a thorough check on my background. I guess they decided I was a loyal American because I was released from camp, reclassified 1-A, drafted, and I ended up serving in U.S. Army Intelligence.

This irony was repeated in numerous accounts of Nisei males who were interned and who eventually served in the armed forces. The "normalizing gaze" of the examination assumed yet another guise in the physical presence of armed "escorts."

> It was late June in 1944 when I received a telegram that my mother was gravely ill. I left Chicago immediately and returned to Amache to get clearance papers so that I could visit my mother in California. I was forced to wait for days to obtain clearance to enter the Western Defense Command area, and during that waiting period, my mother passed away on July 4, knowing that I was on my way to see her. I proceeded on to California anyway so that I could bring her remains back to Amache. . . . At Needles, California, which was a Western Defense Command border, an FBI agent was assigned to me for constant surveillance while I was in California. When we arrived at Los Angeles, I was shocked when we were met by a military MP and SP, and I was marched between them through the Union Station in full view of hundreds of station passengers. I was called "Jap" and other derogatory names by the hostile and curious crowd. I was frightened and humiliated. How ironic that within one month, I was to be inducted into the U.S. Army.

> I remember quite vividly how I spent my last furlough before our regiment went overseas. Of course, I went to see my family in Heart Mountain Relocation Center. There I was for two weeks, locked up once more behind barbed wire, in spite of my uniform. I am sure you can appreciate the irony of that.

> I spent my furlough at the Manzanar Relocation Center, where my fiancee was interned. It was very frustrating trying to locate the camp and after getting there, I was confronted with further aggravation in that I was not allowed to leave the camp without a Caucasian escort. All I wanted to do was go to Lone Pine, a few miles away, for some provisions to celebrate our reunion. Likewise, when we went to Reno, Nevada, to get married, we were escorted by a Caucasian. I feel that my rights not only as a citizen and as a military personnel was rudely violated. I was in military uniform at all times and beg a question: who made these rules and regulations?

Aside from the more obvious contradictions implicated by these circumstances, an equally telling issue lies in the explicit codification of the Nikkei subject that makes possible the "constitution of the individual as a describable, analysable object . . . in order to maintain him in his individual features, in his particular evolution, in his own aptitudes or abilities, under the gaze of a permanent corpus of knowledge" (Foucault, 1979,

p. 190). Hierarchical observation, the disciplinary gaze that functions to totalize a population in the very act and moment of isolating and individualizing subjects, is made flesh in the individually assigned FBI agent, the military MP and SP, the Caucasian escort. Once again, objectification of the subject is served, but in this case, the Nikkei becomes an object through disciplinary practices of totalization and individualization, that is, through the technique of an examination that "manifests the subjection of those who are perceived as objects and the objectification of those who are subjected" (Foucault, 1979, pp. 184-185).

BARRACKS, BARBED WIRE, GUARD TOWERS, SEARCHLIGHTS: DISCIPLINARY TECHNOLOGY AND THE PARTITIONING OF THE JAPANESE-AMERICAN BODY POLITIC

The camps' standardized, physical arrangement itself "interpellated" the interned subjects as marginal. The barbed-wire perimeter of the camp compound, for example, marked off a "margin of safety" (ostensibly for both the Japanese-American community and the general public), a locale securely between the internees' former West Coast homes and the hostility or indifference of the remainder of the country. The relocation center was an institutional site of power, geographically located in the badlands of the United States, in a place neither here nor there, but between, on the fringes, and in the margin.

Indeed, as the internees' accounts vividly reveal, the normalizing order of the evacuation/internment period was realized most directly within the enclosed area of the camp compound, a space partitioned in such a way that the body was subject to close observation and regulation. Spatial constraints on the internees' freedom of movement (constricting both "private" conduct and "public" modes of interaction) were evidenced in both global and local forms. The structural arrangement of the camps, following a conventionalized pattern as prescribed by the Western Defense Command, was designed to maximize surveillance and discipline and to minimize opportunities for aberrant behavior. Thus, the uniform layout of camps emphasized a structural organization of barracks into blocks, and the overall camp design itself enforced regularity and symmetry in movement and patterns of interaction. Centralization of basic activities (e.g., eating, bathing, playing) as well as the absence of privacy in the internees' living quarters brought a concomitant decentering of the family as the primary unit of control and social interaction. In effect, the partitioning of space that effectively deployed a grid of power was also a partitioning of the Nikkei lived-body, as revealed in internment narratives that sometimes captured the humor and absurdities of living conditions but consistently retained a grasp on the indignities, bodily violation, and debasement of the camp experience:

> Many families like ours were separated into different barracks. Because of limited space, many of the smaller families had to share one room with others. We were denied any privacy, and only a partial wall separated us from other families. We were restricted from any personal life or discussions. Any family arguments were heard by the entire barrack. It was a nightly ritual for Mr. Fujimoto to let out an *onara* (flatus) before we fell asleep. (Noguchi in "Rite," 1981, p. 70)

> I was 13 years old when we were at Tule Lake, California. The most upsetting experience happened to me when martial law was declared throughout the camp because of a food riot. We were told that the military police would come to search each one of our families in the barracks. The two MPs looked formidable as they walked in with guns at their side and asked roughly if we had any weapons, liquor or cameras. To be forced to let the MPs in our small, humble quarters seemed like such invasion of personal privacy that the emotional effect of that search still haunts me.

> The Assembly Center was a dusty, hot arid area with barracks put up with four walls, a roof, and divided into four apartments. The fact that our isolation was total from the mainstream of society became crystal clear at this time. The facilities, as such, were the most primitive as far as I could determine. The outhouse had no partition, just a board and holes cut into them. The shower was just that—a long pipe with many shower heads lined up but no partition for dressing rooms. For an individual or group of people who prided themselves on cleanliness and a deep sense of modesty and courtesy, this was the epitome of human degradation. You learned quickly that in order to survive, you must adapt to the standards as set by the Army, that to adhere to your social mores and code of ethics, you would be left with nothing, not even your individuality. . . . The lack of privacy in the barracks made our daily living very stressful, particularly in trying to interact as a family unit.

The barbed-wire demarcation of space articulated onto the enclosed compound a particular grid of power that was manifested in the spatial distribution of internees. As such, the camp compound was an institutional site where the exercise of power was materially displayed, and the ordering of space became a method for managing real and imaginary disorder.

In one sense the camp compound was partitioned into a grid of power that was distributed differentially across the administrative, military, and internee populations, and within this grid all parties were held captive, fixed in and by a set of relations inscribed by the disciplinary technology and discourse of internment. Highlighted by the presence of this partitioning was the constant surveillance made possible and necessitated by the camp's structural layout. The elevated watchtowers that punctuated the barbed-wire camp perimeter actualized in a tangible way the "hierarchical observation" necessary to the deployment of disciplinary order. "The exercise of discipline," according to Foucault (1979), "presupposes a mechanism that coerces by means of observation; an apparatus in which the techniques that make it possible to see induce effects of power, and in which, conversely, the means of coercion make those on whom they are applied clearly visible" (pp. 170-171).

In another sense the absence of partitions within the barracks and washroom/toilet facilities opened a space, literally, in which disciplinary power could be exercised, insofar as otherwise "private" space was no longer inviolable and in fact no longer existed in any meaningful way. Both in personal dealings with other internees and in the constant vulnerability to intrusion by camp authorities, "private" space for camp detainees was annulled. Again, visibility of the subject was augmented, but in this instance the procedure of disciplinary surveillance was operated as much by the internees themselves as it was exercised by camp guards and administrators.

The disciplinary gaze, whether by the sentries in their surveillance of internees in the firebreaks between barrack blocks or by the internees themselves in their constant exposure (both inside and outside the barracks' partitions) to each others' watchful eyes and intrusive ears, was uninterrupted and pervasive in its capacity to define and delimit actions. Power in such a context becomes "a multiple, anonymous and automatic power; for although surveillance rests on individuals, its functioning is that of a network of relations from top to bottom, but also to a certain extent from bottom to top and laterally; this network 'holds' the whole together and traverses it in its entirety with effects of power that derive from one another" (Foucault, 1979, pp. 176-177). Here, then, discipline and surveillance, accomplished in and by the hegemonic disciplinary technology of the internment camps, crossed in such a way that the Nikkei subject was interpellated as a "docile body": a body "subject to someone else by control and dependence, and tied to his own identity by a conscience or self-knowledge. Both meanings suggest a form of power which subjugates and makes subject to" (Foucault, 1983, p. 212).

The former sense of the docile body (i.e., as "subject to someone else by control and dependence") was displayed in those internment stories that drew analogies between the Nikkei subject and caged animals. Beyond the more obvious sense of victimization, there was also at work in these stories a more profound strategy of containment, domination, and domestication of human agency and desire.

On April 4, 1941, we were evacuated from Long Beach. And what a sad day —words cannot describe our apprehension, not knowing what was to come. We felt like pieces of baggage, tagged with numbers and herded together like livestock. Upon arrival we were given some type of inoculation and instructed to fill white bags with straw for our mattresses, which were lumpy, uncomfortable and cold. In our assigned quarters the newly asphalted floor had not hardened, and I recall the Army cots sinking into the floor. It is now unimaginable living in horse stables, drafty and emanating a putrid odor.

In April of 1942 when Executive Order 9066 forced us to evacuate from the West Coast, my sister, Namiko, who was 13, and I, who was 16, packed only what we could carry, and we proceeded to the Santa Anita Assembly Center. The injustices resulting from the war hysteria finally devastated our family, and my sister and I were completely separated from our parents. It was some time later while my sister and I were at Santa Anita that our father was released from Fort Missoula, and he finally joined us at the Assembly Center. We were overjoyed to have our father back with us, but my sister and I will never forget the indignities he suffered. He was hauled into Santa Anita in the back of an open state truck, like so much cattle being herded. He and the others were respected, prominent men before they were imprisoned. There was no justification in taking away their human dignity.

I recall writing a composition in my first English class at Poston in 1942. I wrote about a poultry farmer tending his chickens in a cage. How did that chicken feel? I was that chicken. Incarcerated in a hot, dusty hellhole took tremendous adjustment. And the word *gaman* [endurance] is most appropriate.

Camp life from the time we arrived became highly regimented. We all had to wake up at a certain time, get in line to use the bathrooms, wash basins, and rush to the mess hall to get in line for breakfast, lunch and dinners. . . . Whenever human beings are placed into captivity, for survival we develop a very negative attitude toward authority. We spend countless hours to defy or beat the system. Our minds start to function like any POW, convict or caged animal. (Noguchi in "Rite," 1981, pp. 71-72)

By the time the permanent camp opened, the day-to-day physical and mental survival was something one lived with and passively accepted. When the new camp appeared, the children were delighted, for it had running water in the toilets! And the bathtubs and showers! All these facilities had individual stalls. This was like leaving the flop houses and moving to the Ritz. The individual during this time in the assembly centers lost in many respects his self-esteem, pride, and the ability to aggressively assert his will. Despite the inconvenience of the new centers that still existed with the watchtower, the searchlights at night, the soldiers with machine guns, the fact that one did not have to feel like an animal just to relieve themselves and to keep themselves clean made you look upon your captors as "angels," so to speak.

The constitution of docility in the Nikkei body politic brings with it a normalizing and naturalizing effect, as manifested in these narrative traces: the stories speak of apprehension, uncertainty, adjustment, loss of dignity and pride, passive acceptance, of minds that functioned "like any POW, convict or caged animal," of an almost perverse gratitude toward one's captors, and of *gaman*, a kind of quiet and patient waiting or endurance in the face of difficult circumstances. In the disciplinary technology of the internment camps the Japanese American finds not only a materially realized "iron cage" in the form of a barbed-wire enclosure but also an "iron cage" that discursively penetrates the objectified Nikkei subject, whose human flesh has been transmuted into livestock, cattle, chickens in a coop, caged animals.

These designations are more than nominal, for they point directly to the subjugation of the internee not only by means of overt domination but through disciplinary practices and techniques that come to be accepted as the "norm" (i.e., treatment as nonhuman though sentient beings). This process of subject-objectification is captured well in one internee's account of the immediate and residual effects of the camp's regimen and its normalizing influence:

After things [in camp] had settled down, everything seemed to be taken care of by the rules and regulations. The routine made it boring, and I seemed to sort of drift along, not really putting any effort or thought to the future. We had adjusted, and become dependent, and probably not wanting any change. Therefore, when the war ended, and we were told to leave camp, I felt unprepared and unable to put myself into going. It seemed to be a combination of the shock of the war ending and the fear of going out into or back to the real world. . . . It took me quite a while to come out of my immobilized state.

The routinization of daily life engenders for the internee a dependency and adjustment that becomes over time "normal" and "natural," producing a subject resistant to change. In a site that is removed from the "real world," temporality is compressed in such a way that the future, otherwise considered as an open horizon for human projects, becomes all-but-inoperative: "I seemed to sort of drift along, not really putting any effort or thought to the future." The subjected body, normalized by routinized "rules and regulations," is crossed by a disciplinary network that blocks what Merleau-Ponty (1968) has called the originary power of an "I can" in human existence: the power to realize the open formation of human possibilities. "Immobilized," the internee is "unable to put [him/her]self into going . . . out into or back to the real world." This constitution of docility is made possible in the internment narratives through a delimitation of temporal and existential horizons.

RITUALS OF EXCLUSION, RITES OF SCARIFICATION: THE NIKKEI SUBJECT AS 20TH-CENTURY LEPER/PLAGUE VICTIM

There is a curious tension between isolation and communality, between separation and segmentation, enunciated throughout the internment stories. The camp boundaries, defined by the barbed-wire perimeter, functioned to mark a place that was simultaneously isolated from the "real world" and gathered together as a self-contained (albeit stigmatized) community. The disciplinary technology of the camps bears material witness to these dividing practices and to the spatializing of power, characteristic of exclusion and internment. For in one sense, not unlike the 19th-century leper colony in Foucault's (1979) analysis, the 20th-century internment camp "offers the counterimage of population control through spatial enforcement of power" (Dreyfus & Rabinow, 1983, p. 190). The Nikkei internee, like the leper, "was excluded from society, separated out and stigmatized. He was thrown with his suffering brothers into an undifferentiated mass. The authority to locate and exile lepers into separate communities where they were required to live and die was an act of 'massive, binary division between one set of people and another' [Foucault, 1979, p. 198]" (cited in Dreyfus & Rabinow, 1983, p. 190).

That the relocation center was often referred to as a "colony" by administrators and authorities seems in this regard to be more than a historical coincidence. Structurally, the signifying gap between the leper colony and the Nikkei colony is negligible at most: both are caught up in "rituals of exclusion" (Foucault, 1979, p. 198), quarantined as they are at the fringe or in the "margins" of society. Moreover, the physical marginality of the internees and of the camp locales situates the Japanese Americans, in "an act of 'massive, binary division between one set of people and another,' " in material sites of power where regulation of the body politic can be managed with the greatest efficiency and economy.

Equally, however, the internee, subject to scrupulous control, observation, and regulation, mirrored the condition of the plague victim. In differentiating the plague victim from the leper, Foucault (1979) observes that quite apart from the "massive, binary division" of lepers, the plague "called for multiple separations, individualizing distributions, an organization in depth of surveillance and control, an intensification and a ramification of power" (p. 198). As suggested earlier, these practices of segmentation, individualization, and hierarchical observation of the internees were realized by camp authorities, armed military guards, and, above all, by the anonymous operations of the camp disciplinary technology.

Though these two ways of exercising power are quite different, Foucault notes that not only are they compatible but, over time, they become conjoined. Ultimately, the late-19th century dictum becomes: "Treat 'lepers' as 'plague victims,' project the subtle segmentations of discipline onto the confused space of internment, combine it with the methods of analytical distribution proper to power, individualize the excluded, but use procedures of individualization to mark exclusion " (p. 199). Akin to the leper, the internee "was caught up in a practice of rejection, of exile-enclosure" (p. 198); and like the plague victim, the internee was "caught up in a meticulous tactical partitioning in which individual differentiations were the constricting effects of a power that multiplied, articulated and subdivided itself" (p. 198).

Not unlike the leper and the plague victim, the internee is marked and stigmatized by scars of the flesh, of the psyche, and of the spirit, borne by many Nikkei with anguish, pride, despair, rage, and resignation. A powerful recounting of various rites of "scarification" is articulated in internees' stories of bodily violence and emotional violation, traceable to official negligence, to the harsh and primitive conditions of camp life, and to the unaccustomed climate and often brutal environs of camp sites:

> At the time of my birth, my mother's physician in camp performed a tubal ligation on her. She never gave her consent and was totally unaware of it until 10 years ago when she was examined by her interness for colon cancer. She is not the only one who bears physical scars as a result of our incarceration. I'm married to another victim. He is permanently disfigured due to burns over one-third of his body. Because the barracks we were assigned to had no hot running water, warm water for bathing purposes had to be heated

over a fire. At the age of three, my husband fell into a tub of this boiling water and nearly died. Skin grafts were taken from his pregnant mother's thighs. She miscarried her child from the shock.

I don't know how long we were in Santa Anita before we were taken by train and ended up in Jerome, Arkansas. I recall the sticky heat in the summer and the bitter cold winters and the frostbite on my legs that got infected and left me with the scars I have today.

Father was detained at Camp Livingston in Louisiana. As the eldest in the family, I was granted permission to go and visit him. I was shocked to see him stoop-shouldered, aged beyond his years, as he came shuffling slowly toward me with the help of a cane. He had become a tuberculin, having cared long hours for the other internee patients. With his little background in medicine, he had cared for the sick, who otherwise might have been ne-glected. It was a painful reunion for a father and daughter. After two-and-a-half years, he was allowed to join us at Arkansas camp. He was broken in health and spirit. To see him return to us so changed was the single most painful experience that I bear of the evacuation.

The scarred flesh, the disfiguring burns, the miscarried child, the tubercu-lin elder: All bear more than memories of bodily violation, more than signifiers of their original pain and infliction. Beyond the allegations of physical and emotional abuse, beyond the question of "consent" or coer-cion, and beyond the contingencies of the unintentional or accidental, there is the subjection of those whose bodies are visibly marked as "victims," docile bodies that are "broken in health and spirit." For many internees, their indelible scars remain to this day as lasting emblems of the intern-ment's rites of exclusion and scarification—scars that stand as enduring witnesses to the internees' self-described sense of impotence and dis-ease (i.e., their docility) in the face of carceral practices and a disciplinary order for which no one person could be held accountable.

In the figural traces of the internment's narrative discourse, the in-ternee's body is alter-ed (made into "Other" than what it was/is) through a reordering of lived-space and a particular deployment of power. The relocation results in a dislocation, dispersion, and distribution of Nikkei subjects into inhospitable geographical sites that lacerate and divide the Nikkei body politic. Excluded from mainstream society yet ever the more so included within the grasp of societal (state-authorized) procedures of discipline, the Nikkei body is disfigured in flesh and is deformed in its capacity to act as a subject. The leper and the plague victim in this sense function as both metaphor and metonymy for the disfiguration of the body

and the disqualification of human agency: The dis-abled and deformed
body is a docile body is a disqualified body (politic).

CONCLUSION

The aim of this critical reading of Japanese-American internment
narratives has been twofold: first, to explicate how particular disciplinary
practices operated during the internment in constituting a particular kind
of subject (i.e., a docile and deformed subject); and second, to generate
greater insight into the richness of the internment experience as a watershed
in the sociohistorical formation of the Japanese-American community.

Of the former point, what has emerged from this reading are narrative
representations of a deformation of human subjectivity that enunciates a
fragmentation in space, time, and movement in the evacuee/internee's
lived-experience. Dis-abled in body through an enmeshment in disciplinary technology, the Nikkei internee becomes a 20th-century leper/plague
victim, whose body is excluded, scarred, and partitioned by a barbed-wire
grid of power.

Of the latter point and its relationship to critical thought and to the
heightening of political self-awareness, Antonio Gramsci (cited in Said,
1978) has noted: "The starting point of critical elaboration is the consciousness of what one really is, and is 'knowing thyself' as a product of
the historical process to date, which has deposited in you an infinity of
traces, without leaving an inventory . . . therefore it is imperative at the
outset to compile such an inventory" (p. 25). It is in this spirit that I offer
this essay as a gesture toward a continuing inventory of historical traces,
inscribed in re-collected narratives of internment survivors and articulated in the collective experience of the Nikkei community.

NOTES

1. The term *Nikkei* refers to any ethnic Japanese in the United States, regardless of
generation. The conventional Japanese (American) generational descriptions are as follows:
Issei refers to first-generation immigrants to the United States; *Nisei* refers to second-generation, U.S.-born American citizens; *Kibei-Nisei* refers to second-generation, U.S.-born
individuals, who at an early age went to Japan to receive much or all of their education; *Sansei*
refers to third-generation sons and daughters of the Nisei, thus the grandchildren of the
immigrant, first-generation Issei; and *Yonsei* refers to fourth-generation children of the Sansei.

2. Although many of these narratives are part of the public record, I have chosen to maintain the anonymity of those cited in this essay, based on a prior agreement with the National Coalition for Redress/Reparations, which provided access to videotapes and written transcriptions. Except in those cases where testimonies/narratives have already been published elsewhere, no specific source identifications are given.

REFERENCES

Althusser, L. (1971). *Lenin and philosophy* (Trans. B. Brewster). New York: Vintage.

Bhabha, H. K. (1990a). Introduction: Narrating the nation. In H. K. Bhabha (Ed.), *Nation and narration* (pp. 1-7). New York: Routledge.

Bhabha, H. K. (1990b). The other question: Difference, discrimination and the discourse of colonialism. In R. Ferguson, M. Gever, T. T. Minh-ha, & C. West (Eds.), *Out there: Marginalization and contemporary cultures* (pp. 71-87). Cambridge, MA: MIT Press.

Dreyfus, H., & Rabinow, P. (1983). *Michel Foucault: Beyond structuralism and hermeneutics* (2nd ed.). Chicago: University of Chicago Press.

Foucault, M. (1979). *Discipline and punish* (Trans. A. M. Sheridan). New York: Vintage.

Foucault, M. (1980). In C. Gordon (Ed.), *Power/knowledge: Selected interviews and other writings by Michel Foucault, 1972-1977*. New York: Pantheon.

Foucault, M. (1983). Afterword: The subject and power. In H. L. Dreyfus & P. Rabinow, *Michel Foucault: Beyond structuralism and hermeneutics* (pp. 208-226). Chicago: University of Chicago Press.

Jameson, F. (1975-1976). The ideology of the text. *Salmagundi, 31-32*, 204-246.

Lanigan, R. L. (1972). *Speaking and semiology: Maurice Merleau-Ponty's phenomenological theory of existential communication*. The Hague: Mouton.

Merleau-Ponty, M. (1968). In C. Lefor (Ed.), *The visible and the invisible* (Trans. A. Lingis). Evanston, IL: Northwestern University Press.

Mickunas, A. (1973). Civilizations as structures of consciousness. *Main Currents, 29*, 179-185.

Mumby, D. K. (1987). The political function of narrative in organizations. *Communication Monographs, 54*, 113-127.

Mumby, D. K. (1988). *Communication and power in organizations: Discourse, ideology and domination*. Norwood, NJ: Ablex.

Nakagawa, G. (1990a). "No Japs allowed": Negation and naming as subject-constituting strategies reflected in contemporary stories of Japanese American internment. *Communication Reports, 3*, 22-27.

Nakagawa, G. (1990b). "What are we doing here with all these Japanese?": Subject-constitution and strategies of discursive closure represented in stories of Japanese American internment. *Communication Quarterly, 38*, 388-402.

Rabinow, P. (Ed.). (1984). *The Foucault reader*. New York: Pantheon.

Rite of passage: The commission hearings 1981. (1981). In *Amerasia Journal* (pp. 53-101). Los Angeles: Asian American Studies Center, University of California, Los Angeles.

Said, E. W. (1978). *Orientalism*. New York: Random House.

Said, E. W. (1990). Reflections on exile. In R. Ferguson, M. Gever, T. T. Minh-ha, & C. West (Eds.), *Out there: Marginalization and contemporary cultures* (pp. 357-366). Cambridge, MA: MIT Press.

Therborn, G. (1980). *The ideology of power and the power of ideology*. London: Verso.
U.S. Congressional Commission on Wartime Relocation and Internment of Civilians [CWRIC]. (1982). *Personal justice denied*. Washington, DC: Government Printing Office.

Chapter 7

THE NARCISSISTIC REFLECTION OF COMMUNICATIVE POWER: DELUSIONS OF PROGRESS AGAINST ORGANIZATIONAL DISCRIMINATION

W. Marc Porter and Isaac E. Catt

AGAINST THE PROMISE of human equality there have been increasing reports of racism, sexism, and heterosexism on college campuses (see, e.g., Bernstein, 1990; Boyer, 1990; Clay, 1989; Gibbs, 1990; Magner, 1990; Toch & Davis, 1990; Wiener, 1990). Curiously, though "education" has become a panacea for resolving multicultural differences, educational institutions have become the battleground for rising concerns over racial tension. *Diversity* has become the most recent buzzword used to signify the complexities of people needed to build and sustain a healthy community. Though it is more often understood to mean "multicultural" (e.g., ethnic and racial) differences, diversity is broadly applied to accepting differences among people regardless of gender, race, ethnicity, physical ability, or sexual orientation.

This chapter examines the rhetoric of ethnic-related conflicts on a university campus that led to a civil rights investigation and a large-scale diversity intervention by the institution. This study takes a critical look at the progress of and intervention into a narcissistic discourse on racism. Its contribution rests on two things: (1) few studies adopting an interpretive approach to organizational communication have demonstrated how critical theory can provide a reasonable strategy for understanding and responding to actual human events; and (2) fewer studies have explored from any perspective a long-term organizational diversity intervention.

SELF, OTHER, AND CONTEXT

Both Eco (1986) and Jacoby (1987) assert that university professors in the United States do not demonstrate a proclivity for involving themselves in a community's serious social problems. Surely those of us bold (or arrogant!) enough to call ourselves "scholars" tire of television depictions of professors as benevolent absent-minds or sexless intellectuals. Yet, what about us would offer a motive for change? Into the disorderly dialogue of university life we stumbled, offering well-conceived and long-reflected on ideals for how North State University (NSU) might act and look if it could solve its discrimination problem. To do nothing would have allowed us to disappear anonymously into the monastic life of a university—unburdened by the strife of human affairs surrounding us. Surely, this sounds like idealism or self-congratulatory proselytizing. Though we may have unconsciously begun that way, this is not how the discussion ends.

We claim no pretense of "objectivity," for we were involved in the design and implementation of the diversity intervention at NSU. We were not permitted quixotic theories on equality nor ingenious philosophical dialogues on power and powerlessness surrounding racist and sexist discourse—at least not on the floors of our university halls and in the heat of having to choose an answer. We were, in fact, charged by the university's administration with "solving" racial problems at North State University.

Our approach presents sometimes painful (practical?) experiences of confronting a university's culture, reflecting on and countering narcissistic rhetoric (which tugs at the limits of rational-irrational discourse and at the patience of self-proclaimed rationalists), and facing the real possibility of having our tactics fail and of (more alarmingly) increasing racial tensions. This work is our search for personal meaning; not meaning impressed unethically on historic events, but a discussion of how the events impressed meaning on us. Goodall (1990, p. 288) writes:

> The idea is not to define meaning, but to evoke it; not to claim that it is a source of perfecting discourse, but to admit, outright, that it is imperfect; and not to perpetuate the scientific myth of control, but to advance a post-scientific notion of communication as the process in which and through which self, other, and context make and exchange meaning.

We claim no privileged position over others by asserting some absolute criterion of objectivity, for our position is not superior to the context or the people we "observed"—we, too, lived these events.

Part of our ethical conduct as critical scholars is to contribute actively to community (see Deetz, 1985). When interpretive and critical researchers in organizational communication took issue with functionalism's preoccupation with positivistic methods and managerial propensities (see Pacanowsky & O'Donnell-Trujillo, 1982; Putnam & Pacanowsky, 1983), they were not forsaking the right to improve organizational life. For critical theorists, criticism represents a well-reasoned commentary intended to enlighten and to emancipate people from the systematic constraints of human societies (Geuss, 1981). It seems difficult to imagine a more important discourse needing critical study and reasoned action than racism on university campuses.

The next section discusses the progress of a narcissistic discourse and examines two forms of narcissistic alienation: negation and tolerance. Our report is necessarily a blend of history and historicity; we were participant-interpreters of the discourse on diversity at NSU, so the following mixes the history of events with interpretation.

RHETORIC OF A NARCISSISTIC MOVEMENT

The central argument is that reasoned dialogue against racism ends where narcissistic communication begins. Narcissism forms an important, though largely unseen, ideological background from which the figures of the discourse on diversity arise and on which basis they mirror the logic of those whom they oppose. In other words, narcissism functions as an ideological constraint adversely affecting the possibilities of creating the kind of authentic, pluralistically responsive dialogue that is the prerequisite for emancipation from organizational systems of domination.

Issues of race relations and organizational life have not, heretofore, been associated with the psychoanalytic construct of narcissism. The cultural criticisms of Lasch (1978, 1991) and others (Alford, 1988; Catt, 1986; Fine, 1986; Friedman, 1974; Layton & Schapiro, 1986; Restak, 1982) suggest that the predominant contemporary standard of rationality is the narcissistic consciousness, which is chiefly characterized by its univocity. Narcissistic discourse produces a self that does not have an "other" against whom to measure the lucidity of its thought. Or, when external criteria are used to validate reality, they actually function as a mirror-image of subjective rationality. In either case, the narcissistic gesture issues from the distorted assertion of the self's ability to be the measure of all things. *Where narcissistic discourse flourishes, the diversity of human experience is condensed into a univocal consciousness; narcissism becomes the enemy of communication.*

In general, narcissism may be defined as the experience of an inability to distinguish the boundary or outline of the self—a confusion of the self and the not-self. There are two possible consequences of this undesirable ambiguity. First, the self decides (at some threshold of existential choice beneath explicit cognizance) that there are no differences between external and internal realities, public and private existence. Subsequently, the self becomes dependent on an external reality for self-understanding. Second, the self sees its external reality as a mere extension of the self and therefore exploits it. In either case, the problem is a misrecognition of the radical difference of the distinct other, whether this other is the natural environment or the interpersonal other.

We believe that the current rhetoric against discrimination on the college campus is narcissistic communication and that at least two specific exemplary rhetorical experiences emerge to demonstrate the narcissistic path. *Negation* and *tolerance* amount to two different choices the self may make regarding social interactions. They are also indicative of the historical "progress" we have made in dealing with the problem of human diversity.

THE GESTURE OF NEGATION

Negation refers to both the discrediting and exploitation of difference. In effect, an individual attempts to make real differences between self and others go away by denigrating the significance of these differences. This is the form of narcissism that sees the world as an extension of the self. Like Jacoby's (1975) "social amnesia," the ability to make distinctions is forgotten (i.e., repressed). As extensions of the self, objects of perception, including interpersonal others, assume a property-like character; that is, they are there to be manipulated. This is the self-aggrandizement and exploitation theme of narcissistic experience.

Negation is most easily identified within the dominant community (e.g., white Anglo culture), though it is hardly an exclusive terrain. For instance, white students at NSU commonly provided the following argument:

I'm not a racist.
I haven't seen a racist act.
Therefore, racism doesn't exist on my campus.

The logic is distorted by narcissistic negation. The first statement begins the narcissistic reflection to the extent that the white student declares himself/herself to be "not racist." Whether or not that statement is "true," the next statement assumes that the individual is actually capable of identifying racism. This argument appeared only slightly modified among some white students, as well as some faculty of color after all the "consciousness raising" (e.g., through videotapes, special conferences, student newspaper coverage, and visiting speakers) that took place in the wake of a couple of racial incidents that occurred on campus. The modified argument went as follows:

> I'm not a racist.
> I've seen an example of it, but it was only an isolated case.
> Therefore, racism is not a serious problem on my campus.

The statement begins again with a narcissistic reflection of what the self must be like, and then it reflects back on society that singular reality.

The first two events that prompted NSU administrators occurred in spring 1989; both situations were fueled by negation. In the first event, an African-American grounds custodian was stopped by two white university police officers who demanded: "Drop your weapon." The man was searched and, after a white custodian identified the grounds custodian as a university employee, he was released. University police reported that the incident was not racially motivated but was prompted by a call describing a man who was allegedly cutting bike locks in the area. The yard crew worker was carrying hedge clippers. Campus discussion focused more on the fact that the employee was not wearing any university identification (which was not required) and that perhaps stricter standards regarding badges or clothes were needed to help (police?) identify (black?) yard crew workers as university employees.

The second event was more dramatic. Each spring, the American Indian Club (AIC) and their friends hold their annual Pow-Wow, a popular and spectacular show of Native American culture. However, while preparing for special dances, the AIC alleged that members of the NSU baseball team yelled racial slurs and howled. AIC members skipped all regular channels for reporting harassment and went directly to the provost (vice-president of academic affairs). The AIC charged the university with failing to confront the baseball team and for prohibiting the club from identifying the perpetrators of the slurs. Unsatisfied with the provost's lack of action, the group filed charges with the U.S. Department of Civil Rights.

The objectivity of the U.S. government was compromised in the eyes of university administrators because the Department of Civil Rights sent a Native American Indian to complete the investigative interviews and file the report. Nearly all university officials who spoke with the investigator felt that "she had already made up her mind" and that there "wasn't much you could say at that point." In contrast, AIC members felt partially vindicated by the U.S. government's intervention—an interesting irony. The government had caught the institution doing something wrong—objectively identified as a violation of civil rights—and it aimed to correct the injustice. It took the investigator over a year to complete the report.

The Pow-Wow incident was driven by denial. In this case, the alienation was particularly serious because its origins were clearly linked to one of the highest offices on the campus. The provost would become the first enemy. Also of interest is the type of negation the AIC used. They denied that NSU's harassment and judicial systems could work for them, and they denied the provost a fair discussion by bringing legal counsel to a meeting but only identifying the person after the meeting was in progress. In the end, they had simply flipped the enthymeme to read: "We've been discriminated against by representatives of the university; we know the university is a racist institution; the provost represents the university; therefore, the provost is a racist." The narrative logic suggested that because people on or near campus displayed racism, the institution and its highest-ranking administrators must, therefore, be racist as well. From our point of view (which we realize is simply a different narrative), narcissistic negation created a missed opportunity and sustained what was merely a facade of communication.

REMINISCING

Negation appears to work partially because it is not experienced as a creation of the negative but rather as the creation of the neutral. In other words, the individual is not admitting to the self that he/she is denying the existence of things; instead, the self is accepting neutrality, which is the absence of socially created value and the illusion of a natural order. It appears that the consequence of a community's shared negation (i.e., a kind of collective experience of narcissism) is that human "equality" becomes human neutrality, as if the ignoring of human differences, the blindness of justice visited on the social scene, is itself "equality."

Because of the Pow-Wow and the investigation, the university president requested that the faculty government take up the issue by creating a subcommittee on "diversity and ethnic consciousness." It was clear that the problem was presupposed as "understood" and that the only thing at issue was discovering and applying the correct solution. Furthermore, the correctness of the solution would most clearly, though tacitly, be that which made the "problem" go away.

After the first group meeting, subcommittee members were assigned to investigate reports of campus violence related to discrimination, to examine plans and strategies instigated by other universities, and to develop solutions for NSU. Many of the dialogues in committee began by reminiscing about "what this was like in the '60s." In many respects, the protests of the 1960s were remembered as being far more successful than they probably actually were (Habermas, 1970a). So pervasive is this code of reminiscing that it reappeared one year later in a new committee on culture and student life. This code should not be dismissed as mere nostalgia, for it appears to have significantly influenced the narcissistic alienation of "tolerance" and fed our embryonic replacement narrative of "appreciation." Perhaps it was the very implicitness of the nostalgia that led some to assume that, almost without looking, they had previous knowledge and experience with this problem.

EXPOSING THE SECRET COMMITTEE

Because the subcommittee was part of the faculty government, its meetings and minutes were open and publicly available. Nevertheless, many campus members ignored the actions of the faculty government and let it operate largely unimpeded until some issue came into relief. The racism issue did not simply rise to the top: It exploded. Allegations were levelled by students and faculty that the subcommittee was a "secret committee" operating "behind closed doors" to deal with racism with "no input from people of color." Committee members began to experience (after only 3 weeks in existence) the real weight of the university's conscience.

Negation helps to explain some of the awkward shifting of subcommittee members that followed the group's "exposure." A black-Hispanic male faculty member was assigned to the committee, and a Hispanic female staff member was invited to help with the assessment plan. Yet, the subcommittee chair was a white male faculty member with a discernible

Southern accent. In fact, the committee's complexion was almost entirely white, though half the membership was female.

The attention that the subcommittee received was disproportionate to its importance in the university. It was nothing more than a policy recommending group, the recommendations from which would go to a standing committee, then to the full faculty governing body. Yet, it would become far more than that because of its precarious position and increased public attention. The story about it, as often rehearsed by those who had cause, was that it was to make final decisions concerning the fate of minority groups on campus.

THE "VICTIM'S" PRIVILEGED POSITION

The language of discrimination shifts subtly, inviting those not familiar with the most recent cultural code to blunder across a new label for some cultural group. The difficulty with such restrictive codes is that they are used as the means to assess an individual's sincerity about discrimination. Knowledge of appropriate labels (e.g., African or Afro-American, instead of black; Asian American, instead of Oriental; or Mexican-American, Latino, Hispanic, or Chicano, instead of Mexican) is a prerequisite for access to a discourse community. Communication errors were permitted but only after provisional acceptance.

The challenge to the "whiteness" of the committee was negation in two steps. First, it denied the possibility that some white Anglos had experienced discrimination or could contribute to an open discussion of the problem. In other words, it defined the ability to listen on the basis of a biological accident of birth. Second, it placed "people of color" as having privileged knowledge; thus, heritage or heredity qualified one to judge the efficacy of a diversity intervention. We are not dismissing the experience of an individual or even a class of people, but let us not miss this point: The claim of victimization, a charge against the "ruling class," carries with it the self-assertion that somehow the self-defined victim, if advantaged in no other way, is at least privy to a special place from which to view the totality of a community's limitations. It is from this place, and from no other, that statements of knowledge gain their credulity, but more importantly—and this is the fundamental point—no one else may or even has a *right* to speak who is not a victim, though, again, this status is self-defined.

An African-American student group at NSU exemplified "negation" when it demanded required coursework on racism and sexism. At an academic meeting attended by faculty, staff, administrators, and students, the group's African-American president proclaimed, "We demand the required courses in ethnic diversity, institutional racism, and the politics of racism and sexism *taught by people of color* be instituted immediately" (emphasis added). Further, the group demanded that "all employees of the university . . . be required to attend continuing training sessions on racism and sexism *designed and conducted by people of color*" (emphasis added). White people, therefore, were not qualified to teach the course. It is an interesting reversal of domination: a narrative unaware that it mirrors the logic of that which it, at least in rhetorical content, opposes.

THE RACISM CONFERENCE: ENCOURAGING AND CONFRONTING NEGATION

In October, an educational conference on racism was sponsored by several student-run groups, though mostly organized by ethnic constituencies. The significance of the conference was not reflected in its content but by its very occurrence. Though white students were in attendance, they did not represent their full 86% of the campus population. The conference created no riots (it was not expected to), but encouraged high intensity catharsis.

Former university employees and ethnic students came back to campus to talk about how they had struggled against discrimination at NSU. During the conference one story was told by an American Indian woman. She explained how her two sons had died at NSU under suspicious discriminatory circumstances (some of which had more to do with the city police than with the educational institution). She told how one son might have lived because of his lighter skin, but that he continued to "hang out with his other [darker skinned] Indian friends." Conference planners submitted voluntarily ideas generated during the conference to the faculty subcommittee, fueling (perhaps for the first time) the perception that the subcommittee had significant organizational influence.

Concurrently, the subcommittee chair had drafted a five-step plan with the assistance of the chair of the faculty government. Because of the significant impact these steps would have on the campus, a draft of the plan was shared with the university president before it was submitted to the subcommittee. By now, the subcommittee was attracting the attention of those outside the university's gates, a unique phenomenon for a faculty government's *sub*committee. In brief, the five-point plan called for outside consulting to initiate immediate discussion with the president's cabinet, deans' council, and student government leaders; the collection and expedient communication of all information currently available on racial and sexual harassment, as well as on student judicial processes; and the initiation of "Appreciating Diversity" or "AD Groups" across the campus. The recommendations also called for the postponement of a "principles of community" statement and suggested that AD groups be allowed to generate their own ideas—"let the community make a statement."

The plan received extensive media coverage. The student newspaper, for example, following its own ethnic conscience, assigned its only black reporter (of 65 staff members) to cover this story. What was not immediately known was that the black student reporter was also a member of the Coalition for Racial Unity and the Pan African Union. The latter group was the very one that had called for the educational training of all university employees by people of color, as previously described.

TOLERANCE AND CORPORATE MODELS IN HRD DIVERSITY INTERVENTIONS

In searching current strategies for reducing racial conflict, we discovered far more corporate diversity models than university ones. The corporate models offer in varying prescriptions some form of behavioral, cognitive, or mixed brand of psychology believed capable of achieving multicultural harmony. Corporate diversity programs reflect a minor perspectival shift from human relations thinking to a human resource development approach. The human relations approach assumed a positive correlation (if not a downright causal relationship) between worker satisfaction and organizational productivity, and although the assumption still remains, research findings have proven generally inconsistent. The human resource development (HRD) model represents a modification of the original human relations approach. More specifically, HRD assumes that higher productivity is not so much dependent on worker "satisfaction" as on workers possessing the knowledge, skills, and attitudes that permit them to be satisfied with how they contribute to the organization and to their own lives. The fundamental premise of HRD, then, may be understood causally: Employee satisfaction and organizational productivity are positively related to workplace learning.

It is a commonplace of organizational leadership that "training" has become a panacea for most organizational problems; training is perhaps bandied about as the solution to most organizational problems as often as "communication" deficiencies are identified as the source of most managerial deficiencies. Not surprisingly, then, the shift from human relations to human resource development has coincided with an increase in "diversity training" programs. In fact, the American Society for Training and Development (ASTD), the largest professional organization of HRD practitioners, lists nearly 900 members in its "Multicultural Network," a special-interest group dedicated to enhancing appreciation of ethnic differences in the workplace. Besides countless consultants and facilitators, HRD suppliers (e.g., Copeland-Griggs Productions, CRM Films, and U.S. Learning Corporation) have developed training videos, facilitation packages, or seminars on "valuing" differences in the workplace. NSU, in fact, purchased all seven of Copeland-Griggs's "Valuing Diversity" videotapes as part of its commitment to reducing discrimination and reaffirming a campus population's shared opinion against bigotry (as opposed to being "for" something else).

CHALLENGING THE RHETORIC OF TOLERANCE

The choice to accept perceived differences between people works as a form of social tolerance characteristic of contemporary liberal rhetoric. This choice is not ordinarily seen as problematic. In fact, this choice is most clearly associated with the American ideal of equality, which we interpret as "neutrality" in a narcissistic society.

Tolerance requires community members to "put up with" or "exist with" another class of people. Tolerance therefore objectifies the other. The communicative illness intrinsic to tolerance is that the individual interacts with the other person only to define what the self is not. The narcissistic reflection, then, may be "I'm not like that person." The consequences of this conclusion create two possible conditions in the self. First, the individual may assume that "I'm not like that person . . . so I'm better [or worse] off." This assumption of superiority or inferiority pervades the communication of tolerance. The implicit standard of narcissistic judgment is the self: *Reality becomes a story told to a mirror.*

The second condition emerging from tolerance does not rely on the hardening of the boundaries of the self as with the first condition but rather involves the loss of boundaries. In this case, the communicative act of tolerance overemphasizes the universality and neutrality of the human condition; hence, one concludes that "Though I'm not like you in some respects, generally we are all the same." This is the narrative logic of many current interventions directed to increase "racial harmony."

For example, affirmative action (AA) programs are based largely on the assumption that people are basically similar, but that some were historically denied fair opportunities and are due indemnity; so gross had been these historical violations of basic rights to "minorities" that expedient correction of the problem in ways that could offend, or even deny similar rights of, Anglo males would be considered legislatively and legally justified. AA thus served the grand narrative that depicts "progress" toward eliminating racism. The grand narrative offered hope that a mature society, informed by science and driven by new technology, would continue to take "positive action" toward equity for all. Regardless, AA programs have perpetuated both negation and (especially) tolerance. They encouraged the sort of thinking that suggested "we are all the same." The problem was, however, that the dominant culture became the measure of "sameness," washing away the unique heritages of people of color. Tolerance and cultural assimilation became ideological allies.

In contrast to narcissistic negation, the alienation of narcissistic tolerance supports another and more complicated narrative logic, stated as follows:

I'm not a racist because I am an educated, open-minded person.
I am also an individual who has experienced discrimination *or* understands emphatically and intelligently the subtle forms of discrimination in my society.
Therefore, I will encourage others who are not like me, to be educated in my ways in order for my communication to be improved.

This story begins with a self-assertion, but instead of concluding with the negation of the problem, the individual calls for a reflection on his/her own condition as the measure of how society might be reformed. The self becomes the measure of what society should look like. This is the theme of grandiosity in narcissistic experience.

Regardless of whether it is a condition of negation or tolerance, the general belief that all situations in which people are talking or gesturing is a communicative experience is decentered by the narcissistic illusion of communication. This illusion, reflective of information theory, suggests that the mere exchange of messages is the very same thing as having communicated. What we must realize is that narcissistic communication is a particular neurosis in which people only appear to be engaged in substantive dialogue. The participants in this distorted discourse are unable to "share substance" (Burke, 1969) or achieve shared understanding because their talk is largely a narcissistic reflection attempting to define the self.

The ambiguity of the self's fluid definition in communication with others is simply at odds with cultural demands that we be defined as "individuals" above all else. The promise of the grand narrative—some universally shared story—becomes an experience in individual frustration, for the desire to discover true coherence is challenged by forces the individual is unable to articulate. The narcissistic voice struggles against a linguistic system that gave birth to the "self" and then limited its possibility. Progress toward true meaning, therefore, is a delusion of a narcissistic narrative in which the individual, constrained by the boundaries of the reflected self, comes to believe that his/her narrative is a universal one— an experience reinforced by others who participate in a similar narcissistic delusion (Lasch, 1991). *We are all looking in the mirror at the same time, accepting the uniqueness of ourselves and the ubiquity of our experience.*

THE PROMISE OF APPRECIATION
AND THE IDEOLOGY OF EQUALITY

Our strategy was to change the narrative from one of narcissistic tolerance to what we then perceived as non-narcissistic "appreciation." What we did not, perhaps could not, know at the time was that we had ourselves adopted a mono-narrative design, one that closed off the very possibilities for discourse we sought to open. Our design was technocratically involved. Tactically, we achieved this by the rapid campuswide adoption of the Appreciating Diversity Groups, which in their popularly abbreviated form were known as AD Groups.

Strategically, we had more difficulty convincing community representatives to amend their understanding of racism as psychology to racism as ideology. Racism and other discriminatory systems are popularly understood as an individual attitude or belief in the superiority of one class over another. The problem with this definition is that it seats "racism" in the individual's psychology. The definition becomes problematic in attempts to change "racists" (i.e., those individuals who "suffer" from this mental deficiency or erroneous logic) because the obvious conclusion is that "you can't change peoples' attitudes."

The attitudinal definition of racism was supported by both sides of the debate for a racial harassment policy at NSU. Some administrators argued that such a policy would likely be ineffective because racism is something *in* the individual; special ethnic constituencies responded by saying that the policy was needed as a step toward eliminating "racism" (i.e., eliminating bad or socially unacceptable attitudes). While both sides were working from an assumption of racism as an individual attitude, the debate stalled because they disagreed on how to legislate or punish an "attitude." The logic of the grand narrative of *racism as individual psychology* was failing to achieve a resolution of the enigma.

In order to overcome this psychological definition of racism, we defined it and other forms of discrimination as *ideological systems sustaining communicative acts that intentionally or unintentionally derogate a class of people because of their shared convictions, ancestry, ethnicity, race, origin, gender, and the like.* Ideology operates as a superior structure in the linguistic system of a particular community and in turn works to constrain systematically the possible meanings of a sign within that community (see Althusser, 1970, 1971; Hall, 1985; Mumby, 1988). Ideology, in this respect, represents a superior code that works to produce meaning in human discourse in ways that shape the interpretation of signs. Ideology, for example, builds sexual differences into language and thus influences how our society organizes itself to account for such differences.

Racism, then, is not an individual logic; rather, it is a socially shared logic that works to promote one group above another (see van Dijk, Chapter 5 in this book). It represents an extreme form of ethnocentrism (a narcissistically influenced way of understanding in which one conceives of another's culture only from the perspective of one's own). Pearce (1989, p. 120) writes,

> In ethnocentric communication, whatever "we" are is defined in part by its contrast with "them," and "our" resources include specific ways of dealing with "them" such that those resources are not put at risk. These resources are robust because virtually anything "they" do merely confirms our perception of "their" inferiority or maliciousness. . . . Ethnocentric communication is the norm in contemporary American society. It is, of course, the stuff of racism, sexism, and the like.

Understanding racism as ideology calls one to recognize that racism is socially bound in the fabric of a culture's grammar. It becomes, as Habermas (1970b, 1984) suggests, a "systematic distortion" in communicative acts.

The problem with defining racism as ideology is that some believe it to be an "excuse" for an individual's discriminatory acts. Such a reading misses the point. Certainly, psychological definitions are appealing because they ascribe far more individual free will; that is, one can choose to be or not be a racist, according to the dominant narrative. However, psychological definitions and attitudinal descriptions of racism have failed to yield much in the way of "eliminating" racism or for explaining the rising racial tensions on university campuses. Our approach enables us both to define racism as a structural characteristic of human communication and to expose ideological constraints that previously remained hidden.

THE TACTICS OF APPRECIATION

At once the most successful and the most troublesome tactic of our intervention were the AD Groups. According to Lippitt and Lippitt (1986), the first law of organizational development is to seek approval and support from as high in the organization as possible (a functional maxim that maintains the authority of the dominant narrative). In expected order, the original five-point plan asked that the university president initiate with his cabinet the first AD Group; it was suggested that an outside consultant specializing in diversity interventions be used to facilitate this discussion. The president agreed to support the AD Groups, but after reviewing consulting bids, he rejected the external consultant and with it the need for top-level involvement. In spite of the president and perhaps because of its memorable name, AD Groups stuck and could not be immediately terminated simply because top administrators did not believe they needed to be involved in such activities.

Many of the AD Groups began spontaneously. The department or area workers heard of the idea, asked (sometimes) for a few guidelines, and then sat down to discuss how to improve the campus in regard to multicultural diversity. When requested, the guidelines were kept simple because most of the groups were self-facilitating. Group leaders were told to ask three questions: (1) What do you believe are the central problems in your work area inhibiting one's appreciation of diversity? (2) What immediate and long-term suggestions do you have for improving our campus community and your work area regarding this issue? (3) What would you include as key principles for our community? AD Groups returned reams of suggestions and (in regard to the third question) offered their own "principles of community" statement. Throughout this time (roughly 4 months), no academic unit convened an AD Group. There was no defense against those who angrily criticized the provost and president for not requiring or formally asking deans or department chairs to hold discussions on discrimination. Ironically, it was the *faculty* government that had initiated the plan.

Problematic as these conditions were, the campus discussions continued, and as serendipitous as the AD Groups' successes may have been, they did provide a mechanism for people to talk about discrimination and a means to make specific recommendations affecting their community. Yet, in spite of the broad participation in AD Groups, the more vocal spokespersons of special ethnic constituencies declared before local media their private ownership of the crusade against institutionally protected racism. The politics of ownership worked both to broaden participation across groups and to serve the ambitions of individual faculty, staff, and students seeking "credit" for success.

INDIVIDUALISM AND THE APPRECIATION METAPHOR

We realized (not immediately) that our model suffered the same deep flaw as corporate models. We were encouraging a self-destructive system interested in valuing or appreciating not cultural but *individual* differences. Though we were aware of this possible connection, we believed that we could "manage" the discourse if our ethic was to maintain constant vigilance to protect the integrity of the dialogue. "Appreciating diversity" (or the more popularly known corporate label, "valuing diversity") was not an easy expression to replace or dismiss because it was extended by videos, news agencies, and professional journals: valuing diversity was in vogue (Solomon, 1989).

In many respects the metaphor of appreciation did not escape the centrality of individualism. It too suffered a similar narcissistic logic that resembles (not surprisingly) the alienation of tolerance. The logic of appreciation, expressed below, is a paraphrase of comments spoken by community members stating their commitment to improving the campus. The logic is as follows: "Because I am aware of who I am, I am more open to the differences in people unlike me; and it is important to *value* other people because they can teach me more about myself." The first part of the statement represents the assertion of self-awareness; the second notes how the individual views the economic exchange of dealing with other people. Communication in this instance is not comprehended as a "value" (i.e., something of profound importance) but rather becomes a means for accomplishing the self. The term *appreciation* itself implies an affirmed increase or excess, or a value-added act, a term encapsulated by the economies of contemporary culture.

SUSPICION OF LANGUAGE AND ANTI-INTELLECTUAL PLAY

Although the AD Groups were generally successful, an unforeseen development was an increasing suspicion of language and a challenge to intellectualism. The skillful use of language was a liability for articulate administrators, a gift for ethnic speakers who argued the cause of disenfranchisement. Part of this distrust of language was more deeply grounded in a distrust of the intellectual. This was not a full rejection of intellectualism—people still wanted to appear "intelligent." It was instead a rejection of status, power, and position that an intellectual may hold simply because of rank and status in a university. Surely, rank is not commensurate with intelligence, even at a university. Yet, the appearance of "being intellectual" (i.e., arrogant, verbose, expressive, and fond of reflection) was a signal that one had left the ground of practical reason and was no longer to be trusted, for critical reflection and reason were understood as the veils of racism and sexism.

Implicit allegiance to a deliberative rhetoric prevailed. Such a rhetoric never questioned its own premises and always assumed that the premises of each party to the dialogue were shared. *The* problem had been assumed to be common to all and, to this end, the appreciation model encouraged technical reasoning fostering the promise of *the* solution.

When the subcommittee met for the last time, the faculty rejected the notion of "*a* community statement," demanding instead, "*The* Community Statement." Having been involved all year in the project, they were not satisfied with putting forward the collective statements composed by AD Groups (of staff and students, not faculty) as a *community's* statement. The committee sought the definitive statement, especially one resembling community statements from other universities. The irony was a painful one, for the faculty subcommittee talked of celebrating plurality on the one hand and asserted a universal reality on the other. So strong was the desire for the "one best" community statement, that one faculty subcommittee member raised the issue again in the following academic year. The motion was rejected.

CONCLUSION

The cynical conclusion would be that "nothing worked," which is to imply that something was mechanistically flawed and needed repair. It is also cynical to conclude that in the absence of rational discourse and in the presence of narcissistic talk, that no "solution" could be found because no true problem would ever emerge under such harsh communicative conditions. This position is flawed because it presumes a universal conception of solution/problem; to find the "true" problem, in other words, is to have found the solution.

Certainly, one may question whether organizational development interventions actually produce any predictable results. This should not be understood as a rejection of practical involvement but rather as a challenge to the processual models of intervention, which assume a controlled disruption in the course of human affairs. What ethic does communication hold under these conditions? And, what privileged position do interventionists assume they possess? Is this ethic any different from that of the narcissistic interlocutors whom we have described?

Habermas (1970a, p. 113) warns of a "technocratic consciousness" that is capable of eliminating the distinction between the practical and the technical. Technocratic consciousness emerged in these events when people trusted their ability to control discrimination through the instruments of production and were unable to see how those "solutions" may ultimately control them. The trouble with technocratic consciousness is that even though it bares the ideological face of the practical, it hides the instruments of domination in the technical, thus preventing its own self-destruction. Hence, society convinces itself that technology is the means to solving human problems. Habermas (1970a, pp. 111-112) writes, "For with the veiling of practical problems [technical consciousness] not only justifies a *particular class's* interest in domination and represses *another class's* partial need for emancipation, but affects the human race's emancipatory interests as such." In this way, technocratic consciousness serves as the linchpin in a modern society's grand narrative.

In 1990, the Carnegie Foundation for the Advancement of Teaching distributed its well-publicized study of U.S. universities and colleges: *Campus Life: In Search of Community* (Boyer, 1990). The report calls for a restoration of "community," a commitment to the common good, achieved through educational means. The report's assertion rests on six principles of community: An educational community must dedicate itself to pursuing *purposeful academic goals*, encouraging *open dialogue* while ensuring civility, protecting the "*sacredness of the person*," demanding *responsibility and discipline*, nurturing the *support of others*, and *celebrating* the traditions and future of shared visions. We are not condemning optimism, for it can support worthy ambitions, but the Carnegie report may hold nothing more than the promise of technology as solution. As we examine the rhetoric of a narcissistic movement, we must constantly look back and ask of such a report: Whose community are we restoring or rebuilding? Or, whose interests do we most want to protect in this community?

In the end, we tried not so much to "manage discourse" as to encourage it, for it is the temperament of language-as-spoken—the *value* of communication—that pushes hard against the distortion of narcissistic talk, the latter being a kind of talk that *de-values* the possibilities of communication by identifying it with mere information exchange.

Narcissistic ideological practices are nothing if not uncritical and unreflective. Here, parties exchange information, not to celebrate the many narratives that are possible in a complex and diverse society but rather to flame the passions of vanity, grandiosity, and self-entitlement. The ultimate objective of the narcissistic narrative is not to consider authentically the other group or person's story but is instead an attempt to claim the communicative ground as entirely belonging to one's own worldview, and to none other. Narcissism closes doors through which we might enter and come to know the uniqueness of interpersonal others. Narcissistic narratives support the self-righteous reflections of both dominant *and* subordinate groups; both victims and ruling groups assume their discourse to be privileged above all others. The reality is that the grand narrative is itself a narcissistic narrative and that this narrative works by denying the very progress that it promises. Are we capable as communicative beings of healing the injuries caused by our preoccupation with the self?

The experience of collective life does not entail mitigation of individual identities. It is, rather, through the collectivity that we may discover the resources that give us individual strength. If this is possible, then individuality is accomplished through collective life. Until now, the premise has been that we are individuals first, as if it were an inherited right, and members of a collectivity second. Gergen (1991) understands this bifurcation between the private and collective lives as a postmodern dilemma of the self. He asserts that "meaning is born of interdependence. And because there is no self outside a system of meaning, it may be said that relations precede and are more fundamental than self. Without relationships there is no language with which to conceptualize the emotions, thoughts, or intentions of the self" (p. 157).

Benhabib (1986) acknowledges that the privileging of particular groups (victims or rulers), although typically human, inhibits the growth of a community. She writes,

> The traditional politics of the subject assumes that there is one group of humans whose strategic position uniquely entitles them to represent the plurality. The philosophy of the subject always searches for a particular group . . . whose particularity represents universality as such. The politics of empowerment, by contrast, proceeds from the assumption that there is no single spot in the social structure that privileges those who occupy it with a vision of the social totality. . . .

> Genuine collectivities are formed out of struggle, not out of the logic of substitution that preempts the experience of one social group with the categories derived from the language of another. . . . [Emancipation] is the negation of the existent in the name of a future that bursts open the possibilities of the present. (pp. 352-353)

Perhaps communication becomes the perpetual opening of possibilities, and recognition of its value serves as a precondition for witnessing diverse cultural narratives.

Communication, not self-assertion, makes community possible. For an essential element of a mature community resides in the rich complexity of its relationships. Contradiction and mystery, order and negation, at once feed the development of human communities and host the elements that permit private and collective distortions. Our work is not in the denial or acceptance of a universal narrative or a monoculture but in the protection of our continued discussion of truth and experience of collective life.

REFERENCES

Alford, F. C. (1988). *Narcissism: Socrates, the Frankfurt School, and psychoanalytic theory.* New Haven: Yale Press.

Althusser, L. (1970). *For Marx* (Trans. B. Brewster). New York: Vintage.

Althusser, L. (1971). *Lenin and philosophy* (Trans. B. Brewster). New York: Monthly Review Press.

Benhabib, S. (1986). *Critique, norm, and utopia: A Study of the foundations of critical theory.* New York: Columbia University Press.

Bernstein, A. (1990, March/April). Students on campus: Sex, race, and diversity tapes. *Change,* pp. 18-23.

Boyer, E. L. (Ed.). (1990). *Campus life: In search of community.* Princeton, NJ: The Carnegie Foundation for the Advancement of Teaching.

Burke, K. (1969). *A grammar of motives.* Berkeley, CA: University of California Press.

Catt, I. E. (1986). Rhetoric and narcissism: A critique of ideological selfism. *Western Journal of Speech Communication, 50*, 242-253.

Clay, C. A. (1989, Fall). Campus racial tensions: Trend or aberration? *The NEA Higher Education Journal, 5*, 21-30.

Deetz, S. A. (1985). Ethical considerations in cultural research in organizations. In P. J. Frost, L. F. Moore, M. R. Louis, C. C. Lundberg, & J. Martin (Eds.), *Organizational culture* (pp. 253-270). Beverly Hills: Sage.

Eco, U. (1986). *Travels in hyper reality: Essays* (Trans. William Weaver). San Diego, CA: Harcourt Brace Jovanovich.

Fine, R. (1986). *Narcissism, the self, and society.* New York: Columbia University Press.

Friedman, M. (1974). *The hidden human image.* New York: Dell.

Gergen, K. J. (1991). *The saturated self: Dilemma of identity in contemporary life.* New York: Basic Books.

Geuss, R. (1981). *The idea of a critical theory: Habermas and the Frankfurt School.* New York: Cambridge University Press.

Gibbs, N. (1990, May). Bigots in the ivory tower. *Time*, pp. 104-106.

Goodall, H. L., Jr. (1990). A cultural inquiry concerning the ontological and epistemic dimensions of self, other, and context in communication scholarship. In G. M. Phillips & J. T. Wood (Eds.), *Speech communication: Essays to commemorate the 75th anniversary of the Speech Communication Association,* (pp. 264-292). Carbondale, IL: Southern Illinois University Press.

Habermas, J. (1970a). *Toward a rational society: Student protest, science, and politics* (Trans. Jeremy Shapiro). Boston: Beacon Press. First published 1968.

Habermas, J. (1970b). Towards a theory of communicative competence. *Inquiry, 13*, 360-375.

Habermas, J. (1984). *The theory of communicative action,* Vol. 1. (Trans. T. McCarthy). Boston: Beacon Press.

Hall, S. (1985). Signification, representation, ideology: Althusser and the post-structuralist debates. *Critical Studies in Mass Communication, 2*, 91-114.

Jacoby, R. (1975). *Social amnesia.* Boston: Beacon Press.

Jacoby, R. (1987). *The last intellectuals: American culture in the age of academe.* New York: Noonday.

Lasch, C. (1978). *The culture of narcissism: American life in an age of diminishing expectations.* New York: Norton.

Lasch, C. (1991). *The true and only heaven: Progress and its critics.* New York: Norton.

Layton, L., & Shapiro, B. A. (Eds.). (1986). *Narcissism and the text: Studies in literature and the psychology of the self.* New York: New York University Press.

Lippitt, G., & Lippitt, R. (1986). *The consulting process in action* (2nd ed.) San Diego, CA: University Associates.

Magner, D. K. (1990, June 6). Racial tensions continue to erupt on campuses despite efforts to promote cultural diversity. *The Chronicle of Higher Education*, pp. A1, A29.

Mumby, D. K. (1988). *Communication and power in organizations: Discourse, ideology, and domination.* Norwood, NJ: Ablex.

Pacanowsky, M. E., & O'Donnell-Trujillo, N. (1982). Communication and organizational cultures. *Western Journal of Speech Communication, 46*, 115-130.

Pearce, W. B. (1989). *Communication and the human condition.* Carbondale, IL: Southern Illinois University Press.

Putnam, L. L., & Pacanowsky, M. E. (Eds.). (1983). *Communication and organizations: An interpretive approach.* Beverly Hills: Sage.

Restak, R. (1982). *The self seekers*. Garden City, NY: Doubleday.
Solomon, C. M. (1989, August). The corporate response to work force diversity. *Personnel Journal, 68*, pp. 43-54.
Toch, T., & Davis, J. (1990, April). Separate but equal all over again. *U.S. News and World Report*, pp. 37-38.
Wiener, J. (1990, May/June). Racial hatred rocks campuses. *Utne Reader*, pp. 62-68.

PART IV

NARRATIVE, SOCIAL CONTROL, AND THE MEDIA

Chapter 8

AMERICAN JOURNALISTS AND THE DEATH OF LEE HARVEY OSWALD: NARRATIVES OF SELF-LEGITIMATION

Barbie Zelizer

LIKE ALL SPEAKERS in public discourse, journalists are skilled tellers of events who reconstruct and often displace the activities behind the news. For journalists, the reconstructive work of telling has particular bearing on the legitimacy of their authority as public speakers and their ability to exert social control through narrative. Unlike members of other professional groups, journalists lack recognizable external markers of their authority. Their legitimacy for providing authoritative perspectives on events is instead rhetorically based, with journalists primarily legitimating themselves through the rhetoric they use to tell news-stories.

The following pages discuss one case where journalists have effectively legitimated their positions as credible tellers of one event—the murder of John F. Kennedy's presumed killer, Lee Harvey Oswald. How journalists have shaped their retelling of the role they played in that event is seen here as an exercise in narrative reconstruction, by which journalists have recast the events of that November Sunday in accordance with ongoing discourses about the state of American journalism. More specifically, they have reconstructed the story of covering Oswald's murder as a narrative that celebrates them as professionals. This analysis is based on systematic examination of the public published discourse by which journalists have recollected their part in covering Oswald's murder since it occurred. Narratives were taken from the printed press, professional and trade reviews, television retrospectives, film documentaries, and books.[1] At focus here

AUTHOR'S NOTE: This chapter is an adapted version of material originally published (Zelizer, 1992). © 1992 by The University of Chicago. All rights reserved.

is a consideration of the cultural authority that American journalists have come to embody as authoritative spokespersons for events of the "real" world and the control this gives them over the American public in narratively determining preferred versions of those events.

NARRATIVE, AUTHORITY,
AND RHETORICAL LEGITIMATION

Legitimation through rhetoric is an issue that has traditionally concerned analysts of public discourse. From Max Weber to Jurgen Habermas, theorists have long been concerned with the rational aims that speakers address through language. Habermas, in particular, maintained that speakers use language in order to effect various kinds of consensus about their activity:

> Under the functional aspect of reaching understanding, communicative action serves the transmission and renewal of cultural knowledge; under the aspect of coordinating action, it serves social integration and the establishment of group solidarity; under the aspect of socialization, it serves the formation of personal identities. (Habermas, 1981, pp. xxiv-xxv)

Habermas contended that speakers often use language and discourse to achieve aims related to freedom and dependence, with aims such as social cohesion, group solidarity, or legitimation directly upheld or disavowed by what a speaker says (Habermas, quoted in Wuthnow et al., 1984, p. 190). The ability of communication to uphold consensus in the realization of these aims determines whether true, or effective, communication has been achieved.

Scholars have also argued that narrative provides an underlying logic for implementing more general communicative rules and conventions (Lucaites & Condit, 1985; White, 1981). Narrative is seen as an effective tool for accomplishing community and authority and a means of maintaining collective codes of knowledge. In this light, narrative functions as a meta-code, a point suggested nearly two decades ago by Roland Barthes. It offers speakers an underlying logic by which to implement more general communicative conventions and allows for the effective sharing and transmission of stories within culturally and socially explicit codes of meaning (Barthes, 1977; Lucaites & Condit, 1985; White, 1981). Within the meta-code of narrative, reality becomes accountable in view of the stories told about it. But it becomes accountable only to those who share the codes of knowledge it invokes.

This suggests that journalists, as speakers in discourse, have employed a broad range of stylistic and narrative devices to uphold parameters of their own authority. As Hayden White argues:

> Once we note the presence of the theme of authority in the text, we also perceive the extent to which the truth claims of the narrative and indeed the very right to narrate hinges upon a certain relationship to authority per se. (White, 1981, p. 18)

With all public speakers, questions of narrative have thus come to be regarded as being at least partly entwined with questions of authority and legitimation.

Narrative's role in achieving authority becomes particularly relevant when considering the evolution of particular stories over time. Scholarship by White (1981), Kellner (1989), Canary and Kozicki (1978), and others has shown that, over time, speakers reposition themselves with regard to original events, thereby reconfiguring their authority. Aims having little to do with narrative activity become differentially embedded within narratives over time. In White's view, this has made historical inquiry less motivated by "the necessity to establish *that* certain events occurred than of the desire to determine what certain events might *mean* for a given group, society, or culture's conception of its present tasks and future prospects" (White, 1986, p. 487). Which narrators eventually emerge as authoritative voices of a given story thus reveals much about the practices by which they are rhetorically legitimated and the authority through which they are culturally constituted.

These premises are of direct relevance to journalism professionals, whose work has long been characterized as an entanglement of narrative, authority, and rhetorical legitimation (Carey, 1986; Schudson, 1982). Whereas nearly all professional groups have evolved in association with formalized bodies of knowledge, much of the professional authority of journalists has come to rest not in what they know but in how they represent their knowledge. This means that their rhetoric offers them an effective way of realizing their legitimation as public speakers.

The salience of journalistic legitimation through rhetoric is particularly foregrounded in a mass-mediated age, where media technologies have expanded the range and type of stages available to journalists as public speakers. Journalistic usage of television technology in particular has fostered their self-portrayal as ever present, omniscient tellers of so-called objective events. The aura of rhetorical competence this implies makes analysis of journalistic narrative particularly valuable to our understanding of why journalists are able to present their version of events as authoritative ones.

This suggests that the foundations of cultural authority are embedded within narrative. Through narrative, journalists have held themselves together not only as a profession—a group kept together by credentialing, licensing, and educational procedures—but as an interpretive community—a group kept together by its narratives, tales, and collective rhetoric. Journalistic narratives, in such a picture, offer analysts one example of what James Carey calls the "ritual" side of communication—the patterned activity that draws members of a community together in commonality and community, the stuff that group members use to keep themselves together (Carey, 1975). The notion that narrative promotes a shared lore among journalists thus becomes a focus through which to understand the workings of their rhetorical legitimation as a group. It displays how they work to legitimate their actions through the tales they tell.

All of this has particular bearing on stories of the Oswald murder. The story of John F. Kennedy's assassination, of which the Oswald murder was a part, is seen here as a critical incident among journalism professionals, which journalists have used to evaluate and reconsider consensual notions about professional practice and appropriate boundaries of journalistic authority. At the time, most professional forums, such as the American Society for Newspaper Editors or National Association of Broadcasters, and trade publications, such as *Columbia Journalism Review, Editor and Publisher,* or *Broadcasting,* independently evaluated how journalists covered the story. The Association for Education in Journalism emphasized coverage of the trial of Jack Ruby during a special 1964 plenary session (Official Minutes, 1965, p. 152). As time went on, certain aspects of the story were kept alive while others were dropped from collective memory. Today, approximately three decades later, the story of covering Oswald's homicide is still discussed, albeit in a highly constructed form. How journalists have rhetorically reconstructed the story of their coverage of Oswald's murder to uphold themselves as professionals is thus the topic of this chapter.

THE CONTEXT FOR RETELLING
OSWALD'S MURDER

Retelling the more general story of John F. Kennedy's assassination provided a viable cornerstone against which the reconstructive work of journalists could flourish. Retellings of the assassination produced a huge body of literature, including nearly 200 books within 36 months of his death, hundreds of periodical pieces, television retrospectives, and at least 12 newsletters (Donner, 1979, p. 658). Retelling the Kennedy assassination gave journalists a stage on which to spread tales and gain status for their telling.

To a large extent, the possibility of connecting oneself to the assassination narrative, in all its forms, reflected larger concerns among journalists about journalistic professionalism. During the 1960s, journalists sought to consolidate themselves as a recognized and legitimate profession. Although journalism had been a strong force for decades before Kennedy's assassination, a general movement toward professionalism during the 1960s encouraged journalists to put themselves in their chronicles both as subject and documenter. Reporters were called on to be reflexive about the standards of behavior with which they collected and presented the news. As *Esquire* magazine wrote: "Journalists were part of the problem, part of the solution and always part of the story" (Brackman, 1983, p. 197). Lingering questions about who would define news—the people in positions of power or the people in the streets—challenged journalists to experiment with new standards of professional behavior (Halberstam, 1979, p. 400). At the same time, the emerging validation of television news was creating a new force on the horizon, which was beginning to reshape many givens about journalistic performance. This was not to suggest that television was a recognized and legitimate form of reportage. In fact, a few months before Kennedy's death, television journalists were still denied membership in professional organizations, on the assumption that they did not constitute bona-fide reporters (International Press Institute, 1963, p. 52). Journalists themselves generally felt that the press was the better news medium, with television called a "journalistic frivolity" (Gates, 1978, p. 5).

At the same time, ongoing ties between the journalistic community and Kennedy's administration enhanced the authority of journalism as a profession. Their ties helped set up a framework by which journalists could effectively champion their position as primary spokespersons for events. As *Time* reporter Hugh Sidey observed:

> Has there ever been a more succulent time for a young reporter? I doubt it. It was a golden time for scribes. He talked to us, listened to us, honored us, ridiculed us, played with us, and all the time lifted our trade to new heights of respect and importance. (quoted in Kunhardt, 1988, p. 6)

Everything Kennedy did for journalists, he did in exaggerated form for television journalists, and this solidified the latter's status. Kennedy was seen as having a particular affinity for television, a point suggested by his 1960 TV debates with Nixon, his introduction of the first televised news conferences, informal television interviews, or use of television to convey major political decisions—such as warnings to the Russians during the Cuban missile crisis. These activities gave him the label of "the first television president." So to some extent, the background by which journalists were linked with the story of Kennedy's death already had its roots in ties between his administration and the news media.

The Oswald murder was part of this scenario. Retelling the events around it became a crucial part of establishing the role that journalists played not only in the murder itself but in the larger story of Kennedy's assassination. The rhetoric of journalistic self-legitimation, by which journalists sought to perpetuate versions of the story that cast their own activity as professional behavior, allowed them to conveniently link stories of Oswald's murder with ongoing discourses about journalism, particularly journalistic professionalism and the legitimation of television journalism. The fluctuating state surrounding many givens about what constituted journalism at the time of Kennedy's death worked to their advantage.

COVERING THE MURDER OF OSWALD

Coverage of Oswald's murder took the form of follow-up activity to coverage of Kennedy's death. It began on Friday night, when Dallas police attempted to hold a midnight photo opportunity with Kennedy's accused killer, Lee Harvey Oswald. At the time, over 100 persons filled the halls of the police station, whose conditions were "not too much unlike Grand Central Station at rush hour" (*Warren Report*, 1964, p. 202). Dallas was considered ill-equipped to handle the growing influx of reporters, and the police's attempts that night to address their mounting pressures for information were problematic:

> Cameramen stood on the tables to take pictures and others pushed forward to get close-ups. . . . After Oswald had been in the room only a few minutes, Chief Curry intervened and directed that Oswald be taken back to jail because, he testified, the "newsmen tried to overrun him." (*Warren Report*, 1964, p. 208)

Oswald was to be transferred from the city to the county jail on Sunday morning. Again, the press corps arrived in groups. By 10:00 a.m., an estimated 50 journalists were in attendance in the basement of the city jail, including still photographers, television camerapeople, and reporters from all media (*Warren Report*, 1964, p. 213). Conditions for coverage were among the best available to journalists during the larger assassination story.

The transfer began almost immediately. Reporters pushed and shoved to get a word with Oswald. As one participant recalls:

> All the newsmen were poking their sound mikes across to [Oswald during the transfer] and asking questions, and they were everyone sticking their flashbulbs up and around and over him and in his face. (*Warren Report*, 1964, p. 216)

A few moments later, Jack Ruby stepped out from the group of reporters, drew a gun, pulled the trigger, and watched Oswald slump to the floor. The irony that he was hidden by the very group of journalists trying to record the transfer in collective memory was momentarily lost as the group shifted its focus to record the murder in sound, prose, still photographs, and live television.

How journalists covered the murder was appraised according to two perspectives: One viewed it as the activity of professionals; another cast it as unprofessional conduct. Within both appraisals were concerns for journalistic professionalism and the emerging legitimacy of television as a news-gathering medium.

UNPROFESSIONAL CONDUCT: THE NEGATIVE VIEW

Negative appraisals of journalists' coverage characterized it as professional misconduct. Two clusters of issues motivated this view: physical and legal-ethical. Physical issues—whether and in what way journalists actually facilitated Oswald's death—were uppermost in the mind of one detective, who told of how the "near-blinding television and motion picture lights allowed to shine upon the escort party increased the difficulty of observing unusual movements in the basement" (*Warren Report*, 1964, p. 227). As NBC's Tom Pettit recalled:

> In that throng it was difficult for any reporter to sort out who was who. But for the television reporters the problem was compounded by the need for

> simultaneous transmission. What was recorded by microphones and cameras (either film or live) would go on the air without much editing. What transpired in the hallway was broadcast without much opportunity for evaluation. And the television reporter could not move about freely, since his own movement was limited by the length of his microphone cable. (Pettit, 1965, p. 63)

Journalistic practice was thus seen as being at odds with Oswald's problem-free transport.

When it became clear that Oswald has been shot at close range by Ruby, who emerged from the group of journalists, discussions centered on whether or not journalists had facilitated Oswald's death. The facts that journalists had not easily been identifiable to local police, had possessed intrusive equipment, and had arrived in numbers too large for the police to handle were cited in their disfavor. The *Warren Report* published a special section called "The Activity of Newsmen," where it traced the events leading up to Oswald's murder:

> In the lobby of the third floor, television cameramen set up two large cameras and floodlights in strategic positions that gave them a sweep of the corridor in either direction. Technicians stretched their television cables into and out of offices. . . . Men with newsreel cameras, still cameras and microphones . . . moved back and forth seeking information and opportunities for interviews. Newsmen wandered into the offices of other bureaus located on the third floor, sat on desks and used police telephones; indeed, one reporter admits hiding a telephone behind a desk so that he would have exclusive access to it if something developed. . . . The corridor became so jammed that policemen and newsmen had to push and shove if they wanted to get through, stepping over cables, wires and tripods. (*Warren Report*, 1964, p. 202)

A detective was quoted as saying that "the press and television people just took over" (*Warren Report*, 1964, p. 204).

Similar concerns were voiced by journalists, who publicly questioned the viability of being present without interfering in events. Their discussions centered largely on the instruments of technology—the cables and camera equipment—amid concerns over whether television produced a more truthful and authoritative form of reportage. Marya Mannes penned her complaints at the time in *The Reporter*:

> The clutter of newsmen and their microphones in the basement corridor. The milling and talking, and then those big fat men bringing the thin pasty prisoner, and then the back of a man with a hat, and then Oswald doubled, and then pandemonium, scuffles, shouts and young Tom Truitt and his microphone in and out of the picture trying to find out what happened.

Questions seethed through my mind: How in God's name could the police expose a President's assassin to this jumble of people at close range? (Mannes, 1963, pp. 16-17)

The fact that television was still an uncertain medium for news made many reporters unaccustomed to the cables and camera equipment that television journalists brought with them. As ASNE (American Society of Newspaper Editors) head Herbert Brucker maintained in a *Saturday Review* article, the murder was

related to police capitulation in the glare of publicity . . . to suit the conven- ience of the news media . . . (the problem grew) principally out of something new in journalism . . . the intrusion of the reporter himself in the news. (Brucker, 1964, pp. 75-76)[2]

On the other side of the continuum, television reporter Gabe Pressman came to TV's defense. He complained that his medium was being used as a scapegoat:

Because we have the capacity of telling a story efficiently, dramatically and with a maximum amount of impact—because we have the ability to satisfy the need of the American public for instantaneous journalism in this modern age—does it follow that we have to be paralyzed because people react badly? (Pressman et al., 1964, p. 17)

Published in *Television Quarterly* under the title "The Responsible Reporter," the article asked whether journalists could ever carry out their job without intruding on others. It mentioned that television's newness magnified the irritation that the journalistic community was attributing to television cameras: The camera, said Pressman, "is used as a newspaper- man uses his pad and pencil. And yet, the camera is the most faithful reporter we have. The video-tapes don't lie and the film doesn't lie" (Pressman et al., 1964, p. 15). Thus, at the heart of many comments about this newly evolving medium for news were questions about whether it produced a better journalism. Whether Ruby shot Oswald, for instance, was no longer debatable, for the camera had recorded it. What was unclear was the role it played in facilitating Oswald's death.

Yet another arena of criticism concerned journalistic interpretations of Oswald's guilt. The circulation of half-truths and premature establish- ment of his guilt were frequently mentioned. When *The New York Times* published a banner headline that read "President's Assassin Shot to Death" (*The New York Times*, November 25, 1963, p. 1), one observer lamented the disappearance of the term *alleged*:

Lee Harvey Oswald had not yet legally been indicted, much less convicted, of President Kennedy's assassination. *The New York Times* had no right whatever under American law or the standards of journalistic fair play to call the man the "President's assassin." . . . What did the *Times*' own banner line do if not prejudge without trial, jury or legal verdict? (Tobin, 1963, p. 54)

The headline prompted *Times* editor Turner Catledge to publish a letter where he admitted the paper had erred (Catledge, 1963, p. 36). As one journalist observed,

The central question is whether the best tradition of the press is good enough. . . . The lesson of Dallas is actually an old one in responsible journalism: Reporting is not democratic to the point that everything posing as fact has equal status. (Rivers, 1965, p. 59)

Active discussions along these lines prompted discourse about the legal-ethical standards by which journalists were expected to realize their trade.[3] The *Warren Report* concluded that partial responsibility for Oswald's death "must be borne by the news media," and it called on journalists to implement a new code of ethics (*Warren Report*, 1964, p. 240). Journalistic coverage of Oswald's homicide was seen as making problematic the boundaries around journalistic obligations, rights, and privileges in covering criminal cases. There were plaintive calls for media curbs, which stated that "pressure from the press . . . had set the stage for [Oswald's killing, with] . . . little doubt that television and the press must bear a share of the blame" (Brucker, 1964, p. 76). Trade publications discussed what the *Columbia Journalism Review* labeled "judgment by television" (At Issue, 1964, p. 45). CBS President Frank Stanton offered monies to the Brookings Institute to establish a voluntary inter-media code of fair practices (At Issue, 1964, p. 47). In October of 1964, the ASNE convened a meeting of 17 top news organizations to discuss complaints about journalistic practice. Ten days later, the group issued a statement that warily conceded the influence of the news media over events:

If developing smaller TV cameras is beyond our control, we can certainly try by our own example to teach the electronic newsmen larger manners and a deeper understanding of the basic truth that freedom of information is not an unlimited license to trample on individual rights. (*Report of the Committee on Freedom,* 1964)

Although allowing for pooled coverage under certain circumstances, the statement stopped short of permitting codes or other external bars on media performance.

Thus the negative view of journalistic coverage of Oswald's death ranged from the minute and confined placement of cables to the more far-reaching ability of the media to determine and control reality. Journalistic behavior of both a physical, ethical, and legal dimension was seen as undercutting the professionalism of journalists. Television in particular was seen as changing many of the definitions then-current about the profession. At stake here was a larger discourse about the relationship between professionalism and technology that raised questions about whether journalists constituted "better" professionals by succumbing to technology or by mastering it.

JOURNALISTIC PROFESSIONALISM: THE POSITIVE VIEW

Positive appraisals of covering Oswald's murder provided similarly partial overviews of what had happened. For every violation cited by the negative view, there was an attribute provided by the positive view. The positive appraisal skimmed over the conditions that led up to Oswald's death and focused on what became, in the eyes of certain observers, "a first in television history" (*Broadcasting*, December 2, 1963, p. 46). The recording of Oswald's murder by reporters was cast as a professional triumph for American journalists.

Written accounts concentrated on the incredible fact that Oswald had been shot in full view of the television cameras. Still photographs of the homicide pushed the *Dallas Morning News* into a second edition: The photograph on its front page displayed Ruby clearly pointing a gun at Oswald. Robert Jackson of the *Dallas Times Herald* later won a Pulitzer Prize for his picture of Oswald crumpling under the bullet's impact (Payne, 1970, p. 12). One trade article, entitled "Pictures of Assassination Fall to Amateurs on Street," held that

> the actual shooting down of the President was caught mainly through out-of-focus pictures taken by non-professional photographers. But the actual shooting of his accused assailant was recorded in full view of press photographers with their cameras trained right on him and this produced pictures that may rank with the greatest news shots of all time. (*Editor and Publisher*, November 30, 1963, p. 16)

The juxtaposition of the largely amateur photographic recording of Kennedy's shooting with the professional photographic recording of Oswald's murder was played out in full. As *Editor and Publisher* noted in a moment of professional vindication, "if President Kennedy's death was left for the amateur photographers to record, the situation reversed itself on Sunday, November 24" (*Editor and Publisher*, November 30, 1963, p. 17). Photographic coverage of Oswald's death thus reinstated the somewhat shaky professionalism of news photographers.

Radio reporters called out the news of Oswald's shooting, with Radio Press International broadcasting the sound of the shot to its subscribers around the world (*Broadcasting*, December 22, 1963, p. 37). Ike Pappas was then a reporter for WNEW Radio in New York:

> My job on that day was to get an interview with this guy, when nobody else was going to get an interview. And I was determined to do that . . . I went forward with my microphone and I said . . . "Do you have anything to say in your defense?" Just as I said "defense," I noted out of the corner of my eye, this black streak went right across my front and leaned in and, pop, there was an explosion. And I felt the impact of the air from the explosion of the gun on my body. . . . And then I said to myself, if you never say anything ever again into a microphone, you must say it now. This is history. And I heard people shouting in back of me "he's been shot." So I said the only thing which I could say, which was the story: "Oswald has been shot. A shot rang out. Oswald has been shot." (Pappas quoted in *On Trial*, London Weekend Television documentary, 1988)

But the story of Oswald's murder belonged largely to television:

> For the first time in the history of television, a real-life homicide was carried nationally on live television when millions of NBC-TV viewers saw the November 24 fatal shooting in Dallas of the man accused of assassinating JFK two days earlier. (*Broadcasting*, December 2, 1963, p. 46)

The story played live on NBC. CBS recorded the event on a local camera, where they were able to replay immediate coverage from a videotape monitor. ABC, whose cameraperson had moved to the county jail, had to compensate with non-film accounts of the story (Gates, 1978, p. 254).

A special section of *Broadcasting* magazine, issued a week after the assassination, carried the following description of Oswald's murder:

> Oswald, flanked by detectives, stepped onto a garage ramp in the basement of the Dallas city jail and was taken toward an armored truck that was to take him to the county jail. Suddenly, out of the lower right hand corner of the TV screen, came the back of a man. A shot rang out, and Oswald gasped as he started to fall, clutching his side. (Gates, 1978, p. 46)

A telling feature about this narrative rested in its second sentence, which was repeated verbatim in numerous prose accounts by journalists: "Suddenly, out of the lower right hand corner of the TV screen, came the back of a man." The juxtaposition of reality and televised image, by which Oswald's killer was seen coming out of the television screen, rather than a corner of the basement, paid the ultimate compliment to television's coverage of the event. In the case of Oswald's death, television was featured as offering a reality that seemed momentarily preferable to the real-life situation on which it was based.

More than perhaps other events within the larger assassination story, the presence of journalists was made an integral part of Oswald's murder. A caption under the news-photograph of Oswald sinking to the floor read "Dallas detectives struggle with Ruby as newsmen and others watch" (*Broadcasting*, December 2, 1963, p. 46). Reporters recounted the cries of NBC correspondent Tom Pettit and other reporters on the scene. Replays of Pettit shouting "He's been shot, he's been shot, Lee Oswald has been shot!" legitimated the journalist as eyewitness. It also referenced the presence of news organizations at the event.

The casting of journalistic coverage of Oswald's murder as a professional triumph was also reinforced by professional forums. The *Columbia Journalism Review* hailed the performance of journalists, saying, "Like no other events before, the occurrences of November 22 to 25, 1963, belonged to journalism, and specifically to the national organs of journalism" (The Assassination, 1964, p. 5).

An editorial in *Editor and Publisher* called coverage "the most amazing performance by newspapers, radio and television that the world has ever witnessed" (*Editor and Publisher*, November 30, 1963, p. 6). Broadcast media received special attention. *Broadcasting* magazine claimed that "in those four terrible days, television came of age and radio reasserted its capacity to move to history where it happens" (*Broadcasting*, December 2, 1963, p. 108). The radio-television industry received a special Peabody Award.

At stake in many of these appraisals was the awareness that a new form of news coverage had been born. An editorial in *Television Quarterly* hailed the "full emergence of a televised documentary form (in which) the conditions which define the role and function of the artist and reporter in television journalism have begun to take shape" (Pressman et al., 1964, p. 86).

Positive appraisals of coverage of Oswald's murder were thereby important because such coverage reinstated the uncertain eyewitness status of reporters and photographers in other aspects of the assassination story. It also upheld the ultimate functioning ability of television journalists. Adjunct technologies authenticated journalists as eyewitnesses. The event, now camera-witnessed, emphasized their presence and brought it into chronicles of the event. Reporters replayed the murder across media with the assistance of tapes, recordings, and photographs, their reactions becoming embedded through technology in the murder's retelling. It was within these parameters that telling the tale as a story of professional triumph made sense.

RHETORICAL LEGITIMATION AND THE ENDURANCE OF NARRATIVE

The fact that there existed two active different readings of coverage of Oswald's murder reflected existing tensions within the journalistic community over what constituted the most appropriate and professionally correct way of covering an event such as Oswald's death. To an extent, ambivalence over journalists' reportorial roles emerged from the story's complex nature, coupled with the uncertain but growing legitimacy of television news. As one observer said, the event "gave rise to some of the darker hours, as well as some of the most remarkable accomplishments, of news coverage in Dallas" (Schramm, 1965, p. 12). This displayed the extent to which the acceptable parameters of journalistic professionalism were being debated at the time.

One, personified by the negative view, emphasized the foibles of television. It advanced the perspective that journalistic coverage had overextended itself and that the technological base which television journalists used to ground their struggles for legitimation was more of a hindrance than help. By emphasizing the negative aspects of television technology, the imbroglio about Oswald threatened to upset the shaky legitimacy of practitioners within the new medium. For journalists to agree with the points raised by the Oswald controversy would have invalidated the very qualities that distinguished television journalism from print.

That is why this specific discourse—about journalists facilitating Oswald's death—has simply disappeared over time. The cables, the microphones, the cameras—and the discourse it generated about the appropriateness of television journalism and journalistic professionalism—are no longer referenced in contemporary discussions of the Oswald case. The fact that the technology of television was hailed for producing live coverage of Oswald's murder (by one view) meant that its instruments—the cables, microphones, and cameras—could not be held responsible for facilitating his death (by another view). In other words, it was unfeasible for both positive and negative views of coverage to persist over time, because the same attributes of television were being simultaneously used to both condemn and hail journalism.

At stake was thereby a larger discourse about the relationship between professionalism and technology: Whether journalists constituted better professionals by succumbing to technology or by mastering it inflected debates not only about coverage of the Oswald homicide but also more general discussions about the coverage of Kennedy's assassination. Being a professional meant controlling instruments of technology in an effective fashion. The fact that issues raised by the Oswald homicide about journalistic claims of authority raised questions about television technology and the practices of television journalists meant that it was necessary to recast journalistic memories as narratives legitimating the professionalism of journalists. Because the specific events of Kennedy's death embedded problems of journalistic authority in much of the assassination coverage, retelling the journalists' part in covering the story called for reconstructions of their performances as effective professional triumphs or understandable—but salvageable—professional mishaps on the part of journalistic performers. It was thus necessary for contemporary renditions of the Oswald story to recast it as the professional triumph that was implicit in the scoop of having caught the murder on live camera.

Thus, over time most journalists have preferred the positive view of the Oswald story, which emphasized the attributes of television. That perspective held that journalists had acted professionally in covering the murder. It also, significantly, allowed reporters to generate a narrative that told of their successful adaptation to the new technology of television.

It is fitting to quote from one critic of the time, who held that "broadcasting resembles the little girl in the nursery rhyme. When it is bad, it is horrid. But when it is good, it is very very good" (Brucker, 1964, p. 77). Although the strength of the difference between assessments played a part in generating discourse about covering Oswald's murder, it is the thrust for rhetorical legitimation that gave one assessment an early death. Habermas's suggestion that speakers in public discourse use "street wisdom" as false but effective rationale to exercise their authority makes sense here. Journalists created a sense of their own street wisdom through their reconstructions of the Oswald homicide. Particularly in narratives that persisted over time, speakers reconfigured their versions of the tale in a way that effectively allowed them to present themselves as professionals for having covered the event. They portrayed themselves as having covered Oswald's murder in ways that upheld—rather than detracted from—their own professional positioning inside it, with a special place of esteem reserved for television journalism.

This was not accomplished in an incidental fashion, for narratives about Oswald's murder were linked by journalists with two larger discourses about journalism. One was the authorization of television technology, to the near exclusion of other news-gathering technologies. The other was a regard for the original coverage as professional behavior, by which reporters were seen to act in exemplary fashion. The fact that both discourses— about journalistic professionalism and television journalism—consolidated the more general position of journalists as authoritative spokespeople for events was not incidental. It shed light on how, in the particular case of covering the murder of Lee Harvey Oswald, journalists emerged as more professional through their narratives than warranted by their behavior at the time. Their retellings of the original tale upheld their positioning as professionals through links to larger discourses that were themselves invested in legitimating journalists—and particularly television journalists.

CONCLUSION

What does this tell us about narrative and social control? This discussion raises fundamental questions about the operative modes of social control, as exerted through the narratives of public discourse. The way American journalists have sought and succeeded to shape their own self-image through retellings of Oswald's murder suggests that narrative plays an instrumental role in setting forth preferred constructions of reality. In an age where so few people are able to accomplish primary experience of public events and must instead depend on some degree of mediated experience, the use of narrative to alter realities and construct new ones that better fit the narrator's agenda is a practice with problematic implications. For the success of such a practice is predicated on the acquiescence of publics, publics who accept such preferred constructions as "real" and accurate. The preferred construction of the Oswald tale has become not only an embedded part of histories of American television journalism but a recognized chapter in general American histories as well. In constructing their version of the Oswald tale, then, the media have used narratives of self-legitimation to shape America's collective sense of itself.

Journalists are not the only ones who are capable of exerting social control through narrative. Politicians, lawyers, the clergy, and other public speakers may engage in similar rhetorical practices of self-legitimation. This suggests that retelling is rarely an innocuous activity. If, as suggested here, speakers retell their stories to legitimate their own status and authority no less than to convey content, there is need to more closely explore the workings of such rhetoric in a wide range of discursive arenas. Narratives in public discourse may have as much to do with the self-legitimation of their narrators as with the relay of the information such narratives contain.

NOTES

1. This discussion is taken from Zelizer (1992).

2. Brucker held broadcasting equipment responsible for creating the sense of intrusion, paralleling it with an earlier incident that had surrounded the introduction of radio—the 1937 trial of Bruno Richard Hauptmann for the kidnap-murder of the Lindbergh baby: "The new medium of radio, together with news photographers' flashbulbs made a circus of the trial" (1964, p. 77). Interestingly, new media are often legitimated through discussion of changing borders between private and public space.

3. It is worth noting that legal quarters picked up the controversy about journalistic performance and condemned the press's insistence on the right to know. They claimed that it had seriously interfered with Oswald's right to a free and private trial and had hampered police efforts to transfer the accused.

REFERENCES

The assassination. (1964). *Columbia Journalism Review*, Winter, 5-36.

At issue: Judgment by television. (1964). *Columbia Journalism Review*, Winter, 45-48.

Barthes, R. (1977). Introduction to the structural analysis of narratives. In *Image, music, text* (pp. 79-124). New York: Hill & Wang.

Brackman, J. (1983). The sixties: Shock waves from the baby boom. *Esquire*, June, 197-200; reprinted from *Esquire*, October 1968.

Brucker, H. (1964, January 11). When the press shapes the news. *Saturday Review*, 75-85.

Canary, R. H., & Kozicki, H. (Eds.). (1978). *The writing of history*. Madison, WI: University of Wisconsin Press.

Carey, J. (1975). A cultural approach to communication. *Communication 2*, 1-22.

Carey, J. (1986). The dark continent of American journalism. In R. K. Manoff & M. Schudson (Eds.), *Reading the news* (pp. 146-196). New York: Pantheon.

Catledge, T. (1963, November 27). Until proven guilty. [Letter to the editor]. *The New York Times*, p. 36.

Donner, F. (1979, December 22). The assassination circus: Conspiracies unlimited. *The Nation*, 483, 654-660.

Gates, G. P. (1978). *Air time*. New York: Harper & Row.

Habermas, J. (1981). *The theory of communicative action, Vol. I* (Trans. Thomas McCarthy). Boston: Beacon.

Halberstam, D. (1979). *The powers that be*. New York: Alfred A. Knopf.

International press institute rejects move to admit radio-TV newsmen. (1963, June 8). *The New York Times*, p. 52.

Kellner, H. (1989). *Language and historical representation: Getting the story crooked*. Madison, WI: University of Wisconsin Press.

Kunhardt, P.B. (1988). *Life in Camelot: The Kennedy Years*. New York: Time-Life Books.

Lucaites, J., & Condit, C. (1985). Reconstructing narrative theory: A functional perspective. *Journal of Communication 35*(4), 90-108.

Mannes, M. (1963, December 19). The long vigil. *The Reporter*, 15-17.

Official minutes of the 1964 convention. (1965). *Journalism Quarterly*. Winter. Association for Education in Journalism.

Payne, D. (1970, February). The press corps and the Kennedy assassination. *Journalism Monographs, 15*.

Pettit, T. (1965). The television story in Dallas. In B. Greenberg & E. Parker (Eds.), *The Kennedy assassination and the American public* (pp. 61-66). Palo Alto, CA: Stanford University Press.

Pressman, G. et al. (1964). The responsible reporter. *Television Quarterly 3*(2), 6-27.

Report of the Committee on Freedom of Information. (1964, April 16). American Society of Newspaper Editors.

Rivers, W. (1965). The press and the assassination. In B. Greenberg & E. Parker (Eds.), *The Kennedy assassination and the American public* (pp. 51-60). Palo Alto, CA: Stanford University Press.

Schramm, W. (1965). Communication in crisis. In B. Greenberg & E. Parker (Eds.), *The Kennedy assassination and the American public* (pp. 1-25). Palo Alto, CA: Stanford University Press.

Schudson, M. (1982). The politics of narrative form: The emergence of news conventions in print and television. *Daedalus*, *3*(4), 97-112.

Tobin, R. (1963, December 14). If you can keep your head when all about you. . . . *Saturday Review*, pp. 53-54.

Warren Report: Report of the President's Commission on the Assassination of President John F. Kennedy. (1964). Washington, DC: Government Printing Office.

White, H. (1981). The value of narrativity in the representation of reality. In W. J. T. Mitchell (Ed.), *On narrative* (pp. 1-23). Chicago: University of Chicago Press.

White, H. (1986). Historical pluralism. *Critical Inquiry*, *12*, 480-493.

Wuthnow, R. et al. (1984). *Cultural analysis*. London: Routledge and Kegan Paul.

Zelizer, B. (1992). *Covering the body: The Kennedy assassination, the media, and the shaping of collective memory*. Chicago: University of Chicago Press.

Chapter 9

OPPOSITIONAL VOICES IN *CHINA BEACH*: NARRATIVE CONFIGURATIONS OF GENDER AND WAR

A. Susan Owen

NARRATIVES ABOUT THE Vietnam war long have been a site of ideological struggle in American culture (Ehrenhaus, Chapter 3 of this book; Haines, 1986). In this war more than any other previous to it, American ideographs of "duty, honor, country" failed to maintain hegemony over the experiences of citizen soldiers and civilians alike. As Edelman (1990) put it, " 'Vietnam' is not simply an historical experience that yielded a legacy. Vietnam is a condensation symbol epitomizing sets of conflicting values that polarize late 20th-century America" (p. 6).

The full extent of this ideological crisis can be understood, in part, through an examination of the struggle over representations of the war in American popular culture. Although critics disagree about the aesthetic and political significance of a wide range of literary, filmic, and televisual representations, two points generally are agreed on. First, the most unpopular American war in the 20th century captured public imagination in the years after the war as a genre of popular entertainment. Second, no American cultural forum seems fully adequate to capture the experiences of participants and witnesses.

Two critics in particular focus attention on these taken-for-granteds, and their insights are useful here. Rick Berg (1990) uses the work of Walter Benjamin to explain the apparent contradiction wherein fragmented "remains" of the Vietnam experience—which stubbornly "remain" in American public consciousnes—cannot be "textualized" satisfactorily (read: once and for all) through available technological and cultural modes of representation. Describing the war that will not go away, he writes:

Vietnam *remains*, then, regardless of the ritual cleansings and willed suspensions of memory, regardless of the many memorials for the unknown dead . . . . And while it remains, it stays a problem, or to be more precise, the remains of Vietnam are problematic. What is left of the war, its fragments and its ruins, stays unrepressible and endlessly recuperable. The many mutations mark not merely the continuing effort to misrepresent what has been lost as merely missing and possibly recoverable; they also mark the failure of our modes of cultural representation. None of the transformations satisfy. The illusion, so necessary to particular values, fails. Vietnam succeeds in challenging and foiling the ideological apparatus's modes of production. (Berg, 1990, p. 43)

In a very similar way, William F. Palmer's (1990) essay on Hollywood's Vietnam war films addresses the failure of conventional war discourse (both linguistic and visual codes) to articulate the Vietnam experience. He argues that films produced in the decade after the war failed to capture the symbolic nihilism of the war experience. For Palmer, that nihilism is "the annihilation of the self, the realization of helplessness in the face of evil so all-encompassing that . . . past lives become nothing more than sentimential dreams" (1990, p. 262). Thus, early cinematic efforts to "construct an order out of something as unstructured as the war fails in the face of consistently deconstructing texts" (p. 261). Palmer argues that Oliver Stone's film *Platoon* (1986) marked the first minimally successful cinematic effort to represent the utter abjection of combat experience. For Palmer, then, the problem of translating war into popular entertainment forms is less an issue of ideological struggle and more one of creative imagination.

In spite of both the technical difficulties and ideological constraints involved in representing the Vietnam experience, various attempts have been made to do just that. In the past 20 years, we have seen the development of a genre of literature and film about the Vietnam war and its consequences. But we must remember that literature and film are relatively elite and privileged mass media. Perhaps the most challenging test of the capacity to represent Vietnam to a mass audience is the success of programming in the televisual medium. One series stands out in this regard—*China Beach*. First broadcast in 1987, this melodramatic series ran for three seasons and garnered both viewer loyalty and critical acclaim. My purpose in this chapter is to explore both the constraints and possibilities for representing Vietnam in prime-time, fictional television. I will do so through an analysis of the narrative and semiotic structures of the series. In particular, I will examine the gendered subjectivities of the series and the tension between mainstream and marginalized voices as represented in the major characters.

CONSTRAINTS AND POSSIBILITIES
OF WAR NARRATIVES

Compared with the actual sights and sounds of the front, the word *shit* is practically genteel. (Fussell, 1975, p. 331)

Three constraints, minimally, are crucial to understanding any attempt to represent the Vietnam War. Respectively, these concern the ability to represent the actual experience of combat, social conventions governing the propriety of discussing those experiences, and media-specific constraints on content. First, the experience of warfare cannot be translated easily, accurately, or comprehensively. As noted, in particular, by Benjamin (1968), Fussell (1975, 1989), Kristeva (1984) and O'Brien (1990), the horror and abjection of war creates for its witnesses a series of inchoate experiences. In *The Things They Carried*, O'Brien describes his own experience in Vietnam this way:

The angles of vision are skewed. When a booby trap explodes, you close your eyes and duck and float outside yourself. When a guy dies . . . you look away and then back for a moment and then look away again. The pictures get jumbled; you tend to miss a lot. . . . Sometimes it's just beyond telling. (1990, pp. 78-79)

A related difficulty, of course, is that no preexisting societal schemata of values and beliefs prepare witnesses and participants for what they experience in or near combat—the lived reality of warring as an active, crushing, destroying, brutalizing experience (see Hansen, Owen, & Madden, 1992). This is particularly true of modern warfare. Writing about the hermeneutics of storytelling, Walter Benjamin (1968) draws one of his examples from his recollections of the First World War. Emphasizing the difficulty of articulating the horrors of war, he observes with a frustrated incredulity:

Was it not noticeable at the end of the [First World] war that men returned from the battlefield grown silent—not richer, but poorer in communicable experience. . . . For never has experience been contradicted more thoroughly than strategic experience by tactical warfare. . . . A generation that had gone to school on a horse-drawn streetcar now stood under the open sky in a countryside in which nothing remained unchanged but the clouds, and beneath these clouds, in a field of force of destructive torrents and explosions, was the tiny, fragile, human body. (p. 84)

Paradoxically, the fractured sensibilities and psychic shattering consequent to participation in war only can be reclaimed in a story. Yet, the narrative format falsifies that experience because it creates order out of chaos. Even as the narrative delivers the storyteller from the horror of abjection—the collapse of meaning—it belies the most irreducible element of war, fragmentation.

Even if it were possible to give voice to the abjection of war, social conventions of "polite society" historically have precluded the public examination of those experiences. Fussell (1975) notes that it was not until the 1960s and 1970s that the "concept of prohibitive obscenity, a concept which has acted as a censor on earlier memories of 'war,' " (p. 334) lost its totalizing grasp on public memory. Perhaps for the first time, American mass society was confronted with cinematic, literary, and televisual representations that explored taboos such as the shattered body, ravaged landscape, massacred civilian populations, and the psychic consequences of warfare for the warrior. O'Brien (1990) succinctly captures these points in the following poignant passage:

> You can tell a true war story if it embarrasses you. If you don't care for obscenity, you don't care for the truth; if you don't care for the truth, watch how you vote. Send guys to war, they come home talking dirty. (p. 77)

Finally, we must consider the constraints on content and technology under which the television industry operates, as well as the cultural contexts within which specific programming arises. Above all else, American television is an economic institution. Aesthetic, artistic, and substantive choices concerning content and placement of programs are determined primarily by ratings and sponsorship dollars. Because sponsors are interested in "buying" particular demographic groups, they typically wish to purchase time on programs deemed noncontroversial. In addition, television is guarded more carefully than cinematic vehicles, ostensibly because it is consumed directly in the private domestic spaces. For these reasons, then, television is the most conservative mass medium in American culture.

It is reasonable to presume, therefore, that the obscenities of war would defy the forms and formulas of this medium. Indeed, Todd Gitlin (1983) predicted that Vietnam would not be assimilated easily into the great episodic flow of prime-time television. Writing about the foibles of American television programming, Gitlin notes that in the late 1970s and early 1980s there was a great deal of interest in Vietnam among major network chiefs. He writes:

> [I]t was . . . inevitable that, once the air had cleared, the networks would sidle up to the subject. The war had usurped an enormous part of the consciousness of millions, especially the generation who, by the late seventies, were

moving into middle management at the networks and starting to make a name for themselves as producers. After the war finally ended, without resolving, in 1975, they went to see *Coming Home*, read books like Michael Herr's *Dispatches* and Robert Stone's *Dog Soldiers*, and observed their considerable if not blockbuster success. Finally, *Apocalypse Now* and *The Deer Hunter* broke commercial ground. As Grant Tinker said, "The Vietnam thing lasted so long, it's such a hunk of our recent history, that it isn't surprising that everybody finally got around to it." (p.227)

But the brooding preoccupation with Vietnam never evolved into a bankable series. Gitlin (1983) attributes two reasons for the failure to bring a series to broadcast. First, in order to "distance [themselves] from the grinding horror of combat itself," (p. 227) the networks approached the topic through the situation comedy genre. This approach backfired; writers and producers shrank from the possibility of "taking something as important as Vietnam and trivializing it with a twenty-two minute sitcom" (p. 236). In addition, network officials vacillated over the political ramifications of a television series on Vietnam. Gitlin reports that CBS, in particular, articulated the importance of "balancing" *market* positions ("reach the most number of people in a wholesome manner") with *moral* positions about the uses of television. Gitlin summarizes tartly, "Hollywood's movers and shakers are more committed to saving precious metals than to saving souls." (p. 224).

Gitlin's detailed account of how the Vietnam experience confounded the conventions of television meshes well with the insights of Berg and Palmer and supports the central thesis of this essay: War does not play well on television. And yet, Gitlin overlooked the fragments of the Vietnam experience surfacing in the vast flow of television programming.

Since the end of the war, the veteran had surfaced paradigmatically as a category for character development—far too often as semiotic coding for deranged or debilitated individuals—but also as fully functioning, likable characters in the detective genre and the action-adventure series. *Magnum, P. I.*, for example, was the first prime-time television narrative about "well-adjusted" veterans whose friendships were forged in part through the shared subtext of Vietnam. Recuperated through familiar forms and formulas, the characters of this series constituted a mainstream composite of the returned warrior. War, itself, was represented as the ultimate male adventure/quest; the training and experiences of war were reconstituted as useful vocational skills in a civilian context. In this discourse, the veteran was rehabilitated via mainstream liberal democratic ideologies: War is hell, but it is both a necessary evil and the ultimate adventure where men bond, learn, grow, and profit from their shared experiences (Haines, 1990).

Other producers and writers have negotiated the constraints of the televisual medium in their efforts to explore contemporary warfare. The most obvious example is the phenomenal success of the series *M*A*S*H*, a "dramedy," ostensibly about Korea, which voiced "liberal outrage" (Berg, 1990, p. 40) and explored decidedly antiwar sentiments and storylines. Amid the general trend of "social awareness" programming of 1970s television (e.g., *All in the Family*, *Maude*), *M*A*S*H*'s commentary on war gave American viewers some insight into the carnage of war, privileging the involuntarily conscripted "civilian" perspective of the Army Medical Corps. The medical motif of the series enabled the producers to explore representations of the traumatized human body and psyche consequent to war. In addition, this series gave us a look at war from the private spaces of the characters' personal lives. The domesticity of the *M*A*S*H* unit foregrounded the tension between private lives and the public spaces of policy-making. Although *M*A*S*H* was limited to a predominantly white, male perspective, its liberal bourgeois critique of the Korean War familiarized American viewers with a thinly disguised commentary on American imperialism and militarism.

The phenomenal success of Oliver Stone's *Platoon* ushered in an era of "realism" in the developing genre of Vietnam films (see Dionisopoulos, 1990). Few could have anticipated the explosion of cinematic representations of Vietnam following in its footsteps. In conjunction with this move to "realism" (e.g., *Full Metal Jacket*, *Hamburger Hill*), *Magnum, P. I.*, as the first coherent televisual narrative about Vietnam, and *M*A*S*H*, as allegorical exploration of Vietnam, helped to create the cultural context within which *China Beach* appeared.

Respectively, these two programs typify relatively "closed" and "open" television texts (see Fiske, 1989; Hall, 1980). *Magnum, P. I.* invited the viewer to participate in a preferred reading of the Vietnam War. Each week's show concluded with a voice-over narration by its main character, in which the moral and meaning of the episode was made explicit; the price of liberty is eternal vigilance and blood. *M*A*S*H*, in contrast, created more flexible spaces for understanding the Korean (read: Vietnam) War as ultimately senseless and wasteful, institutional claims of national purpose notwithstanding (see Barker, 1987).

What *Magnum, P. I.* and *M*A*S*H* demonstrate, then, is that although televisual texts operate within pronounced constraints, they also contain enabling possibilities. In both of these portrayals, we see evidence of the ideological struggle to determine how we are to think about war, generally, and how we are to remember Vietnam, specifically. A polysemic reading of *China Beach* should locate both the conventions of dominant, mainstream culture and the possibilities for reading against the grain. As McKerrow (1989, p. 108) reminds us, a polysemic reading "uncovers a subordinate or secondary reading which contains the seeds of subversion or rejection of authority, at the same time that the primary reading appears to confirm the power of the dominant cultural norms."

"Subordinate" readings that contain "the seeds of subversion" are possible even within mainstream televisual texts. William Broyles, Jr., and John Sacrett Young, executive producers of *China Beach*, wove a tale of Vietnam with broad appeal for mainstream American popular culture. The relative success of the series proves that Broyles and Young were able to offer an "acceptable" translation of the Vietnam experience into prime-time American television. But perhaps more significant, the series provided glimpses of the "dark side" of the war experience: cynicism, despair, greed, murder, wanton destruction, pornographic violence, rage, cultural oppression, cultural bigotry, and human exploitation.

In its desire to avoid being cast as "just another war melodrama," *China Beach* incorporated moments of "high drama." Whether by design or accident, these moments function as openings, ruptures in the text that breach the limitations imposed by American culture's essential conservatism. These interludes were created through manipulation of the paradigmatic spaces of the central narrative; moments of radical insight and critique arose in the structured tensions between and among the series's central characters. The disruptive potential of these interludes was tempered by the distractions of a large cast and intersecting storylines. Consequently, although viewers encountered glimpses of radical critique, essentially fissures in the conventions of melodramatic storylines, they could take comfort in the familiarity of the conventional that largely characterized the series (e.g., episodic structure, stories centered on traditional gender relationships and the struggle between good and evil).

NARRATIVE CONFIGURATIONS OF *CHINA BEACH*

A true war story is never moral. It does not instruct, nor encourage virtue, nor suggest models of proper human behavior, nor restrain men from doing the things men have always done. If a story seems moral, do not believe it. If at the end of a war story you feel uplifted, or if you feel that some small bit of rectitude has been salvaged from the larger waste, then you have been made the victim of a very old and terrible lie. There is no rectitude whatsoever. There is no virtue. As a first rule of thumb, therefore, you can tell a true war story by its absolute and uncompromising allegiance to obscenity and evil. (O'Brien, 1990, p. 76)

The narrative configuration of any text is a function of three major concerns. First is the nature of the medium. I have already discussed in some detail how the televisual medium imposes cultural constraints on the possibility of storylines. As the most conservative mass medium, due to its "location" in the private spaces of the home, the representations television offers must not rupture the cultural sanctity of those spaces. Second is the syntagmatic structure of the message, the events that occur throughout the unfolding of narrative time. Finally, narrative configuration is constituted through paradigmatic complexity—*how* interaction among the characters gives shape to the unfolding master (or "meta-") narrative.

SYNTAGMATIC STRUCTURE AND CULTURAL CONSTRAINTS

Precisely because *China Beach* is located in the extraordinary conditions of wartime, the constraints imposed on the televisual plots it develops are all the more apparent. Syntagmatically, *China Beach* is highly conventional, "advancing the genre of recombinant melodramatic representation . . . in a self-conscious way, [illustrating] how humane collectivities cope" with chaos (Haines, 1992). Plots across episodes center on melodramatic themes of heterosexual romance, conventional role-related gender tensions, and traditional notions of good and evil, all contextualized by the Vietnam War.

Significantly, gender is the primary organizing concept in the syntagmatic flow of the narrative. This cultural imperative shapes all episodes. Moreover, through its reliance on traditional gender relationships as its central organizing theme, the series places itself safely within the conventions of the medium. (It is noteworthy that the Lifetime network markets its reruns of *China Beach* by focusing on heterosexual entanglements in the series, and it advertises the program in conjunction with "the hunks" on *L.A. Law*.)

The pilot episode of *China Beach* marked what many mainstream journalists heralded as a "woman's point of view" of war. Publications as disparate as *Rolling Stone* and the *Wall Street Journal* described the series as a story "about women in war" (Bales, 1988; Morrison, 1988). Similarly, both the *Los Angeles Times* and *The New York Times* claimed that the series brought viewers a woman's point of view (O'Connor, 1988; Rosenberg, 1988). These assessments are all the more significant because all portrayals of war historically have been from the dominant male perspective.

Although I would agree that *China Beach* is mediated through feminized subjectivity, *the series is not about women and their experiences*. Rather, the producers of the series have *feminized the discourse of war* in order to create a text within which the warrior can articulate his experience. The combat veteran views his experience as hermetically sealed (see Hansen et al., 1992); he cannot, therefore, speak directly for himself. But the combat veteran rejects "official" explanations of the war. Consequently, the feminized voice is an effective choice for articulating the warrior's narrative. Women are not contained by the ideological constraints of masculinity. Where war is concerned, women's historical roles have been as "outsider" and "caregiver." As outsiders to traditional war discourse, women bring to the experience both a moral compass and a humane perspective. In the act of wartime caregiving lies profound grief, sacrifice, loss, bitterness, and an unusually intimate examination of the human costs of war. These capacities, plus the presumed moral superiority of the nurturing female, render the feminine voice a viable vehicle for the brotherhood, to whom all others, categorically, are outsiders. This makes *China Beach* significantly different from other televisual and filmic portrayals of the war. *China Beach* is intensely domestic politics—a relocation of the public platform for examination of public virtue.

Perversely, however, the master narrative of *China Beach* employs traditional gender constraints to illustrate how even the "best" of women are flawed mediators for warriors. This is made manifest in two ways: first, men colonize the spaces of feminized subjectivity; and second, women are created in the image of the veteran's needs (see the Appendix for character descriptions and status).

To begin, both men and women share "feminized" spaces. Positions of masculine subjectivity are filled only by warriors and by those who signify corrupt masculinity, such as industrialists, politicians, capitalists, most military officers, and war technologists, all of whom exploit the warrior. Noncombatant males and medical officers occupy "feminized" subjectivity. Since warriors are inchoate, they cannot be positioned as narrator or narratee but simply as "actors" who utter simple truths that must be understood by and through the feminized characters. Only the feminized voices "reflect." Warriors pass briefly before us, uttering terse, enigmatic statements. The feminized characters reflect at length on these statements, demystifying them and adding their own insights in support of the warriors. For example, the feminized warrior Boonie or the black mortician Beckett often speak for the warriors, as does Dr. Richards, the noncombatant physician. The corrupt masculine roles are undeveloped, one-dimensional characters; they rarely are drawn sympathetically, and if we are invited as viewers to identify briefly with them, it is only to understand their tragic flaws.

Second, this exclusionary tale of the brotherhood positions all female characters in the image of the veteran's needs. Regardless of their positions in the master narrative—whether "the girl next door," "the innocent virgin," "the minx," "the whore," or "the spinster-bitch"—all women find themselves contained by masculine discourses as plots develop (see Meehan, 1983). In the pilot episode, for example, McMurphy is described by another female character (who clearly envies her ability to compete for male attention) as having "Hair like silk, a body like Monroe and a heart probably as big as all America." McMurphy rejects this description, replying that she simply is "one of the boys." Yet, McMurphy's sexuality is a prominent feature of her character and is held systematically in contradiction with her ability to be a team player (i.e., "one of the boys"). Ironically, the heterosexual desire of soldiers for McMurphy renders her defective, denying her the possibility of bonding with those with whom she strives to identify.

The gender constraints that contribute to what I believe is the central flaw of *China Beach* long have been with us. One contributing factor to the dominance of the male perspective in war narratives is that women's experiences in war have not been well documented. Recent work done by feminist historiographers and other critical scholars helps us envision the many ways in which women's lives have been, and are, touched by war (see Hanley, 1991). Given the vast silence of women's voices in conventional accounts of war, it is understandable that its narrative traditions are structured from masculine perspectives. By implication, then, discourses of war necessarily are "gendered." And as a consequence, we need to examine the social formations that legitimate these discourse practices. One such route is the careful examination of narrative logics.

Twentieth-century narrative traditions in American culture have popularized three stereotypical roles for women during wartime. In descending order of perceived virtue and public value, these are: domestic icons of patriotic zeal (those for whom wars are fought, e.g., mothers, wives, sweethearts, sisters, daughters); nurses and support personnel (those who comfort and sustain); and whores (the quintessentially disposable distraction for the warrior) (see Honey, 1984; Rupp, 1978).

Although most war narratives simply exclude the feminine, those that include women generally are moved along by themes of romantic entanglement between warriors and their love interests. The primary dramatic tension in these heterosexual liaisons is that women seek to tame warriors, and true warriors must resist being tamed. This sets up a fundamental contradiction that results in perpetual antagonisms between the genders: The feminine, defined by the dominant male voice, is characterized as a perceived threat; women's sensibilities inherently are corrupting of warriors. Moreover, regardless of the female role or relationship to the male, the appearance of the female in the male domain of war always is portrayed as flawed. For example, the presence of non-native (i.e., American) women in a war zone always is reducible to a matter of their choice. For American warriors, there is no choice. In addition, women often are portrayed as too weak or too virtuous to be "team players."

Two contiguous scenes in the pilot episode of *China Beach* (which I shall refer to as "The Funeral Procession") are pivotal for exemplifying these constraints and for illustrating how gender constrains the paradigmatic spaces of the narrative, as well. Both scenes establish for the viewers key character relationships, the central character of the series, the logic of gendered relationships, and some of the major themes that the series explored across its three seasons (see the Appendix).

The first scene centers on the arrival of a commercial aircraft bringing a variety of personnel to Vietnam (e.g., fresh recruits, elaborately coiffed female USO entertainers, and U.S. embassy staff). The closing moments of this scene are crucial for establishing a key semiotic device of the series—the movement into intense light and wind to signify "the Nam." As the stylishly clad female USO entertainers move to the opened airplane portal, they are enveloped in that light and blowing air, which wreaks havoc with their carefully arranged hairstyles. Implicitly, then, these devices signify "the Nam's" capacity to disrupt order. Vietnam is destructive, in the sense of "de-structuring." Hence, concerns with superficial matters of appearance (e.g., fashion, hairstyles, preening) disintegrate in "light" of the harsh realities of Vietnam.

The second scene is juxtaposed with the first and introduces us to McMurphy. The contrast to the female entertainers is startling. McMurphy's hair is unkempt, her face shows fatigue and strain, and her surgical smock is saturated with blood. The syntagmatic relationships in this scene are influenced greatly by movement on the "x-axis" (which concerns horizontal movement on the television screen). We watch McMurphy journey from surgery to the morgue, accompanied by two corporals, wheeling a war casualty on a gurney. The manifest composition of the text suggests that they are escorting a dead soldier, much like an honor guard might escort the casket of someone greatly revered. The audio track reinforces this visual with Aretha Franklin's tune, "You Make Me Feel Like a Natural Woman"; more than merely soulful, its halting, deliberate cadence sets the pace at which McMurphy and the escorts move into "the morning sun." The illusion of a funeral procession is reinforced further as McMurphy and her escorts move left on the x-axis; their route is lined with soldiers, some of whose faces we see, others whose backs are turned toward the camera, and all of whom appear to be standing at attention. We never actually see the dead soldier, only a bloodied sheet covering a large, truncated lump, with bloody imprints on the sheet where legs ought to be. McMurphy smoothes the sheet and ever so briefly caresses the still figure.

As she and the "honor guard" pass from the hospital to the morgue (from life to death), they pass through a helicopter landing pad, which is being used by off-duty soldiers as a softball playing field. She pauses to "play ball" with the soldiers who, for the most part, ignore the still form on the gurney. In the ensuing dialogue between McMurphy and Boonie (a "retired" warrior and now-recreational director of China Beach), we learn that McMurphy's tour of duty is almost completed and that Boonie wants her to "renegotiate her contract." McMurphy emphatically declines, pauses briefly to field (bare-handed) a fly ball (amid cheers and whistles of approval), and continues moving left toward the morgue. The procession is interrupted once more, this time by a pilot whose interest in her is explicitly sexual. She tells him that she doesn't get involved with pilots, "any more." He replies, "Forget him . . . I'll help." Using the refrain of a familiar song, McMurphy snaps, "But will you still love me tomorrow?" She resumes her movement left, signaling the end of the conversation, and exits off camera. The camera closes in on the pilot, who looks directly at the still form on the passing gurney and wonders aloud, "Who says there'll be a tomorrow?"

An abrupt shift of the camera next places the viewer inside the dimly lit morgue, watching with Beckett and the war dead as the doors burst open with the arriving procession. At this point, motion on the x-axis virtually stops, and an important conversation between Beckett and McMurphy is blocked on the z- axis, enhancing the illusion of depth and spatial arrangement in order to showcase Beckett's frenzied, ironic speech about the dead:

Beckett: So, what's on today's menu?
McMurphy: [Business-like] Ahhh, traumatic amputation, multiple lacerations, through and through fragment wounds.
Beckett: [As if savoring good food] Mmmm, mmmm, *mmmm*. And that's the way it is on patrol today in the vicinity of Da Nang, in the Republic of Vietnam.
McMurphy: [Softly, visually stunned] Beckett . . .

McMurphy's demeanor shifts from self-controlled, self-awareness to a concern for Beckett. She is sympathetic, and yet, bewildered by the intensity of Beckett's reaction to this latest arrival at the Graves Registration Unit—that there is simply no more room, that he will accept no more death. As Beckett delivers his empassioned monologue, McMurphy merely reacts. In a series of close-up reaction shots, we are invited to share their pain, grief, and shock. We listen with McMurphy as Beckett rants on about the scent of formaldehyde that he can't wash off his hands, and the absurdity of sending home semi-nude corpses because there is a shortage of dress military pants. In the final seconds of the scene, the camera takes the point of view of yet another still figure positioned inside an opened body bag. We see a low angle shot of Beckett's face as he says good-bye to the dead soldier and begins to zip the bag. "We'll miss you," he says, and the screen fades to black. The sound of zipping continues after the scene has ended visually, positioning us in the body bag with the dead soldier.

Taken together, these scenes establish the key thematic elements in the syntagmatic flow of the series: gender; the injured body; collective, ritualized grieving; and death. Gender is used to signify relationships as sexual or nonsexual and to create expectations for interaction between and among the characters. In the interaction between McMurphy and the pilot, we see the affirmation of heterosexual relationships and the cultural assumption that whereas men seek adventure, women are fundamentally wary of that untamed impulse. We also glimpse that women cannot tame men, especially men who are warriors, precisely because the warrior must remain untamed to be effective. Yet we also see that warriors seek sex with women as a distraction from the dangers of their craft. And perhaps most important, the flirtation between McMurphy and the pilot is contextualized by the presence of the gurney bearing the corpse; it is a montage constructed of images of heterosexual desire, conventional gender norms, despair, and the ravages of war.

The expressly nonsexual interaction between McMurphy and those playing softball implicitly raises the question of whether a female can ever be a member of the brotherhood. The answer comes in McMurphy's self-observation, "Good field, but no hit." In the brief exchange between McMurphy and the "retired" and now-feminized Boonie, we see a more "fraternal" relationship between men and women. Baseball metaphors, with their attendant gender-role assumptions, structure possibilities for nonsexual interaction between men and women in a war zone. In response to her observation and her attendant declaration that she has "hung up" her "spikes," Boonie replies, "Just a slump. It's a long season." Boonie acts much like a fellow team player, exhorting McMurphy to persevere in the face of what we are to infer as discourse about "burn out." Friendly exhortation between "teammates" presumes their equality, possible only because Boonie has removed himself from the warrior class of the brotherhood. McMurphy may "play ball" as well as any female can, but she will always be "only" a female. Her insights can never equal those of the brotherhood, both because of her sexuality and because she is in Vietnam voluntarily. The latter point is underscored later in the pilot episode when a drunken, cynical McMurphy, who is ready to throw in the towel, is confronted by Richards, her immediate superior, a noncombatant male surgeon. He berates her, calling attention to the chasm that always will separate her from the brotherhood:

> Just remember, though, you're not a politician, you're a nurse. See, I was drafted. You volunteered. You wanted this. Well, you got it. You found a place where you'll never be more valuable. So, get out, or finish sucking on your baby bottle and feeling sorry for yourself and come back in the time you got left and help us save some teenagers.

McMurphy's reaction to this tirade is one of weary resignation and reflection. Rather than challenging Richards's chastisement and the assumptions on which it was founded, her response reinforced the location of the character in a position of perpetual subordination and marginality. As my analysis of paradigmatic structure will show, *China Beach* may offer limited critique of the Vietnam War (and through it, of the American capital system), but never by questioning social conventions of constructed gender norms and the role that they play in perpetuating and legitimating war.

The "Funeral Procession" scene also introduces two other major themes of the series: grieving and death. The procession with the gurney sets up both conceptual and visual representations of collective, ritualized grieving for the dead. Death is explored in surgery, but the morgue is the chief locus of the discourse of death, with its flickering pattern of shadows and bright lights filtering through from the "outside" (Reflective discourse on the metaphysics of death occurs apart from the glaring light and brute realities of "the Nam"). Beckett's concern for "his men," and his ironic monologues on the difficulties of embalming the war dead, draw our attention to the injured body and to the taboo topic of mutilation. His discourses, as well as those uttered by the surgeon, confront our sensibilities with the nature of war wounds: traumatic amputations, sucking chest wounds, "mix and matches" (injuries from booby traps), "crispy critters" (burn victims), and "veggies" for the "vegetable patch" (those who will never recover consciousness or those who will be forever emotionally or cognitively impaired).

These themes give structure to the unfolding storylines in *China Beach*. Many of them stake out new territory for commercial broadcast television; many of them are safe and familiar. Quite reasonably, those that are safe, such as the emphasis on heterosexual entanglements, temper the disruptive potential of themes such as the mutilation of human bodies in war. But in commercial television, even themes that acknowledge the "realities" of war are constrained from exploring them in ways that fundamentally challenge or disrupt the social and institutional arrangments in American society that legitimate and naturalize war. Only in specific interactions between characters—characters who, themselves, are marginalized—are there any opportunities in this forum for the serious expression of oppositional positions. This leads us to consider key paradigmatic relationships between characters in *China Beach* who give voice to ideological crisis and who speak in voices of critique.

PARADIGMATIC STRUCTURE AND CULTURAL RUPTURE

In television narratives, the range of interpretive possibilities lies in the paradigmatic complexity of character relationships that shape the master narrative. As Robert C. Allen (1992, p. 112) states, "*who* tells *whom* is just as important as *what* is being related." Characters in narratives are not merely "individuals." Each character is the embodiment of a "type," a social category defined by the expression of a particular constellation of social norms and attitudes. The paradigmatic complexity of a narrative is determined by its "network of character relationships" (p. 112). In *China Beach*, we find three general categories of character in the regular cast. These I have labeled Warrior, Women in the War Zone, and Feminized Males. Within each category, characters instantiate either mainstream, conventional values or they personify marginalized positions (see the Appendix for character description and paradigmatic status). The unity of this system of character categories is anchored by McMurphy. As its central character, McMurphy embodies mainstream sensibilities. Her presence in the narrative denotes conventionality; what she sees, *and how we are asked to see*, conforms to culturally dominant interpretive frames. However, her absence from the narrative creates openings in the text where marginalized voices are privileged.

For example, McMurphy often is placed in dialectical tension with two marginalized characters, K.C. and Beckett. In the structured narrative logic of the series, McMurphy—a nice middle-class, white, Catholic girl from Kansas (with great legs and tight-fitting Army tee shirts)—is plunked down in Vietnam where she nurses wounded and dying American boys. She struggles to reconcile her state-side values and experience with an increasingly insane situation. Neither her middle-class upbringing nor her brief Army training have prepared her adequately for the madness she encounters at the China Beach Army Hospital.

K.C. and Beckett, however, are far less bewildered by the fragmentation and incoherence of the war; for them, Vietnam is much more a continuation of the forms of oppression that they experienced in their "civilian" lives. They give voice to the discourse of recrimination, cynicism, and despair. Referring to themselves, interchangeably, as "niggers," they articulate the experience of disenfranchised, marginalized veterans of the war. McMurphy listens to their voices—sometimes in sympathy, sometimes in anger, shock, and dismay, and always with anguish.

McMurphy's responses generally resonate with mainstream, middle-class morality. Consequently, the paradigmatic pairing of McMurphy with K.C. or Beckett serves to domesticate the rage and potential for social disruption contained in their discourses. Significantly, however, when K.C. and Beckett are paired without McMurphy's moderating presence, radical critique of American capitalist culture can emerge in the text.

Collectively, all characters in *China Beach* participate in shaping the ideological character of the narrative. As I have indicated, McMurphy functions to moderate radical discourse, while not suppressing its emergence altogether. All characters participate in shaping the narrative through one of three functions. They may serve as reasons or excuses for ideological crisis in the text. They may shape that rupture by their discourse (which, by definition, locates them as marginalized characters). Or, they may function to suppress or establish boundaries on that discourse (which locates them as mainstream).

In view of these functions, particular character pairings structure both the circumstances under which oppositional voices can emerge in the narrative as well as the extent to which those voices will be contained by the hegemonic constraints of culturally and/or institutionally dominant positions. To appreciate the implications of paradigmatic pairings for narrative development, the character categories of Warrior, Women in the War Zone, and Feminized Males require brief elaboration.

The Warrior

This character category represents "the brotherhood," often discussed, but rarely seen. The only regularly seen Warrior is Dodger, the quintessential "bush" fighter, comfortable in the jungle and ill-at-ease in any conventional social setting. The Warrior engages the viewing audience only indirectly, through the reflective talk of Women in the War Zone and Feminized Males. The warrior is defined by four characteristics: he has killed or witnessed killing; he has been drafted or he has volunteered to serve because of ideological imperatives of masculinity and patriotism; his experience cannot be understood by outsiders; and he has been betrayed by his government (which is duplicitous) and his nation (which is ignorant and indifferent).

Women in the War Zone

Here we find the usual collection of female character types: nurses, Red Cross volunteers (donut dollies), whores, career military personnel in support positions, unseen wives and lovers back home, entertainers, and journalists. Although these "types" are "typical," they constitute the implied audience for the series. Through them, the American public is instantiated in the text.

The women's roles are played against each other to dramatize various aspects of American political consciousness. McMurphy, our central character, is the all-American girl next door. She is white, middle-class, and raised Catholic. She is conventionally attractive, sexually selective, and socially modest. She is nurturing, caring, supportive, and possessed of decency and integrity. In short, McMurphy embodies the idealization of American political consciousness: fundamentally decent and desirable, tattered and battered, but still caring and responsive to the needs of the downtrodden. One measure of the cultural attractiveness of this position is evidenced by the multiple Emmy Awards given to Dana Delaney for Best Actress in a dramatic series. The master narrative positions us with her, this anguished, yet controlled and beautiful woman. And since McMurphy's presence in the narrative signifies preferred readings, her reactions suggest how we should "see" the Vietnam experience and, by implication, how we should "read" the veteran.

K.C. often is set in opposition to mainstream female characters. She is the calculating hooker without a heart, who occasionally falters to reveal her humanity. Although she occupies a privileged position in the text, she speaks the discourse of the disenfranchised. K.C. is cynical and relentlessly mercenary. However, her oppositional voice is tamed in certain situations. In one episode, for example, when K.C. was placed in opposition to McMurphy, we learned (by her comparative shortcomings) of the importance of decency, courage, and honesty in the face of death and uncertainty.

A relatively short-lived, mainstream character, the virginal Cherry was killed off in the middle of the series. Cherry embodies the innocence and naïveté of the American public regarding Vietnam. Blonde, diminutive, and sweet, she is altogether out of her element as a Red Cross volunteer in a war zone. An Iowan (like Radar O'Reilly on *M*A*S*H*), Cherry goes to Vietnam to locate her brother, Rick, who has been listed "Missing In Action." Through her, we come to understand how ill-prepared the American public was for the brutalities of this war. When Cherry is paired with K.C., we see just how naive she is (and Americans were) for believing in the patriotic platitudes of "duty, honor, country." In one scene, K.C. gives Cherry "the truth":

K.C.:   Duty? Honor? Country? I know all about honor . . . I honor MasterCharge, BankAmericard, and American Express. . . . What do *you* give them? Some nice chit-chat. Then you send them out there to be shot at, or shafted, or maybe to begin a life-long relationship with a green piece of plastic that zips? [Long pause] Take off the invisible white gloves. Open your eyes. We do the same thing. Except, I perform a real service. [Speechless, Cherry leaves. K.C. smiles smugly and takes a leisurely drink of whiskey.]

Despite K.C.'s antagonism, her cunning enables Cherry to locate her brother, in an opium den, selling black market drugs for the corrupt Saigon regime. Rick has "crossed over" and can never return to "the world." He is as much a casualty of the war as the still forms on the gurneys and in the body bags. Through Cherry's mainstream, feminine innocence, we learn that Vietnam can consume the warrior's soul, just as well as his life. Using the license of melodrama, Cherry is killed "in the field," when the fire base she is visiting is attacked. Her death embodies the loss of innocence, an important theme in the series.

Three supporting female characters constrain radical ruptures in the text. Lila, the career officer, generally insists on strict compliance with military codes of conduct. She clings to a rational worldview in the face of Vietnam's insanity and represents the "absurd" voice of the military. However, when Lila does see the incongruities of the war, she serves as reluctant witness to the institutionalized madness around her. Likeable despite her rigidity, this historian of "wars past" often laments that war isn't what it used to be. The narrative often pairs Lila with K.C. in competition for the attention and approval of high-ranking military officers. K.C. subverts the American military system and exploits its corruption, currying political favors in exchange for sexual encounters and black market goods; Lila strives to excel on merit, earned by hard work and fair play.

Lorette and Wayloo are the most frivolous and least complex of the female characters, especially evident when paired with McMurphy or K.C. Although Lorette leaves the series as Wayloo arrives, their roles are functionally equivalent. Lorette is an entertainer and Wayloo is a broadcast journalist. Much is made subtextually of the parallels between the two women's career choices; both create illusions, both "distract," and both are pivotal parts of the fictions about Vietnam constructed for the American public. Because these characters are so conventionally drawn, they function as shorthand devices to close off ruptures in the text.

Feminized Males

This category includes all male characters who are not Warriors or corrupt representatives of dominant institutions. Only three, however, are essential to the master narrative. Boonie and Beckett are marginalized; Dr. Richards is not.

Boonie is named for his past exploits as a Warrior "in the boonies." Although he is a key character from the outset, we do not discover until the second season why he is a "retired" Warrior; at that time the narrative reveals that while on a reconnaissance patrol, Boonie "fragged" a CIA special forces operative who was slaughtering Vietnamese civilians. Boonie's desire to "tell the truth" conflicted with institutional pressures to conceal what happened, "for the greater good." Ultimately, he is pressured into accepting a medal for valor in order to "build morale after Tet." Because of what he has seen and what he has done, Boonie can neither go home nor return to the bush. Like Rick, only with moral compass intact, Boonie literally is a mis-placed person. At China Beach, he creates meaning as "lifeguard," literally preserving human life. Boonie's story emphasizes how fictionalized representations of the Vietnam War were created by the media, politicians, and the military to advance their own purposes. Reflecting on the abjection of war experience (the collapse of meaning), Boonie gives voice to the long-silenced wisdom of the veteran: "There's no truth. There's what happened and what people need to think happened. Either way, it won't change anything." Or, as many combat veterans put it, "Fuck it. It don't mean nuthin."

Like Boonie, Beckett lives "in the rear." He is marginalized by race and by occupation. His most common pairing is with McMurphy. She cares for the mortally wounded warriors until they die; then she relinquishes them to Beckett. He refers reverentially to the dead as "his men." As a measure of his connectedness to them, he occasionally sleeps in the morgue, sometimes in a body bag. Beckett appears most frequently alone or in the company of women. Warriors, in particular, avoid him. He reeks of embalming fluid; a black man, his hands have bleached white. Beckett ruptures the text by his indictment of the waste of human *lives*. Beckett is intimately tied to the particular, to the value of *each* human life, and his diatribes rail against a system that treats them as "acceptable losses." Paradoxically, as K.C. observes, Beckett refuses to allow his disillusionment and despair to transform into cynicism and a wholesale indictment of that system.

When K.C. and Beckett are paired, their cynicism and despairing hopefulness create the greatest ruptures in the master narrative; no clear cues indicate which discourse should be privileged. In one key scene, Beckett confronts K.C., after learning that she is selling the votes of dead American soldiers. Her mercenary cynicism collides with Beckett's maternal protectiveness of "his men" and his enduring faith in the principles of democratic idealism. The scene is set at night, during a monsoon. It takes place in K.C.'s quarters. The entire scene is composed of tight shots; its feel is claustrophobic. What begins as a confrontation transforms into a revelation of ideological commitments. As Beckett challenges K.C. with his sense of violation—with his anger, disgust, astonishment, and finally, his disappointment in her—K.C. responds by joking about necrophilia, and laying bare her utter lack of faith in a world defined by capitalism and the illusion of democratic pluralism. In the climax of the scene, Beckett justifies his allegiances to that world in terms of sacrifices already made (much as American involvement in Vietnam was justified by citing the "supreme sacrifice" of those already killed in combat). In the following exchange, we see the ideological tension between their worldviews:

Beckett: [Extreme close-up shot] You know, where I come from, my daddy had to take a literacy test to vote. You know what a joke that was? [K.C. breaks off eye contact] A white man walks into voter registration and they hand him a book and ask him to read, "See Dick run. See Jane run after Dick." Okay, you can vote. A Negro walks in and they hand him a Chinese newspaper and ask him, "Can you read the headlines, nigger?" The Black man says, "Yeah, it says Black men don't vote in North Carolina."

K.C.: [Agitated, begins backing away from Beckett] You think democracy makes America? It's capitalism . . . cash, that's what makes America hum, and that's why I love it. What other country on God's earth lets a poor girl with a 10th-grade education make a decent buck and get out of the sewer she was born into? Huh? If my grandfather had stayed in Poland, I'd be harvesting beets right now, eating black bread and raw onions. We're both niggers. [Music begins, bass strings] I believe in the U.S. of A.! Uncle Sam, Uncle . . . Hamilton, Uncle Jackson, Uncle Abe, Uncle George. [She gestures with a handful of bills] I have a chance. [Sarcastically] In America, a poor girl can be a queen.

Beckett: Even if that's true, I'll never stop believing that there can be another America. [He exits the room, and the camera lingers on K.C.'s face. She laughs]

Though both are marginalized by their culture, Beckett clings to—and is the voice of—faith in the promise of the American dream. For K.C., that "promise" is little more than a distortive hallucination of greed and exploitation.

The final Feminized Male is the surgeon, Dr. Richards. Consummately mainstream, he is a "liberal," lecherous, wisecracking, golf-playing, cocktail-sipping, suburban physician of high skill. In many respects, he is "Hawkeye," one war removed. Although Richards rails against the war, he functions ideologically to constrain McMurphy's developing critical consciousness. The exchange between Richards and McMurphy presented earlier in this essay epitomizes that function. Paradigmatically, his browbeating of the drunken and exhausted McMurphy reveals his reliance on the "ultimate" gendered basis for trivializing women in a war zone— McMurphy chose to be there, and Richards was drafted against his will.

CONCLUSION

> To articulate the past historically does not mean to recognize it "the way it really was" (Ranke). It means to seize hold of a memory as it flashes up at a moment of danger. . . . Only that historian will have the gift of fanning the spark of hope in the past who is firmly convinced that *even the dead* will not be safe from the enemy if he wins. (Benjamin, 1968, p. 255)

There is much in this series that moves us closer to a painful understanding of the human costs of war. In spite of the constraining conventions of the medium, the series places us squarely in a discomforting examination of the dark side of war. We are asked to view American capitalism in the context of greed, wanton waste, and exploitation. We are confronted with the paradox of pairing war and medicine to implement foreign policy: technologies that fragment and technologies that re-assemble. Through McMurphy's lapsed Catholicism and the series's reliance on themes of mysticism, we are asked to understand that no institutional religion can cope with human evil of this magnitude. The series is both a poignant, wishful tale of compassion, integrity, and decency and a shrieking, sobbing, ranting clarion call to look carefully at the fundamental moral depravity of war.

The series offered a public forum for oppositional voices to critique institutionally sanctioned and culturally popular narratives about war. Through an elaborately structured narrative logic, the veteran was enabled to "tell" his story to a sympathetic, supportive audience. And yet, the unexamined cultural imperatives in the narrative render the series fundamentally flawed. Earlier, I argued that the constraints on any televisual representation of war are so compelling that certain "distractions" are necessary to conceal any serious textual openings. Put bluntly, without McMurphy's nipple shots and themes of romantic entanglement, the economic constraints of the medium would preclude broadcast of such a series. Clearly, this series cleverly manipulated conventional themes to make a place for textual ruptures such as monologues by Beckett, tirades by K.C., and thematic examination of anguish, the destruction of private lives, and death. And yet, the series ignores the ways in which the discourses of war are "gendered." Close textual examination of the series illustrates that traditional masculinity (and its implied role for femininity) are crucial to the Warrior image. As long as representations of war fail to examine social formations that naturalize war and make it desirable, attractive, and even erotic, no serious social critique is possible.

APPENDIX: KEY CHARACTERS OF *CHINA BEACH*

CHARACTER STATUS

Character Type	Mainstream	Marginalized
Warrior		Dodger
Women in the War Zone	McMurphy	K.C.
	Cherry	
	Lila	
	Lorette	
	Wayloo	
Feminized Males	Dr. Richards	Beckett
		Boonie

CHARACTER DESCRIPTIONS

McMurphy: Central character of *China Beach*; surgical nurse; paragon of middle-American morality.

K.C.: Prostitute and black market entrepreneur; former Red Cross "donut dolly"; disillusioned and cynical.

Boonie: Self-retired warrior; lifeguard and recreational director at China Beach; nice guy, emotionally scarred by Vietnam.

Beckett: Ethnic minority (African American); runs morgue at China Beach; prepares bodies of dead for return to U.S. for burial; disillusioned and filled with despair, yet eternally hopeful.

Dr. Richards: China Beach surgeon; drafted; maintains sanity through humor and sexual innuendo and verbal play.

Lila: Career officer; chief of nursing staff; works "by the book"; conventionally patriotic; middle-aged spinster.

Cherry: "Donut dolly"; youthful, blonde, virginal, naive.

Lorette: USO entertainer; out for a good time; goes to Vietnam for personal adventure and "men-o-rama."

Wayloo: Replaces Lorette in series; aspiring broadcast journalist of limited competence and large breasts; daughter of congressman.

Dodger: Quintessential combat veteran; reticent; emotionally brittle; stoic; "thousand yard stare."

REFERENCES

Allen, R. C. (Ed.). (1992). *Channels of discourse, reassembled: Television and contemporary criticism.* 2nd. Ed. Chapel Hill, NC: University of North Carolina Press.

Bales, M. (1988, May 16). TV: A distaff view of Vietnam. *The Wall Street Journal,* p. 15.

Barker, D. (1987). Television production techniques as communication. In H. Newcomb (Ed.), *Television: The critical view.* 4th ed. New York: Oxford University Press.

Benjamin, W. (1968). *Illuminations* (Ed. H. Arendt; Trans. H. Zohn). New York: Schocken Books.

Berg, R. (1990). Losing Vietnam: Covering the war in an age of technology. In L. Dittmar & G. Michaud (Eds.), *From Hanoi to Hollywood: The Vietnam War in American film* (pp. 41-68). New Brunswick, NJ: Rutgers University Press.

Dionisopoulos, G. (1990). Images of the warrior returned: Vietnam veterans in popular American films. In R. Morris & P. Ehrenhaus (Eds.), *Cultural legacies of Vietnam: Uses of the past in the present* (pp. 80-98). Norwood, NJ: Ablex.

Edelman, M. (1990). Introduction. In R. Morris & P. Ehrenhaus (Eds.), *Cultural legacies of Vietnam: Uses of the past in the present* (pp. 1-6). Norwood, NJ: Ablex.

Fiske, J. (1989). *Reading the popular.* Boston: Unwin Hyman.

Fussell, P. (1975). *The great war and modern memory.* New York: Oxford University Press.

Fussell, P. (1989). *Wartime.* New York: Oxford University Press.

Gitlin, T. (1983). *Inside prime time.* New York: Pantheon.

Haines, H. W. (1986). "What kind of war?" An analysis of the Vietnam Veterans Memorial. *Critical Studies in Mass Communication, 3,* 1-20.

Haines, H. W. (1990). The pride is back: *Rambo, Magnum, P. I.,* and the return trip to Vietnam. In R. Morris & P. Ehrenhaus (Eds.), *Cultural legacies of Vietnam: Uses of the past in the present* (pp. 99-123). Norwood, NJ: Ablex.

Haines, H. W. (1992, February). *Bringing up the rear: China Beach and ideological closure.* Paper presented at the annual meeting of the Western Speech Communication Association, Boise, ID.

Hall, S. (1980). Encoding/decoding. In S. Hall, D. Hobson, A. Lowe, & P. Willis (Eds.), *Culture, media, language* (pp. 128-138). London: Hutchinson.

Hanley, L. (1991). *Writing war.* Cambridge, MA: University of Massachusetts Press.

Hansen, J. T., Owen, A. S., & Madden, M. P. (1992). *Parallels: The solider's knowledge and the oral history of contemporary warfare.* New York: Aldine de Gruyter.

Honey, M. (1984). *Creating Rosie the Riveter: Class, gender, and propaganda during World War II.* Cambridge, MA: University of Massachusetts Press.

Kristeva, J. (1984). *Powers of horror: An essay on abjection* (Trans. L. S. Roudiez). New York: Columbia University Press.

McKerrow, R. E. (1989). Critical rhetoric: Theory and praxis. *Communication Monographs, 56,* 91-111.

Meehan, D. (1983). *Ladies of the evening: Women characters of prime-time television.* Metuchen, NJ: Scarecrow Press.

Morrison, M. (1988, May 19). "China Beach" salutes the women of Vietnam: Let's hear it for the girls. *Rolling Stone,* pp. 75-79.

O'Brien, T. (1990). *The things they carried.* Boston, MA: Houghton Mifflin.

O'Connor, J. (1988, April 26). "China Beach," women at war. *The New York Times,* p. C18.

Palmer, W. (1990). Symbolic nihilism in *Platoon*. In O. W. Gilman, Jr., & L. Smith (Eds.), *America rediscovered: Critical essays on literature and film of the Vietnam War* (pp. 256-274). New York: Garland Publishing.

Rosenberg, H. (1988, April 26). Women in war. *The Los Angeles Times*, VI, p. 1.

Rupp, L. J. (1978). *Mobilizing women for war: German and American propaganda, 1939-1945*. Princeton, NJ: Princeton University Press.

NAME INDEX

SUBJECT INDEX

Affirmative Action, 137-138, 175-176
Agency, 17-22, 25, 27, 28, 127
Authority, Hayden White on, 191

Barthes, Roland, on narrative, 190
Behaviorism, 20
Benjamin, Walter, on the hermeneutics of
    narrative, 209
Bureaucracy, 16
    structure of, 102

China Beach, 207-228
Communication:
    and covert control, 104
    and emancipation, 183
    and ethics, 181-183
    and narrative, 2
    and value, 182
    as domination, 88
    as social control, 83-85, 87, 89, 90
    as social integration, 83, 84, 87-88, 93
Community:
    and individualism, 182-183
    educational, 181-182
Consensus, 16, 33, 79, 83-84
    Habermas on, 190
Conversation analysis, 31-32
Crisis of representation, 1-2

Culture, organizational, 101-103

Discipline, 143-161
    and marginality, 153, 158-159
    and normalization, 149-151, 152, 157,
        158
    and ordering of space, time, and move-
        ment, 148-149, 153-155, 158
    and rites of scarification, 159-161
    and rituals of exclusion, 158-159
    Foucault on, 155
Discourse Analysis, of racist stories, 129-
    139
Discrimination, and narrative, 164-183
Diversity, 164, 172, 173
    and affirmative action, 175-176
    and narratives of tolerance, 174-176
Domination:
    Mumby on, 145
    Weber on, 101-102

False consciousness, 17, 25, 32-33
Family:
    Monolithic, 51-55
        ahistorical nature of, 52-53
        and gender, 52
        and generation, 52
        and social science, 54

Lyotard, Jean-Francois:
  on legitimation, 3
  on narrative, 3

Mobilization of bias, 22-23
Mouffe, Chantal, on social theory, 5
Mumby, Dennis, on domination, 145

Narrative:
  about minorities, 125-141
  agency and responsibility, 127
  and evidence, 126, 139-141
  and narratibility, 126-127, 132
  and stereotypes, 127, 140
  argumentation, 126-127, 129, 136, 139
  counterstories, 139
  minorities as "threats," 127-128, 133-
    134, 136, 138-139
  and authority, 191
  and concealment, 17-18, 32, 37, 42
  and consensus, 190
  and covert control, 97-115
  and critical analysis, 79, 80, 90, 93, 94
  and discipline, 143-161
  and discrimination, 164-183
  and diversity, 172
  and docile bodies, 147-161
  and ethics, 114
  and everyday life, 16, 31-34, 42
  and family, *see* Family storytelling
  and functionalism, 32
  and gender, 207-228
    and feminized males, 225-227
    and stereotypes of women, 215-217
    constraints, 216-217, 225, 228
  and ideology, 17, 78-80, 82, 85-89, 105
  and language, 31-42
  and narcissism, 166-173, 182
  and postmodernism, 3-4, 79-80
  and power, 15-42, 83-89
  and power/ethnic dominance, 122, 125,
    140
  and production of subjects, 149-161
  and racism, 121-141, 176-178

and re-positioning, 189, 191-194. 202-
  205
and revelation, 16-17, 32, 37, 42
and self-understanding, 143-144
and social cognitions, 121-123, 140
and social theory, 15-42
and sociology, 15
and speech act theory, 61-63
and truth claims, 105-107
and values, 109-111
and Western Marxism, 32
and the workplace, 97-115
and/of tolerance, 173-176
as a form of reminiscing, 169-170
as exemplars, 107
as meta-code, 190
as natural, 144-145
Barthes on, 190
categories of narrative schema, 122,
  132-138, 140
Fisher on, 1
Fragmentation of, 78-83, 89-94, 207,
  210-211, 222
Jameson on, 144
journalistic use of 189-205
Lyotard on, 3
mental models of, 124-125
of courtship, 70-73
of Japanese American internment, 143-
  161
of marital conflict, 69-70
of self-legitimation, 189-205
of war, 207-228
  and character, 208, 211-213, 221-222,
    224-227
  and television, 208, 210-215, 221,
    228; Gitlin on, 210-211
  cultural constraints, 208, 214-221
  media constraints, 208-214, 228
  open/closed text, 212
  oppositional voices in, 222, 224, 228
  possibilities of critique, 208, 212-213,
    220, 222, 228
  social convention, 209-210, 213, 220,
    223
socio-cultural functions of, 125

ABOUT THE CONTRIBUTORS

ISAAC E. CATT (Ph.D., Southern Illinois University at Carbondale, 1982) is Professor and Chair of the Department of Communication and Theater at Millersville University of Pennsylvania. He has extensive teaching and administrative experience. His published research has been influenced by his intensive study of Continental philosophy, especially semiotic and phenomenological approaches to the study of human communication. Of particular relevance has been his analysis of narcissism as a distinct and pervasive problem of interpersonal experience inherent in the postmodern era.

STEWART R. CLEGG (Ph.D., Bradford University, 1974) is Professor in the Department of Management at the University of Western Sydney-MacArthur. The early 1990s were spent as Professor of Organization Studies at the University of St. Andrews, Scotland. Most of his career has been spent in Australia. He was Professor of Sociology at The University of New England in Armidale, New South Wales, from 1985 to 1989 and spent a formative period from 1976 to 1984 at Griffith University, Brisbane. He has published 11 books, including *Power, Rule and Domination* (1975), *Frameworks of Power* (1989), and *Modern Organizations: Organizations in the Postmodern World* (1990), and has written many articles and chapters.

PETER EHRENHAUS (Ph.D., University of Minnesota, 1979) is Associate Professor of Speech Communication at Portland State University. His work for the past several years has centered on the politics of representation as it pertains generally to shaping public memory and the social value of warfare and, more particularly, as it relates to contesting definitions, lessons, and interpretations of the meaning of America's Vietnam

241

experience. In addition to essays in *Argumentation and Advocacy, Communication Monographs*, and *Journal of Communication*, that have focused on the Vietnam Memorial and the politics of remembrance, he is co-editor (with Richard Morris) of *Cultural Legacies of Vietnam: Uses of the Past in the Present* (1989).

KRISTIN M. LANGELLIER (Ph.D., Southern Illinois University at Carbondale, 1980) is Associate Professor of Speech Communication at the University of Maine. She is Editor of *Text and Performance Quarterly*, and her recent publications include essays in *Doing Research on Women's Communication, Uncoverings, Women Communicating*, and *Text and Performance Quarterly*.

DENNIS K. MUMBY (Ph.D., Southern Illinois University at Carbondale, 1985) is Associate Professor of Communication at Purdue University. He is the author of *Communication and Power in Organizations* (1988) as well as numerous articles in journals such as *Communication Quarterly, Communication Monographs*, and *Academy of Management Review*, and he serves on the editorial boards of *Communication Monographs, Quarterly Journal of Speech*, and *Communication Studies*. Mumby's research focuses on the relationship between power and discourse in institutional contexts. He is currently examining the possibilities of a postmodern feminist account of organizational communication.

GORDON NAKAGAWA (Ph.D., Southern Illinois University at Carbondale, 1987) is Associate Professor of Speech Communication at California State University, Northridge (CSUN). His academic interests include postmodern and poststructuralist philosophy, feminist theory, cultural and discourse studies, and ethnic/racial identity formation (with particular attention to the relationship between identity formation and communication practices). In addition to teaching speech communication courses, he has also taught for the Asian American Studies department at CSUN. In 1991, he received CSUN's Distinguished Teaching Award. He helped to initiate the formation of the Asian/Pacific Caucus in the Speech Communication Association, and he is active in Asian American community organizations in the Los Angeles area.

A. SUSAN OWEN (Ph.D., University of Iowa, 1989) is Associate Professor of Communication and Theater Arts at the University of Puget

Sound, Tacoma, Washington. Her work investigates both the social construction of gender in mass media texts and representations of warfare and the warrior. She is co-author, with the late Michael Madden and Tim Hansen, of *Parallels: Soldiers' Knowledge and the Oral History of Contemporary Warfare.*

ERIC E. PETERSON (Ph.D., Southern Illinois University at Carbondale, 1980) is Associate Professor and Chair of the Department of Speech Communication at the University of Maine. His recent publications include essays in *Critical Studies in Mass Communication, Communication Education, Communication Quarterly,* and *American Behavioral Scientist.*

W. MARC PORTER (Ph.D., Ohio University, 1990) is Assistant Professor of Organizational Communication at California State University, Chico. His research adopts interpretive and critical approaches in studies of the ideology of workplace learning videotapes, corporate diversity programs, corporate environmental public affairs campaigns, and corporate ethics codes. In the human resource/training and development profession, he has earned a national reputation for his leadership and contributions to the design of three large international training and development conferences. He has also worked as a quality circle facilitator and HRD consultant and regularly leads seminars for profit and nonprofit organization leaders on such topics as multicultural diversity and team building.

TEUN A. VAN DIJK (Ph.D., University of Amsterdam) is Director of the Program in Discourse Studies at the University of Amsterdam. He has authored or edited over 30 books, including *Communicating Racism* (1987), *News as Discourse* (1988), and *Racism and the Press* (1991) and *Elite Discourse and Racism* (1993). He is founder and editor of the journals *TEXT* and *Discourse & Society.* He has lectured in numerous universities in Europe and the Americas.

MARSHA WITTEN (Ph.D., Princeton University, 1992) is Assistant Professor of Sociology at Franklin and Marshall College. She is the author of *All Is Forgiven: The Secular Message in American Protestantism,* and *Guarding the Castle of God: The Secular Discourses of Contemporary American Protestantism* (forthcoming) and of articles and book chapters on ideological features of religious and organizational texts. Her doctorate is in sociology.

BARBIE ZELIZER (Ph.D., University of Pennsylvania, 1990) is Assistant Professor of Rhetoric and Communication at Temple University. A former journalist, she is author of *Covering the Body: The Kennedy Assassination, the Media, and the Shaping of Collective Memory* (1992) and co-author (with Y. Roeh, E. Katz, and A. Cohen) of *Almost Midnight: Reforming the Late-Night News* (1980). She has published extensively on journalism as cultural practice, and her articles have appeared in *Journal of Communication, Critical Studies in Mass Communication, Semiotica,* and elsewhere.